DIVIDING THE SPOILS

Ancient Warfare and Civilization

SERIES EDITORS:

RICHARD ALSTON   ROBIN WATERFIELD

In this series, leading historians offer compelling new narratives of the armed conflicts that shaped and reshaped the classical world, from the wars of Archaic Greece to the fall of the Roman Empire and Arab conquests.

Dividing the Spoils: The War for Alexander the Great's Empire

Robin Waterfield

ROBIN WATERFIELD

DIVIDING THE SPOILS

*The War for Alexander
the Great's Empire*

OXFORD
UNIVERSITY PRESS

OXFORD

UNIVERSITY PRESS

Oxford University Press is a department of the University of Oxford.
It furthers the University's objective of excellence in research, scholarship,
and education by publishing worldwide.

Oxford   New York
Auckland   Cape Town   Dar es Salaam   Hong Kong   Karachi
Kuala Lumpur   Madrid   Melbourne   Mexico City   Nairobi
New Delhi   Shanghai   Taipei   Toronto

With offices in
Argentina   Austria   Brazil   Chile   Czech Republic   France   Greece
Guatemala   Hungary   Italy   Japan   Poland   Portugal   Singapore
South Korea   Switzerland   Thailand   Turkey   Ukraine   Vietnam

Oxford is a registered trade mark of Oxford University Press
in the UK and certain other countries.

Published in the United States of America by
Oxford University Press
198 Madison Avenue, New York, NY 10016

Library of Congress Cataloging-in-Publication Data
Waterfield, Robin, 1952–
Dividing the spoils : the war for Alexander the Great's empire/Robin Waterfield.
p.   cm. — (Ancient warfare and civilization)
Includes bibliographical references and index.
ISBN 978-0-19-539523-5 (hardcover); 978-0-19-993152-1 (paperback)
1. Greece—History—Macedonian Hegemony, 323–281 B.C. 2. Macedonia—History—Diadochi,
323–276 B.C. 3. Generals—Greece—Biography. 4. Generals—Macedonia—Biography. 5. Greece—
Kings and rulers—Biography. 6. Macedonia—Kings and rulers—Biography. 7. Mediterranean Region—
History, Military. 8. Mediterranean Region—History—To 476. I. Title.
DF235.4.W38   2011
938'.070922—dc22   2010030834

Printed in Canada by Marquis Book Printing
on acid-free paper

FOR MY FATHER
AND IN MEMORY OF MY MOTHER

Contents

Preface

This book tells the story of one of the great forgotten wars of history. It took more or less forty years after the death of Alexander the Great for his heirs (the *Diadokhoi*, the Successors) to finish carving up his vast empire. These years, 323–281 BCE, were filled with high adventure, intrigue, passion, assassinations, dynastic marriages, treachery, shifting alliances, and mass slaughter on battlefield after battlefield. And while the men fought on the field, the women schemed from their palaces, pavilions, and prisons; this was the first period of western history when privileged women, especially from the royal families, began to play the kind of major political roles they would continue to play throughout the future history of Roman, Byzantine, and European monarchies.

My period has a natural starting point—the death of Alexander in June 323—and an equally natural end. The year 281 saw the violent deaths of the last two direct Successors of Alexander, those who had known and ridden with him. The next generation—the *Epigonoi*, as Nymphis, a historian of the second century BCE, called them in a lost work—may have been just as ambitious as their fathers, but the world had changed. It was no longer realistic to aim for dominion of the whole of Alexander's empire; instead, their first aim was to hold on to their core territories—Macedon for the Antigonids, Asia for the Seleucids, and Greater Egypt for the Ptolemies. Of course, they and their descendants would regularly attempt to take over some of a neighbor's territory, but no individual any longer realistically aspired to rule the whole known world. There would never again be a time like the time of the Successors, forty years of almost unremitting warfare aimed at worldwide domination.

In their day, the Successors were household names, because they held the fate of the world in their hands. If their fame has become dimmed over the centuries, that is a result of historical accident (the loss of almost all our sources for the period) and of our perennial obsession with Alexander the Great, in whose shadow they have been made to stand. My main purpose in this book has been to revive the memory of the Successors. A narrative account is enough on its own to demonstrate that the early Hellenistic period was not an anticlimax after the conquests of Alexander, and certainly not a period of decline and disintegration. In fact, Alexander had left things in a mess, with no guaranteed succession, no administration in place suitable for such an enormous empire, and huge untamed areas both bordering and within his "empire." A detailed and realistic map of Alexander's conquests would show him cutting a narrow swath across Asia and back, leaving much relatively untouched. So far from disintegration, then, the Successors consolidated the Conqueror's gains. Their equal ambitions, however, meant that consolidation inevitably led to the breakup of the empire and the foundation of lesser empires and kingdoms.

Military narrative features prominently in the book, but has been broken up by "asides" on cultural matters. For, astonishingly, this period of savage warfare was also characterized by brilliant cultural developments, especially in the fields of art, literature, and philosophy. The energy released by world conquest was not all absorbed on battlefields, and the culture the Successors brought in their train flourished, thanks especially to royal patronage. Although they were warlords, the Successors were not uncultured. Alexander himself was said to have slept with a copy of Homer's *Iliad* under his pillow—along with a knife.[1] Without the consolidation the Successors brought to Alexander's gains, the spread of culture would have been impossible; there is no civilization without structure.

So as well as an account of the military action, this book also contains an outline of its cultural impact. A new world emerged from the dust and haze of battle—a world with distinct territories each ruled by its own king, but with a common culture. That common culture is what entitles us to speak generally of "the Greek east," distinct from "the Roman west," and it was the Successors, therefore, who set up the world-changing confrontation between these two power blocs. The result, of course, was Roman dominion over the entire Greek world. The takeover culminated in 30 BCE with the annexation of Egypt, and this date is generally taken to mark the end of what scholars call the "Hellenistic" period—the period, starting with the death of Alexander, when the Greek culture that the Successors fostered came to dominate the world from the Mediterranean to Afghanistan.

My main intention has been to write an accurate and enjoyable book—to make sense of a very difficult period of history. The overarching story is implied by my title and subtitle. The spoils *were* divided. We see the emergence, out of Alexander's single empire, of a multistate political order and of a developing balance of power. At one time or another, all the Successors tried to emulate their dead leader and conquer the entirety of the empire, but none of them succeeded. We witness what realist historians would describe as a law of history: contiguous powers with imperialist ambitions are bound to clash and so limit those ambitions. At the beginning of our forty-year period, grand imperialism was a possibility, but not at the end. The action of this law is the thread that runs through the book.

If an empire is the political, economic, and military domination of disparate populations by a distinct ruling class, with the whole administered from a geographically remote center, Seleucus won an empire (large chunks of the former Achaemenid empire of Persia), Ptolemy won an empire (Greater Egypt, as I call it from time to time in the book), and the Antigonids won a kingdom, as well as hegemony (the ability to command obedience on the basis of a real or implied military threat) over much of Greece. Very few, then, of the fifteen or so Successors succeeded in fulfilling their ambitions with any degree of stability or endurance. The law of history I mentioned just now plays itself out in various ways. Empires can be won or lost by caution, luck, treachery, military brilliance, megalomania. The forty years of the Successors display all of these dramas.

There had been empires in the world before. The Persian empire of the Achaemenids (550–330 BCE) was the one of most significance for the neighboring Greeks; it was preceded in its turn, on a far smaller scale, by the Neo-Assyrian empire (934–610), which was preceded by the Hittite empire (1430–ca. 1200) and the Akkadian empire (late third millennium). Farther east, there may have been something describable as an empire in northern China during the Shang and Zhou periods (1766–1045; 1045–256), though the evidence is difficult to assess. But Alexander's Successors created the first empires whose rulers and dominant culture were European; the so-called Athenian "empires" of the fifth and fourth centuries were not really empires, above all because subjects and rulers shared a common ethnic background.[2]

Of course, Alexander himself was the conqueror in whose imperialist footsteps the Successors trod, but his empire was cut short by his death after a mere ten years, and can hardly be described as an empire anyway, for the reason I have already given: he was too busy conquering to give much thought to the perpetuation of his rule. It was the Successors who created the first stable empires with a European flavor. This was indeed a significant period of history, and it has been overlooked only because of the difficulties in recovering it. Historians of imperialism simply skip from Alexander to Rome; I aim to set the record straight.

In order to make the book as accessible as possible, I have chosen to focus on individuals; while maintaining a forward thrust, chronologically speaking, most of the chapters hinge on the adventures of one or two of the protagonists. To some readers, this may seem an old-fashioned approach. In emphasizing the role of individuals like this, am I not following the bias of ancient historians and writing "great man" history? History, it is said, is not driven by individuals so much as by economic, technological, and other, more abstract imperatives; individuals do not make society, but society makes individuals. There is truth in this, and I have tried to bring out at least some of the economic aspects of the Successors' warfare. At the same time, however, it needs to be remembered that these men were absolute rulers, a hard fact that many critics of "great man" history tend to ignore. The Successors' egos and desires could and did alter the course of history.

As soon as Alexander died, his empire began to crumble; he, not economic forces, had been holding it together. If Antigonus had not desired to emulate Alexander, if Demetrius the Besieger had not succumbed to megalomania toward the end of his life, if Seleucus had not had the courage to reclaim Babylon with a minimal force . . . a hundred such "ifs" could be written, each demonstrating that the Successors' personal ambitions and passions could and did determine what happened. History is not made only by great men, it is true, but nor is it made entirely by profit–loss calculations. More irrational and less predictable factors often play a part (as satirized in Joseph Heller's *Catch-22*), and they certainly did in the early Hellenistic period covered in this book. The very ideology of early Hellenistic kingship, as we shall see, encouraged individual ambitions. I make no apology, then, for having chosen to focus on individuals. It may or may not be true that "The history of every country begins in the heart of a man or a woman."[3] At any rate, a surprising amount of the history of many countries, from Greece to Afghanistan, began in the hearts and minds of the Successors of Alexander the Great. Their stories deserve to be better known.

Acknowledgments

I gathered a great deal of research material by writing out of the blue to scholars around the world and asking for offprints of articles. I met with nothing but kindness during this process, and so I first thank collectively all those who helped me in this way. Much research was carried out in Athens, where the staff of the Blegen Library of the American School of Classical Studies at Athens, and of the Library of the British School at Athens, were their usual helpful selves. I am grateful to James Romm for early sight of a late draft of his book *Ghost on the Throne* (we swapped), and to William Murray likewise for sending me a chapter of his forthcoming book on Hellenistic warships. The comments of Oxford University Press's anonymous reader were very useful, and I also profited from improvements suggested by my editor Stefan Vranka, my friends Paul Cartledge and Andrew Lane, and my wife Kathryn Dunathan. There are, of course, so many other reasons why I am in Kathryn's debt.

Lakonia, Greece, January 2011

PICTURE CREDITS

3. Ptolemy I of Egypt. British Museum no. CGR 62897. © The Trustees of the British Museum.

4. Seleucus I of Asia. The National Archaeological Museum, Naples. Scala 0149108g. © 2010 Scala, Florence, courtesy of the Ministero Beni e Att. Culturali.

5. Demetrius Poliorcetes. The National Archaeological Museum, Naples. Scala 0149109g. © 2010 Scala, Florence, courtesy of the Ministero Beni e Att. Culturali.

6. A Lysimachan "Alexander." British Museum no. AN 31026001. © The Trustees of the British Museum.

7. The Taurus Mountains. © Robin Waterfield.

8. The Acrocorinth. © Kathryn Waterfield.

9. The Temple of Apollo at Didyma. www.irismaritime.com.

10. The Arsinoeion. From A. Conze, *Archäologische Untersuchungen auf Samothrake*, vol. 1 (1875), pl. 54. © The British Library Board (749.e.4).

11. Indian War Elephant. © Hermitage Museum, St Petersburg.

12. Salamis Commemorative Coin. British Museum no. AN 3179001. © The Trustees of the British Museum.

13. The Lion Hunt Mosaic, Pella. Bridgeman 332175. © Ancient Art and Architecture Collection, Bridgeman Art Library.

14. Ivories from Vergina. © Ekdotike Athenon s.a.

15. Wall Painting from Vergina (detail). Bridgeman 60120. © Bridgeman Art Library.

16. The Fortune of Antioch. Vatican Museums. Scala 0041467M. © 2010 Scala Archives, Florence.

List of Illustrations

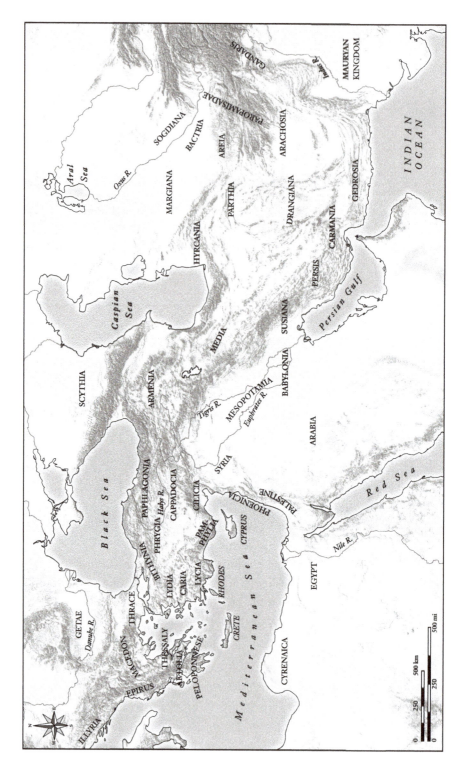

A. Alexander's empire

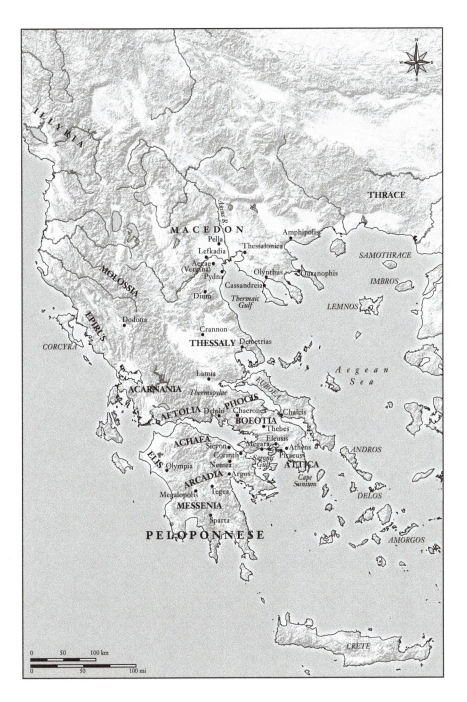

B. Macedon, Greece, and the Aegean

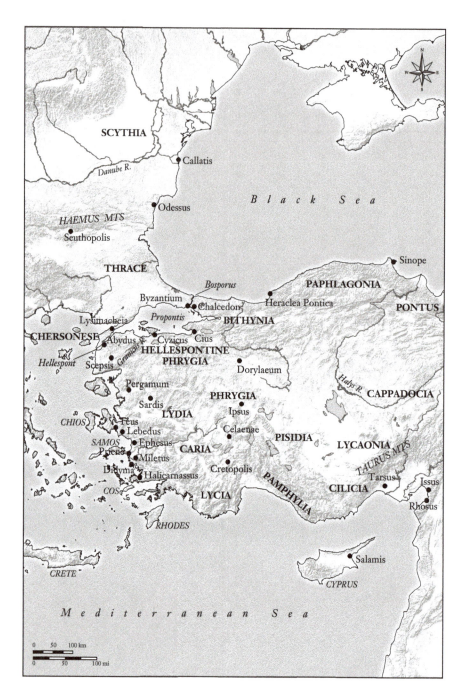

C. Asia Minor and the Black Sea

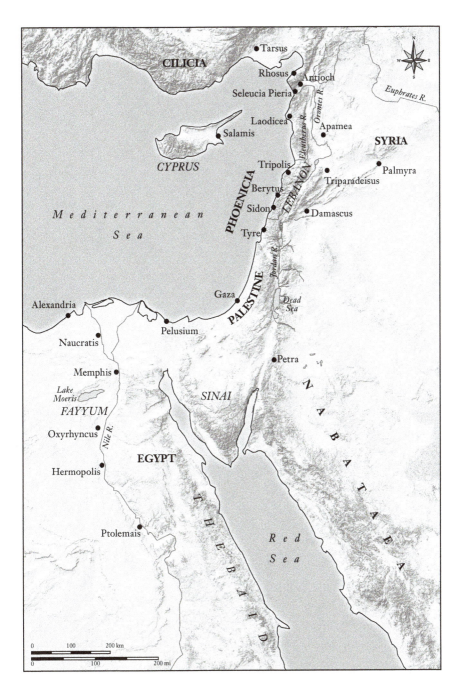

D. Syria and Egypt

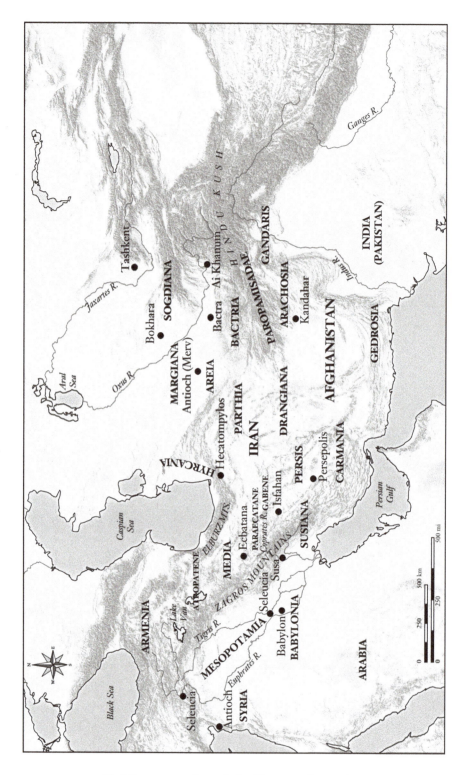

E. Mesopotamia and the Eastern Satrapies

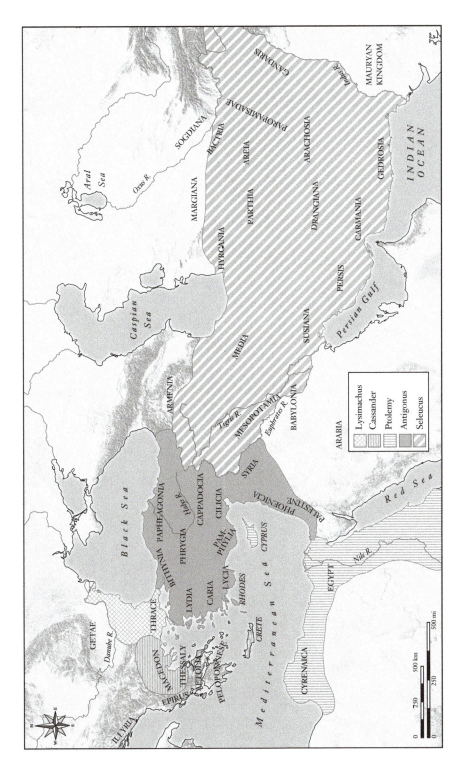

F. The Empire after the Peace of the Dynasts (311 BCE)

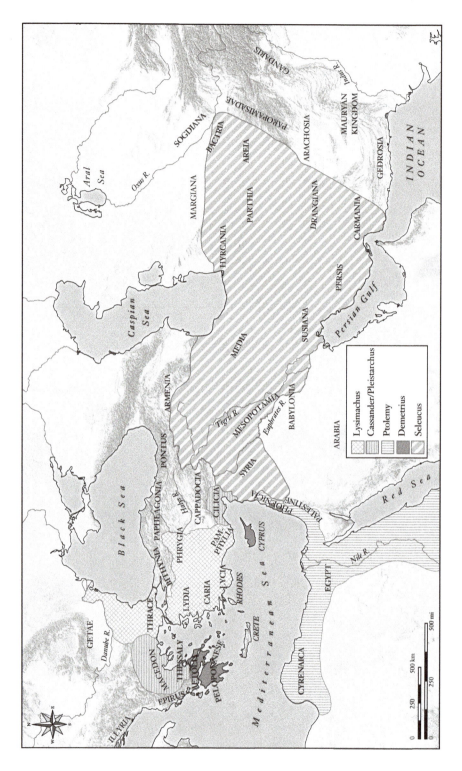

G. The Empire after Ipsus (301 BCE)

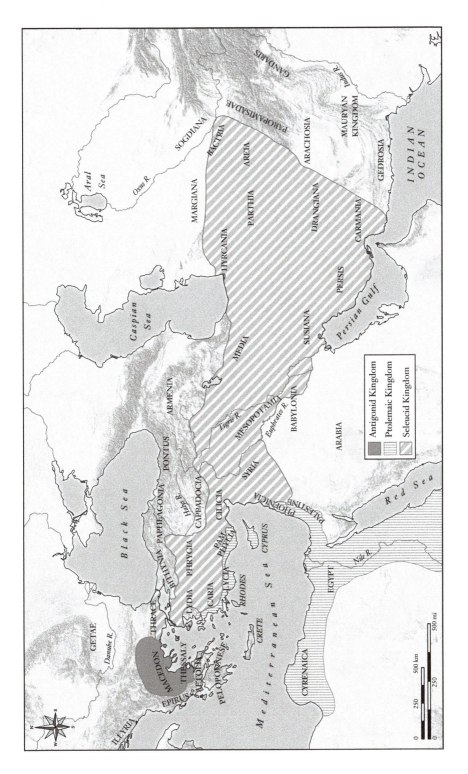

H. The Empire ca. 275 BCE

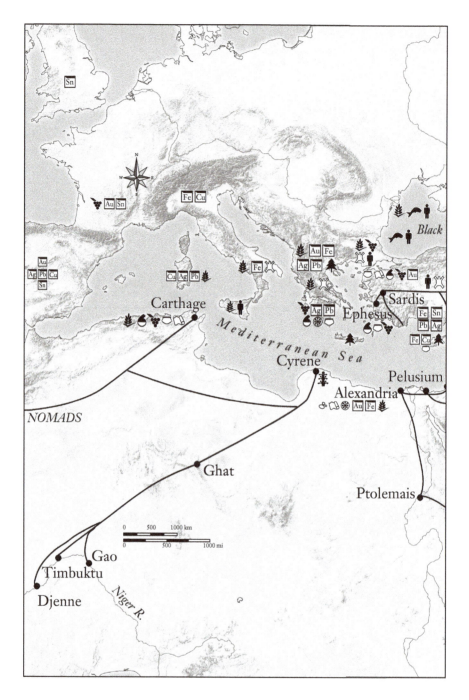

I. Roads and Resources

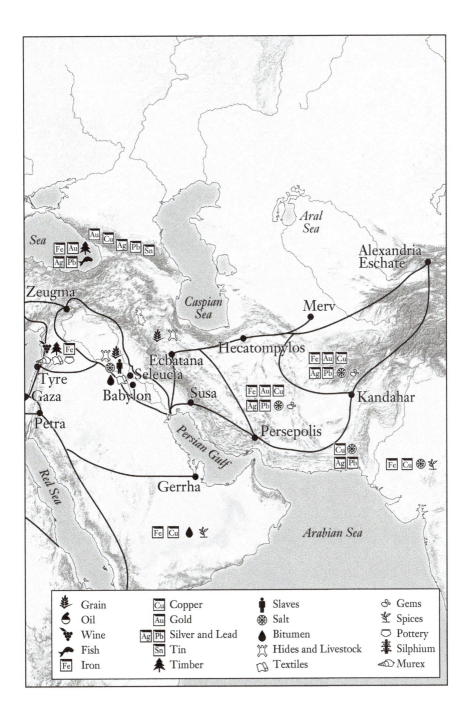

Sea

Aral
Sea

Caspian
Sea

Au Cu Ag Pb Sn
Fe Au
Ag Pb

Zeugma

Alexandria
Eschate

Merv

Hecatompylos

Fe Au Cu
Ag Pb

Fe

Tyre

Ecbatana
Seleucia

Babylon

Susa

Fe Au Cu
Ag Pb

Kandahar

Gaza

Petra

Persepolis

Cu
Ag Pb

Fe Cu

Red Sea

Persian Gulf

Gerrha

Arabian Sea

Fe Cu

🌾 Grain	Cu Copper	👤 Slaves	⚙ Gems
🫒 Oil	Au Gold	✵ Salt	🌿 Spices
🍇 Wine	Ag Pb Silver and Lead	⬤ Bitumen	⌣ Pottery
🐟 Fish	Sn Tin	Hides and Livestock	🌲 Silphium
Fe Iron	🌲 Timber	Textiles	🐚 Murex

DIVIDING THE SPOILS

The Legacy of Alexander the Great

THE WORD SPREAD rapidly through the city of Babylon and the army encampments around the city: "The king is dead!" Bewilderment mingled with fear, and some remembered how even the rumor of his death, two years earlier in India, had almost provoked mutiny from the Macedonian regiments. They had been uncertain as to their future and far from home; their situation was not much different now. Would the king stage yet another miraculous recovery to cement the loyalty of his troops and enhance his aura of divinity? Or was the rumor true, and was bloodshed sure to follow?

Only two days earlier, many of his men had insisted on seeing him with their own eyes. They were troubled by the thought that their king was already dead, after more than a week of reported illness, and that for complex court reasons the truth was being concealed. Apart from rumors, all they had heard were the bland bulletins issued by Alexander's staff, to the effect that the king was ill but alive. Knowing that he was in the palace, they had more or less forced their way past his bodyguards. They had been allowed to file past the shrouded bed, where a pale figure waved feebly at them.[1] But this time there was no contradictory report, and no waving hand. As time passed, it became clear that this time it was true: Alexander the Great, conquering king and savior god, was dead.

At the time of his death in Babylon, around 3.30 p.m. on June 11, 323 BCE, Alexander was just short of thirty-three years old. He had recklessly exposed himself to danger time after time, but apart from war wounds—more than one of which was potentially fatal, especially in those days of inadequate doctoring—he had hardly been ill in his life and was as fit as any of the veterans in his army.

How had such a man fallen ill? True, there had been a lot of drinking recently, both in celebration of the return to civilization and to drown the memory of Hephaestion's death (which, ironically, had been brought on or caused by excessive drinking). This boyhood friend had been the only man he could trust, his second-in-command, and the one true love of his life. But heavy drinking was expected of Macedonian kings, and Alexander had also become king of Persia, where, again, it was considered a sign of virility to be able to drink one's courtiers under the table. If anyone was inured to heavy drinking, it was Alexander, and his symptoms do not fit alcohol poisoning. Excessive drinking, however, along with grief and old wounds (especially the lung that was perforated in India), may have weakened his system.

The accounts of his symptoms are puzzling. They are fairly precise, but do not perfectly fit any recognizable cause. One innocent possibility is that he died of malaria. He had fallen ill ten years previously in Cilicia, which was notorious for its malaria up until the 1950s. Perhaps he had a fatal recurrence of the disease in Babylon.[2] More dramatically, the reported symptoms are also compatible with the effects of white hellebore, a slow-acting poison. The incomprehensibility of Alexander's death to many people, and its propaganda potential, led very quickly to rumors of poisoning, especially since this was not an uncommon event among the Macedonian and eastern dynasties. And, as in an Agatha Christie novel, there were plenty of people close at hand who might have liked to see him dead. It was not just that some of them entertained world-spanning ambitions, soon to be revealed. It was more that Alexander's recent paranoid purge of his friends and officials, and his megalomaniacal desire for conquest and yet more conquest, could have turned even some of those closest to him.

Now or later, Alexander's mother stirred the pot from Epirus, southwest of Macedon. For some years, Olympias had been in voluntary exile from Macedon, back in her native Molossia (the mountainous region of Epirus whose kings, at this moment in Epirote history, were the de facto rulers of the Epirote League). On his departure for the east, Alexander had left a veteran general of his father's, Antipater, as viceroy in charge of his European possessions for the duration of his campaigns—Macedon, Thessaly, Thrace, and Greece. Unable to be supreme in Macedon, and irrevocably hostile to Antipater, Olympias returned to the foundation of her power. But she never stopped plotting her return to the center. She was widely known to have been involved in a number of high-profile assassinations, and was a plausible candidate for the invisible hand behind the murder of her husband, Philip II, in 336, since it seemed as though he was planning to dislodge her and Alexander from their position as favorites.

Olympias, then, knew exactly where to point the finger over her son's death. And she had a plausible case: not long before his death Alexander had ordered Antipater replaced, largely on the grounds of his "regal aspirations."[3] Like many of Alexander's actions in his last months, this order was not easily justifiable: already over seventy-five years old, Antipater had served three Macedonian kings and, despite limited resources, he had done a good job of leaving Alexander free to concentrate on eastern conquest. He had defeated the Persian fleet at sea and quelled a Thracian rebellion and a major Greek uprising (though even then, in 331, Alexander had sneeringly dismissed this as a "battle of mice").[4] Nevertheless, Antipater was to be relieved by Craterus, Alexander's favorite since the death of Hephaestion, and was to bring fresh Macedonian troops out to Babylon.

Recently, however, such summonses had acquired the habit of turning into traps. Antipater had good reason to think that he would be executed on some charge or other, just as other powerful and seemingly loyal officials had been. Unhinged by Hephaestion's death in October 324, Alexander had instigated a veritable reign of terror against even incipient signs of independence among his marshals. Moreover, to strengthen Olympias's case, two of Antipater's sons had long been in Babylon—and one of them, Iolaus, was well placed to act as a poisoner, since he was Alexander's cupbearer. And Alexander's fatal illness had begun immediately after a heavy drinking session. Indeed, shortly after news of Alexander's death reached Athens, the anti-Macedonian politician Hyperides proposed honors for Iolaus precisely for having done away with the king. Yet another of Antipater's sons, Cassander, had arrived only a few weeks earlier, presumably to plead for his father's retention in Macedon. His mission had not gone well. Unfamiliar with the changes that had recently taken place in Alexander's court, he had fallen out with the king over his insistence on obeisance from his courtiers, and Alexander had publicly humiliated him in return.[5]

Whatever the facts, it was a perfect opportunity for Olympias to sow mischief against her chief enemies. Antipater was compelled to respond: before long, someone in his camp published an account of Alexander's last days that was supposed to be the official diary of the king's secretary, Eumenes of Cardia. The document downplayed the idea that the king had died an unnatural death, and stressed the heavy drinking, while appearing to suggest that this was nothing unusual; it hinted at Alexander's grief over Hephaestion, and at an unspecified fever that carried him off.[6]

But even if Olympias was wrong about Antipater and his sons, there were plenty of others who could feel uncomfortable if people started speculating and looking for motives. And even if she was wrong that Alexander's death was part of a power play by certain individuals, she was right that his death would free the ambitions of those who had been closest to her son—those, at any rate, who were still alive after thirteen years of hard campaigning and ruthless purges. As it turned out, even bloodthirsty Alexander would have been proud of the scope of their ambitions: they embroiled the known world in decades of war.

THE CONQUESTS OF ALEXANDER

Philip II came to the Macedonian throne in 359. Within four or five years, by a combination of diplomacy, assassination, and military force, he had warded off internal and external threats and united the various cantons under his autocratic rule. It became clear that the Greek states to the south were his next target. He improved on Greek infantry tactics and developed the army until he had a stupendous fighting force at his personal command. He could call on two thousand cavalry and thirty thousand soldiers trained to high professional standards and equipped with superior weaponry. Many Greek states would have to unite in order to field an army of comparable size. Their failure to do so meant that he could pick them off one by one, or league by league.

Athens became the focus of what little resistance there was to Macedon, but it was the last gasp of traditional Greek city-state autonomy. War, financed in part by Persia, was waged in a ragged fashion by Athens and its allies against Philip, until in 338 he marched south. Alongside Boeotian troops, Athenians faced the Macedonians at Chaeronea in Boeotia. Numbers were almost equal. The battle was so hotly contested that the elite Theban Sacred Band died nearly to a man, and the Athenians too suffered crippling casualties.

Almost the first action Philip took as ruler of southern Greece was to form the conquered states into a league, the Hellenic League or League of Corinth, with himself at its head. Interstate conflict was outlawed, and so Philip, a Macedonian king, took the first step toward

Greek statehood, finally attained over two thousand years later. In return for votes on the league council, every state was obliged, when called upon, to supply troops for military expeditions. He next got the league to appoint him supreme commander for the long-promised "Greek" war against Persia, in retaliation for a century and a half of Persian interference in Greek affairs and two destructive invasions, in 490 and 480 BCE. Though that was distant history, the Greeks had never forgotten or forgiven; Persia was the common enemy, and public speakers ever since had fanned the flames of Greek supremacism and revenge.

But Philip was murdered in 336, on the eve of his journey east, at his daughter Cleopatra's wedding party. It is a sordid tale, but worth repeating for the insight it affords into the Macedonian court. The killer, Pausanias, was one of Philip's Bodyguards and his lover. He had aroused the ire of Attalus, one of Philip's principal generals, and Attalus allegedly arranged for Pausanias to be gang-raped.[7] Philip refused to punish Attalus at this critical juncture, when he was about to lead a division of the army of invasion. Pausanias therefore killed the king. The water is further muddied by the fact that Attalus was a bitter enemy of Olympias and Alexander; it is not implausible to suggest that Olympias encouraged Pausanias's desire for revenge.

In any case, both the Macedonian throne and the eastern expedition devolved on Philip's son, Alexander III, soon to be known as "the Great." In 334, Alexander crossed the Hellespont into Asia. His first act was to cast a spear into the soil: Asia was to be "spear-won land," his by right of conquest. In a series of amazing and closely fought battles, he crushed the Persians and took control of the empire.

The battle at the Granicus River in 334 took care of the Persian armies of Asia Minor; four satraps (provincial governors), three members of the king's family, and the Greek commander of the Persians' mercenaries lay dead on the battlefield. The remnants of the king's western army were ordered to fall back to Babylonia, where a fresh army was mustering. In 333 Alexander annihilated the Persians near Issus, not far from the border between Cilicia and Syria. It was a notable victory: not only were Persian losses serious, but eight thousand of Darius's mercenaries deserted in despair after the battle, the Persian king's immediate family were captured, and Alexander enriched himself with the king's war chest.

Alexander returned to Phoenicia and protected his rear by taking Egypt in 332. By the time he returned from Egypt and marched east again, Darius had had almost two years in which to gather another army. Battle was joined near the village of Gaugamela, close to the Tigris, on October 1, 331. As usual, in addition to the formidable Macedonian fighting machine, both luck and superior strategy were on Alexander's side, and despite its vastly superior numbers the Persian army was eventually routed. It was the end of the empire; it had been ruled by the Achaemenid house for over two hundred years. The king fled to Ecbatana in Media, and Alexander proclaimed himself Lord of Asia in Darius's stead. Babylon and Susa opened their gates without a fight, and the rest of the empire lay open to his unstoppable energy. A minor defeat near Persepolis hardly delayed his taking the city, the old capital of the Persian heartland. In the summer of 330 he marched on Ecbatana. Darius fled before him with a scorched-earth strategy, but was killed by some of his own satraps and courtiers.

The conspirators fought on, in a bloody and ultimately futile war, basing themselves in the far eastern satrapy of Bactria. By 325 Alexander had pacified Bactria and extended the empire deep into modern Pakistan (ancient "India"), but his troops had had enough and he was forced to turn back. An appalling and unjustifiable desert journey decimated his ranks and undermined his popularity, which was further weakened by measures that were perceived as an attempt to share power with native elites. In Susa, in April 324, he and all the senior Macedonians and Greeks in his retinue took eastern wives. Alexander, already married to a Bactrian princess called Rhoxane, took two further wives, daughters of the last two Persian kings. But to many Macedonians and Greeks, all non-Greeks were by that very fact inferior beings.

By the time of his death, Alexander's empire of about five million square kilometers (roughly two million square miles) stretched patchily from the Danube to the Nile to the Indus. Modern terms show immediately the extraordinary nature of his achievement: the empire incorporated Greece, Bulgaria, much of Turkey, Lebanon, Syria, Israel/Palestine, Egypt, Iraq, Kuwait, Iran, Afghanistan, western Pakistan, and parts of Turkmenistan, Tajikistan, and Uzbekistan, and he had received the submission of further kings and chieftains within and on the borders of the empire.

His territory was so vast that it helps to think of it in terms of a few major blocks of territory, defined not just by the geographical features such as mountain ranges or seas that formed their borders, but also by the fact that ripples spread by events within one block did not necessarily reach neighboring blocks. The European territories—Macedon, Greece, and Thrace—constitute one such block, separated from Asia by the narrow and critical Hellespont; Asia Minor is another, bordered to the east and southeast by formidable mountains. With its natural defenses of desert and sea, Egypt always considered itself a separate unit, and even under Achaemenid rule often strove for independence. Syria west of the Euphrates was caught between Asia and Egypt, and was long a bone of contention. Finally, east of the Euphrates the eastern satrapies stretched all the way to the Indus River in Pakistan.[8]

DIVINE KINGSHIP

The astonishing energy of the campaigns was due entirely to Alexander's character. He was a driven man, and world conquest was his focus. He slaughtered by the thousands those who stood in his way. He thinned the ranks even—especially—of those closest to him at the slightest suspicion of conspiracy, or even disagreement with major policy decisions. One erstwhile close friend he ran through with a spear in a drunken rage. He exposed himself recklessly to danger on numerous occasions, not as a calculated way to win his troops' devotion (though it certainly did that) but because he was sure of his destiny, and certain that the king of the gods, Zeus, would protect him until that destiny had been fulfilled. No wonder he was so furious when his troops mutinied in 325 in India and his will was for once thwarted.

Such rage, feigned or not, was part of Alexander's new image. Shortly after the victory at Gaugamela in 331, Alexander was proclaimed "Lord of Asia," but this did not mean that he felt he was merely replacing the Achaemenids. That would have been tactless, and poor propaganda, since he had come to eliminate the hated Persian rulers, not to replace them. In fact, in styling himself Lord or King of Asia, he was marking a break between himself and the Achaemenids, whose title had been "King of Persia." By the same token, he adopted at this time the diadem—a plain hair band—as the symbol of his kingship, not the Persian upright tiara.

In addition to these symbolic differences, Alexander took practical steps to present himself as a different kind of king, not quite in the Persian or the Macedonian mold. He adopted at least some of the regalia of Achaemenid kingship, and took over other Persian practices as well, such as limiting access to his presence, having his subjects salaam or make obeisance before him, and seating himself on a golden throne (totally unfamiliar to Macedonian tradition) for official meetings. This was all cunningly done. He adopted enough Persian customs for him to be acceptable to his new subjects (and it helped that, at least as a temporary expedient, he allowed some easterners privileged positions in his court), while at the same time sending a clear message to the Macedonians: I am no longer quite a Macedonian king. They could only see him as an eastern king—that is, a despot—and that is exactly what he intended. He was deliberately developing Macedonian kingship toward a more autocratic model, in how he presented himself and how he expected his subjects to respond to him.[9]

It is hard to avoid the conclusion that power and success had gone to his head. He began to present himself as Heracles, the ancestor of all the Argeads, and he chose to blaze like Achilles, from whom he was descended on his mother's side. Both these heroes had carried out legendary missions in Asia, and he saw himself also as an avatar of Dionysus, who was said to have single-handedly conquered India. Alexander allowed himself to be called the son of Zeus, and Olympias had encouraged him from an early age to think of his true father as Zeus, not the mortal Philip, so that he would have the same dual mortal and immortal parentage as Heracles of legend. There is no doubt that Alexander exploited the idea of his godhood for political reasons, but there can also be little doubt that he found the idea attractive in itself.

The practice of obeisance (*proskynēsis*) was particularly infuriating to his Macedonian and Greek courtiers. They bowed to no one except the gods—but that was the point: Alexander now felt himself to be a god. To say that Alexander was larger than life is to state the obvious, but he broke the bounds of both humanness and humaneness because he was convinced that he was on a god-given mission. Many of his subjects were also ready to acknowledge his godhood, not just because they had a tradition of regarding kings as gods or the gods' instruments, but because Alexander's achievements were incredible, and incredible achievement was precisely the mark of divinity. The petty worldview of the Greek states with their pocket handkerchief–sized territories and focus on "our sea," the Aegean, was exploded forever. Alexander opened up the whole known world and tore down barriers. Boundless opportunities emerged for Greeks to improve their lives of poverty.

The world would never be the same again, and such total transformation was naturally taken to be the work of a god—not just in Alexander's case but, as we shall see, in the case of his Successors too. The gods brought benefits, as Alexander, for instance, freed the Greek cities of the Asia Minor seaboard from the threat or reality of Persian rule, and so the Asiatic Greeks were the first to worship him as Savior.

Not long before his death, Alexander himself had also ordered the Greek cities of the Balkan peninsula to follow suit; Athens and others complied. Alexander's deeds made everything about him talismanic. The history of the next thirty or forty years is, from certain perspectives, the history of his influence, of the lingering presence of his ghost.

THE SUCCESSION PROBLEM

Succession to the Macedonian throne was often an untidy business, littered with coups and corpses, but even by Macedonian standards this one was far from straightforward. Succession depended on birth into the royal house, nomination by the outgoing king (if he had time), the agreement of the king's inner circle or council of Companions, and the approval of the citizen or army assembly.

In the first place, there was no obvious heir. It was unthinkable that the next king should not be an Argead, born from a male Argead, for the house had ruled Macedon for over three hundred years, but there were few candidates. Alexander had left few rivals alive. He had a half brother Arrhidaeus, roughly the same age as himself, from another of Philip's many wives, but Arrhidaeus suffered from some mental defect—not enough to incapacitate him, but enough to make him liable to embarrassing behavior on public occasions.[10] We will never know all the details, but that he *was* defective in some way is clear from the facts that Alexander had let him live and that, even though he was an adult, the question of his succession to the throne was always accompanied by debate over who should be his "protector." He seems never to have acted of his own accord rather than being manipulated by those close to him.

Then there was a four-year-old boy called Heracles, a good Argead name, since Heracles of legend was supposed to be their remote ancestor. His mother was Alexander's former mistress, Barsine. No one doubted that Heracles was Alexander's son, but Alexander had never married Barsine or formally acknowledged the boy as his own, and so he was an unlikely candidate. Besides, he had the black mark against him of being not fully Macedonian, since his mother was half Iranian. Of Alexander's three wives, Rhoxane was pregnant, and due to deliver in a couple of months' time. If she came to term—she had already miscarried once—and if the child was male, he would become a serious claimant to the throne, though again he would be a half-breed.

In the second place, Alexander left no will, or rather failed to make his will known. A will appeared some years later, but it was certainly a forgery, cleverly designed for propaganda purposes.[11] But why did he not write one in those last days, when he must have suspected that he was dying? Either he was too weak (he seems to have lost the power of speech, but he was able, as already mentioned, to gesture at his men), or it was suppressed by schemers close to him, or he was just irresponsible. But in his dying moments he silently passed his signet ring to his second-in-command in Babylon, Perdiccas, as though to assign him the responsibility for whatever would happen next.

In the third place, the crisis had blown up in Babylon, but Babylon was only one of three centers of power. Roughly the same number of Macedonian troops were to be found in mountain-girt and mineral-rich Cilicia and in Macedon itself. Craterus was in Cilicia, where he had an army of more than ten thousand veterans and the armament that Alexander had been building up for his next world-conquering project. He also had access to the financial resources of one of the main treasuries of the empire, secure in the mountain citadel of Cyinda (location unknown). And then, scarcely less wealthy in natural resources than Babylonia, there was Macedon itself, where Antipater ruled supreme. Whatever solution was found to the succession problem was going to have to take account of many disparate interests.

THE THREAT OF CHAOS

Even apart from the specific problem of the succession, which urgently needed to be addressed by the senior officers and courtiers assembled in Babylon, there was the general background problem. Alexander's "empire" was an unstable and unformed entity. As it stood, it was an artificial aggregate of the twenty satrapies (often nation-sized in themselves) of the Achaemenid empire and a multitude of minor principalities, tribal unions, confederacies, city-states, and so on, with varying relationships and strategies toward the central power. If it was to be a whole, it was critically in need of organization, or at least official endorsement and maintenance of the status quo, but Alexander's exclusive focus on campaigning and conquering had precluded his doing much beyond a little tinkering. For instance, while taking over the existing satrapal structure of the Persian empire, he divided administrative from military functions within the satrapies, so that each could check the other and there would be at least one senior Macedonian in each place. But, generally speaking, Alexander's empire had not advanced beyond the stage of military occupation; there was no capital city, little civil service, and little administration beyond the emergency preparations any commander takes to protect his rear while he continues on campaign.

Alexander did, however, have a loyal and intelligent secretary, Eumenes of Cardia. The Greek had also served Philip II in the same capacity for the last seven years of the great king's life. All the official correspondence of the empire came through his office. He could keep the empire running, short of emergencies, but he could not make the critical decisions, which needed a king's attention. Alexander had also created a central finance office, run by his long-trusted friend Harpalus. But when Alexander returned from the east, Harpalus absconded. He had been setting himself up almost as a king in Babylon, and he saw how Alexander was treating even those whom he merely suspected of independent ambitions. Harpalus took with him five thousand talents (with the spending power of about three billion dollars)[12] and six thousand mercenaries. Even worse, he took his expertise. For all intents and purposes, then, there was no administration beyond the will of the king himself. *L'état, c'est moi*, as a later absolute monarch was to claim; Alexander was the administration, but he was dead.

Shortly after Alexander's death, Eumenes gave Perdiccas Alexander's "Last Plans," sketched out over the past few months—at any rate, before Alexander knew he was dying, since all the plans had him at their helm.[13] The only important one, militarily and politically speaking, was the plan to conquer all of North Africa, including the flourishing Phoenician-founded city of Carthage (and then Spain, Sicily, and southern Italy); this involved not just amassing a huge army and solving its supply problems, but the construction of a vast fleet of one thousand warships in Cilicia and Phoenicia and laying a trans-African road along the north coast from Egypt to Carthage and beyond. Other plans focused on piety: grand temples were to be constructed, an enormous pyre was to be raised in honor of Hephaestion, a pyramid was to be built for Philip II. A final set of plans involved the foundation of further cities. Alexander had already founded a number of cities—Alexandria in Egypt being the most important, but there were others in the eastern provinces[14]—but this time there was a new twist: any city founded in the west of the empire was to gain a portion of its population from the east, and vice versa, to encourage intermingling and intermarriage, and presumably also to break up potentially troublesome populations.

None of these plans seems to have as their purpose the stabilization of the empire. On the contrary, the most significant of them would, in the short term, destabilize it. What provisions would Alexander have taken for the administration of the notoriously rebellious satrapies of the east while he was thousands of miles away attempting to conquer the western Mediterranean? How would he persuade people to move from their homes and populate his new foundations? The movement of native populations would surely have required military force, or its threat, just as Adolf Hitler's *Lebensraum* program of the displacement of native populations in Eastern Europe by Germans was predicated on German military superiority. It seems that Alexander had chosen to conquer the world rather than consolidate his vulnerable gains.

The brilliant youth who had set out to conquer the east in 334 had, as we have seen, come to adopt a more autocratic, Persian style of kingship. Perhaps the most immediately disruptive of the new acts of autocracy was the so-called Exiles Decree.[15] The league of Greek cities that Philip had put in place in 338 was hardly a league of equals, since Philip himself was the leader and arranged things so that his wishes would be carried out. Nevertheless, the setup was that every member state had a voice, and decisions were reached by consultation and approval at one of the league's regular meetings. This may have been a charade, but it was one which all the parties were prepared to work with. Despite this, early in 324 Alexander took a unilateral decision that would have a drastic effect on a number of Greek states.

All the Greek states were to take back their exiles. This would create, at the very least, administrative and judicial chaos, and possibly even political turmoil, since a lot of the exiles had been banished for political reasons. Many had been working abroad as professional soldiers. Moreover, Alexander threatened recalcitrant states with military action: "We have instructed Antipater to use force in the case of cities that refuse to comply."[16] Alexander was behaving like a tyrant toward the very cities in whose interests he had claimed to conquer the east, and was riding roughshod over the conditions of the league. The decree was an attempt to address a genuine problem: there were large numbers of rootless men, who threatened disorder all over the Greek world. But it would also ensure that every Greek city had people within it who had reason to be grateful to Alexander personally.

Alexander was right to anticipate trouble. It was not just the high-handed manner in which he issued the directive, but also the fact that at least two states would be particularly severely affected by the decree. The Aetolians had forcibly taken over Oeniadeae, a port belonging to their Acarnanian neighbors, expelled its inhabitants, and repopulated it with their own people; the Athenians had done the same with the island of Samos, over thirty years previously. Not only would they have to find some way to accommodate their returning citizens, but they would lose these important gains. When, during the course of his flight, Harpalus arrived in Athens (where he was an honorary citizen), the mood, as a result of the Exiles Decree, was ripe for rebellion, and he immediately offered to finance their war effort.

Trouble was looming, then, in Greece. In fact, it is possible that one of the reasons for Alexander's displeasure with Antipater was that, nine months later, he had not yet shown much interest in enforcing the Exiles Decree. Antipater was a hard ruler of Greece, and had preferred to see oligarchic administrations in the Greek cities, backed up where necessary by garrisons. In one sense, then, the Exiles Decree undermined Antipater, since a number of the returning exiles would be precisely men who had been sent into exile by his puppets. One of the tasks Craterus had been given, once he had replaced Antipater, was to ensure the freedom of the Greeks; a strategy of noninterference meant that he would be able to stand on the sidelines and watch as rival factions and feuds tore the cities apart.

But Greece was likely to be only one trouble spot. Alexander's despotism also created the conditions for the brutal and divisive warfare that followed his death. By Macedonian tradition, the main check on the absolute power of the king was his entourage of Companions (or "Friends," as subsequent kings called them), noble or ennobled Macedonians and a few Greeks; Alexander had added a few easterners. They acted as his advisers, and carried out whatever administrative duties were required of them; they served as staff officers in time of war, ambassadors, governors of provinces, representatives at religious festivals, and so on. In other words, they formed the basic structure of the Macedonian state. At the very least, then, one might have expected Alexander to have ensured that his Companions formed a tightly knit and harmonious cabinet. Instead, he sowed dissent.

One aspect of the problem was that, in acting autocratically, he left his Companions with less responsibility, and was beginning to make flattery rather than friendship the criterion for inclusion in the inner circle of his court. Any given decision would therefore meet with approval from some of the court and disapproval from the rest. The most divisive issue was Alexander's increasing orientalization. Many, including Craterus, agreed with Cassander and did not think it right that Alexander should demand the humiliating rite of obeisance from

Macedonians and Greeks, even if his eastern subjects were prepared to go along with it. Many more were disturbed by his explicit demand that he should be accorded divine honors.

Then there was the purge. Of the twenty satraps of the empire, Alexander had just killed six and replaced two more within a few months. Four more conveniently died, of illness or wounds; two more provinces had changes of governor, without our knowing the circumstances. Those who replaced the dead or deposed satraps were often yes-men.

By the end of the purge, only Egypt, Lydia, and Phrygia had long-standing governors. Alexander had left an old Egyptian hand, Cleomenes of Naucratis, in charge of the province in 331, where he had proved an effective milker of its resources, and in 334, on his way east, he had entrusted Phrygia, and protection of the route back to Macedon, to Antigonus. Known as Monophthalmus, the One-Eyed, for an old war wound, Antigonus was a sixty-year-old former Companion of Philip II. He had served Alexander well, by protecting his rear as he advanced east, and above all by repelling a Persian counteroffensive after Issus. As the years went by, his governorship of Phrygia had expanded into a supervisory role over all Asia Minor. But if Antipater could be replaced in Macedon, neither Cleomenes nor Antigonus, nor Menander in Lydia, could be sure of his position. Alexander had made every man of power in his empire afraid of his peers and envious of others' success. At the time of his death, a number of satraps, old and new, were either in Babylon or on their way, summoned by Alexander to bring fresh troops or for other, unknown purposes—to act as judges, perhaps, in Antipater's case.

Like all despots, Alexander was showing signs of living in fear of effective men, in case they should turn against him. But despite the purge and the war losses, there were still men of destiny around him. Naturally so, for they had conquered the east with him, and many had been with him from the start. Most of them had grown enormously wealthy; many had courts and courtiers of their own. They had no desire to lose either their wealth or their power, and they had become used, in the manner typical of courtiers, to competing with one another for power. "Never before that time did Macedon, or indeed any other nation, produce so rich a crop of brilliant men, men who had been picked out with such care, first by Philip and then by Alexander, that they seemed chosen less as comrades in arms than as successors to the throne."[17] Many of these men had known each other since childhood; all of them had bonded in the way soldiers do in the course of a long, hard campaign. But such sentiments could be crushed by personal ambition.

So Alexander sowed the seeds of the civil wars that followed his death. Later, a rumor arose that on his deathbed he invited a deadly struggle over his empire by bequeathing it to "the strongest" and, punning on the tradition of holding an athletic competition to commemorate a great man, by saying, "I foresee funeral contests indeed after my death." Though capturing the spirit of macho Macedonian culture, the story is hardly likely to be true. But it was written by someone who saw clearly that the hounds of the wars that followed had been unleashed by Alexander.[18]

The Babylon Conferences

IMMEDIATELY AFTER ALEXANDER's death, while the embalmers got busy with his body, those of his senior officers who were present in Babylon met and began to make arrangements for the future. The power play began. The marshals of the empire, each with his own network of alliances, considered their own and their rivals' prospects. There were no guarantees of success. A bid for power was as likely to end in violent death as it was in a slice, or the whole, of the empire.

The Macedonian king was protected by special units within the army, but "Bodyguard" was also an honorary post, a way of rewarding and describing his closest advisers and protectors. As his father had before him, Alexander restricted the number of Bodyguards to seven, with losses immediately made up. Peucestas, however, became an honorary member for saving Alexander's life in India; unlike the others, he was also awarded a satrapy. There were eight, then, but after Hephaestion's unexpected death in 324 his place in the inner circle was not filled by anyone else. Who would have dared suggest a candidate to grieving Alexander? Since Peucestas, along with other satraps, had been summoned from his province to bring fresh troops, all the Bodyguards were together in Babylon: Aristonous, Leonnatus, Lysimachus, Peithon, Perdiccas, Peucestas, and Ptolemy. All of them were roughly the same age as Alexander, in the prime of their lives. Five of them would strive to become kings in their own right; two would succeed; only one would establish a dynasty.

It was both Macedonian and Persian tradition that kings should be generous to their closest companions; it was a form of display, of confirmation of power, as well as serving to secure valued relationships.[1] These were the men Alexander had felt the greatest need to have around him, and they had been rewarded with wealth and power, earned by conspicuous bravery and loyalty in the course of the campaigns. They had become accustomed to living with privilege.

In any case, they had long been familiar with wealth and power: Leonnatus and Perdiccas were royal in their own right, from the princely houses of cantons of Upper Macedon; Ptolemy had been brought up in Philip's court alongside the heir; Perdiccas had been Alexander's second-in-command and chief cavalry officer since Hephaestion's death; all were from the very highest echelons of Macedonian society. By virtue of their elevation by Alexander, each of them was the head of his clan, and therefore a potential dynast. Their personal ambitions were bound by an oath of loyalty to Alexander, but the bond had dissolved on his death. Now, given the certainty of a troubled succession, each of them had to decide where to place his loyalty and that of his subordinates, or whether to make a bid for power himself.

There were also senior men present who were not Bodyguards. Seleucus had for the past seven years been the commander of the crack infantry regiment, the Shield-bearers, three thousand strong. Eumenes of Cardia, Alexander's secretary and archivist, was joined, as a Greek, by Nearchus of Crete, the admiral of Alexander's Indian fleet, based in Babylon. Nor were there only Macedonians and Greeks; as a matter of policy (largely insurance policy), Alexander had included a number of easterners in the highest court circles. But they will play little part in what follows—such an exiguous part that it is clear that, as far as almost everyone was concerned apart from Alexander, they were there on sufferance. After Alexander's death, they were never going to be contenders; all the principal resources were in the hands of the new conquerors.

Some very important people were not in Babylon. Apart from Olympias, brooding in Molossia, two leading men were absent, though they were on everyone's minds. These two were Antipater and Craterus. By virtue of his viceregal position, Antipater was the most powerful man in the empire after Alexander—or at least he had been until Alexander had ordered him replaced. Craterus, as we have seen, had been given two specific jobs: he was to take back home ten thousand Macedonian infantry veterans and 1,500 cavalry, and he was to replace

Antipater as viceroy in Europe and head of the League of Corinth. Antipater, meanwhile, was to bring fresh Macedonian troops east to replace those Craterus had repatriated.

But Alexander's death found Craterus still lingering in Cilicia, halfway home, some months after he had been sent on his way. Why? The silence of our sources has attracted a few more or less sinister answers, but the probable truth is relatively banal. In the first place, when Craterus set off for Macedon, he was so ill that there was some doubt whether he would even get there, so he may have been recuperating for a while. At any rate, he had certainly recovered enough to play a vigorous part in what followed. If he had died, his replacement would have been Polyperchon, another senior officer who was being repatriated.

In the second place, Cilicia was to be the headquarters of Alexander's planned conquest of the western Mediterranean, but it was not entirely stable. The traitor Harpalus, for instance, had recently made Tarsus his temporary home. Craterus, then, had been busy ensuring the stability of the region and supervising the preparations for the conquest of the western Mediterranean. But even if this was the main reason for his delay, he might also have been unwilling to carry out his mission. After all, it was not impossible that Antipater, relying on his long-established power base, would simply refuse to be deposed, in which case Craterus's arrival might provoke civil war in his homeland.

So Antipater and Craterus were on everyone's minds. What would happen to Antipater now? How would Craterus react to the news of Alexander's death? Would either or both of them make a bid for power? Antipater had Macedonian troops and the money to hire mercenaries; in Cilicia, Craterus had the men and the money and the armament, several experienced officers who would certainly side with him, and the Cilician fleet, commanded by Cleitus. And he was enormously popular with the Macedonian troops.

There were somewhere between ten and fifteen thousand Macedonian troops stationed in Babylon at the time. There were also thousands of native troops and mercenaries (with tens of thousands more scattered around Asia and Asia Minor, chiefly on garrison duty), but it was the Macedonians, and the soldiers trained in the use of Macedonian weaponry and tactics, who made the difference. Not only were they the most powerful fighting force in the known world, and therefore a critical resource for an ambitious man, but they represented the end of the chain in the Macedonian process of selecting a king. What normally happened was that the outgoing king nominated his successor, by word or by deed, and his choice was debated and fought over by his inner circle of Companions until consensus was reached. Since the Companions ruled all or most of the country, and had the loyalty of their forces, that was effectively the end of the matter, but the decision was finally presented to an assembly of however many ordinary, landowning, Macedonian citizens could be rounded up at relatively short notice, who vocally acclaimed the new king.

The sequence could, in theory, be broken at two points—the approval of the Companions and the acclamation of the assembly. On the bloody occasions when such a breach happened, it was invariably the result of noble disapproval rather than refusal by the assembly to give its acclamation. But the possibility was there, and in Babylon in June of 323 BCE the Macedonian troops were the assembled Macedonian people. Moreover, as the years of the eastern campaigns had passed, even the Macedonian troops had begun to behave more and more like mercenaries. Factors such as military prowess and the ability to enrich them might, or might soon, weigh as heavily with them as Argead blood or the king's and his councilors' approval. If any of Alexander's successors was to succeed, he would need the wealth and military charisma to gain and keep troops, as well as the ruthlessness to use them against fellow Macedonians.

CONFRONTATION AT THE CONFERENCE TABLE

The night after Alexander's death was spent in mourning by Macedonians and Persians alike. All fires were ritually extinguished to mark the extinction of their king.[2] The next morning, the Bodyguards and Companions met in the palace; there may have been as many as fifty men present. The whole business reeks of haste. Someone, probably Perdiccas, the recipient of the ring, was pushing things along fast, without waiting for Craterus and Polyperchon to return to Babylon to attend the meeting, or to see if aged Antipater would make the long journey from Macedon. By the time they even got to hear of Alexander's death, the decisions taken in Babylon would have become established facts.

Perdiccas was worried about how long the troops would abide a period of uncertainty. They were far from home, under the blazing sun, with no leader or paymaster, and with idle time on their hands. He could also argue that wherever the king was—or, in this case, had been—was the administrative center, and so that they had the right to meet and make unilateral decisions that would hugely affect others' lives.

It was meant to be a private meeting, more council than general assembly, and it was meant, in typical Macedonian fashion, to be followed by an army assembly. The senior officers would come to a decision about the succession, and they would put it to the assembly for acclamation. But a large number of junior officers and rank-and-file soldiers pushed their way into the palace compound too, agitated, grieving, numbed by the enormity of what had happened. The soldiers' cries were an audible reminder to those inside the palace that their decisions would generate either calm or chaos, and information about what was going on inside the palace percolated outside, while the views of the mob were also able to influence the meeting inside.[3]

Perdiccas had stage-managed the meeting in high ritual fashion. The noble Companions were to deliberate in the presence of Alexander's empty throne, which was adorned with the royal robes and armor, and the diadem, the simple hair band that Alexander had made the symbol of kingship. And he opened the meeting with a moment of silence in which he added to the display the signet ring that Alexander himself had handed him not long before his death.[4] Reverence for the symbols of kingship was a Macedonian tradition. It was a solemn moment, but they had to put aside such feelings and get down to some hard negotiation.

The critical assumption of the meeting was that the task for the foreseeable future was to keep hold of all of the territories acquired by Alexander, and the corollary of this was that those areas within the empire that remained unsubdued should be brought into line, and borders and other trouble spots should be secured. There was work to be done, but also a hierarchy to be established, with Alexander's heir at its head. The existing administration was bound to be shaken up, and there would be plum jobs available for those who played the game of power well. But above all they had to determine whose domain it was in the first place.

Perdiccas used the weight of his authority to argue that they should all wait and see whether Rhoxane's unborn child was a boy, and then make it king. She would come to term in a couple of months, and he hoped and expected not only to hold the reins of power until then, but to act as regent afterward, until the boy came of age—if the boy were allowed to come of age. No doubt Perdiccas remembered that Philip

II had gained the Macedonian throne after acting as regent; no doubt he was already hoping that Rhoxane would give birth to a girl, so that power could more easily remain in his hands.

The first hint that Perdiccas was not going to have things all his own way—and of the tensions just below the surface of the meeting—came from Nearchus. He agreed that it was unthinkable to consider anyone but a boy with Argead blood a legitimate successor, but argued that the situation was too tense to wait even the few weeks until Rhoxane should give birth. He proposed, then, that Heracles should be made king. This was Nearchus's bid for power, since at the Susa weddings of the previous year he had gained as his wife Heracles' half sister. Eumenes, who had gained Heracles' aunt, was silent; he was Perdiccas's man, or at any rate an Argead loyalist who was naturally inclined to favor Rhoxane's offspring. Nearchus's suggestion was shouted down, on the grounds that Alexander himself had never acknowledged the child as his own and therefore as a possible heir.

Ptolemy pointed out the problem with both Heracles and Rhoxane's unborn son: they were not full-blooded Macedonians, and therefore would not be acceptable in all quarters. Some would wonder what had been the point of conquering the east, if an easterner was then given the throne. Ptolemy suggested a compromise solution. He wanted to see the inner circle of Alexander's advisers become a junta of marshals; they had been Alexander's council in war and peace, and so they should continue to meet in the presence of Alexander's famous golden throne, and to deliberate and issue decrees for the empire, just as they always had done. This suggestion was an attempt on Ptolemy's part to gain at least equal power with the other members of his proposed junta for himself and his allies, chiefly Peithon and Leonnatus. Otherwise, and especially because he and Perdiccas were not on the best of terms, he could see himself becoming sidelined. The proposal was not as republican as it looked; spelled out, it meant that Alexander's Bodyguards and senior Companions would be assigned satrapies and other positions of responsibility, so that the most powerful of them, at least, would each in a sense be monarchs of their own kingdoms, but they would meet as a council when decisions had to be taken for the empire as a whole.

Ptolemy's impractical solution met, to Perdiccas's irritation, with considerable approval, presumably because more people present saw it as a way of gaining a slice of the pie themselves. An impasse was rapidly developing, created by the mutual distrust of the senior officers. Aristonous tried to tip the scales in Perdiccas's direction by suggesting that the unconstitutional irregularity of any kind of period without a true king could be avoided if Perdiccas himself were to succeed to the throne. This idea too was warmly welcomed; perhaps that is what Alexander had meant by handing his ring to Perdiccas, who was, after all, royal in his own right, even if not an Argead.

Perdiccas was tempted, but he was intelligent enough to realize that confrontation would inevitably follow his assumption of kingship. There were many who were loyal to the Argead line, and it would be easy for someone to challenge his right to the throne once Rhoxane's child was born. At the same time, if he had Rhoxane and her unborn child killed, he would court massive unpopularity. So he could not be king, but it appeared that he could not be regent of an unborn child either, and that any kind of interregnum might be unacceptable and unworkable. Even while he was hesitating and considering his options, Meleager, a respected infantry officer, was arguing against his or any other man's sole regency, on the grounds that it would be equivalent to non-Argead kingship.

So far, if our confusing sources have preserved at least in outline some traces of the actual debate, Alexander's half brother Arrhidaeus had not been mentioned as a candidate for kingship. But Arrhidaeus was, to put it patronizingly, a kind of mascot for the infantry, and a royal presence in their religious rituals. It became clear to those inside the palace that those outside would like to see Arrhidaeus on the throne: he was an adult, fully Macedonian Argead, and he was there in Babylon. He may even have already been given the honorary title of King of Babylon by Alexander.[5] There was no need for an interregnum.

Peithon, however, spoke for many in dismissing the idea that a half-wit should occupy the Macedonian throne. He suggested a less radical way out of the impasse than had been mentioned before, and one that recognized his friend Leonnatus's stature: Perdiccas and Leonnatus, as the two with the highest credentials, should act in Asia as regents for the boy king, Rhoxane's child, when he was born, while Antipater and Craterus should similarly be the guardians of the kingdom in Europe. After a little more debate, this was the position on which this first meeting settled.

PERDICCAS'S CHANCE

It is commonly said that a camel is a horse designed by committee; certainly Alexander's Companions had produced a camel. If anyone had stopped to think, it must have been obvious that the existence of four regents for the next eighteen years or so (or three regents, once aged Antipater had died) was no recipe for peace. And, although Perdiccas's lobby in the meeting had been powerful—in addition to Aristonous and Eumenes, he had the support of several very highly respected senior officers, including his younger brother Alcetas and Seleucus—he was not likely to be happy with the outcome. He had glimpsed and laid claim to sole power, only to be denied it. In short, the outcome of the first meeting looks like a temporary measure. Scheming undoubtedly continued behind the scenes.

Nevertheless, the Companions behaved as though they had found a solution. Delegates were chosen to present the decision of the meeting to the cavalry and the infantry. The cavalry made no demur, but the infantry was incensed. The officers who were sent to win them over, led by Meleager and a respected senior officer called Attalus, met with the overwhelming demand that Arrhidaeus be made king. The loyalty of the Macedonian infantry to the Argead line was impressive, and the fact that the cavalry was prepared to go along with the meeting's decision would hardly have weighed with them at all. Every ancient commander had to come to terms with the fact that his forces consisted of two groups who were perennially divided: the cavalry and all the senior officers came from the highest social classes, while the infantry was made up of peasant farmers. The two did not always see eye to eye, and sometimes even had to be coerced into making up a single fighting unit.

Meleager and Attalus saw an opportunity for themselves. As matters stood, they were not going to be major beneficiaries of the new dispensation. But perhaps the passion of the infantry could sweep them to power. Instead of merely reporting the decision to the troops for their acclamation, they threw in their lot with the infantry. Before long, they returned to the palace at the head of an armed mob, insisting that Arrhidaeus be made king; they had chosen the name "Philip" for him, to remake him in the image of his heroic father, so that he would be Philip III, King of the Macedonians. Meleager had Arrhidaeus prominently displayed beside him, dressed as Alexander, while he himself wore the insignia of a Bodyguard of the new king. Disturbingly, the infantry had usurped the barons' role and turned kingmaker, for the first time in Macedonian history. They had the right to acclaim a king, but never before had they effectively chosen one. Alexander's death had shaken fundamental structures.

The cavalry, however, remained loyal to their officers and refused to accept the infantry's choice. They were still committed to Rhoxane's unborn child. Civil war was about to erupt between the cavalry and the infantry, as it almost had in India two years earlier, just at rumors of Alexander's death. Within a day or two of his actual death, the champions of two rival candidates for the throne were poised to come to blows, and a mob was in the process of elevating a man who was not fully competent to kingship. These were not good omens for the future.

Perdiccas and a number of others took refuge in the vast palace with its hundreds of chambers, but it was not hard for Meleager's men to force their way in. There was no way that Perdiccas could win this confrontation, so he surrendered. Leonnatus led the cavalry units and the war elephants out of the city. Perdiccas stayed in an attempt to patch things up, but, feeling uncertain whether he would remain alive long in Meleager's Babylon, he soon joined Leonnatus in camp outside the city.

Meleager's brief moment had arrived. He was the king's right-hand man, he controlled Babylon, and he had possession of Alexander's talismanic corpse. But this was illusory power. Leonnatus's flight with the cavalry did not serve only to prevent Macedonians killing fellow Macedonians, but was also a tactical move. Their mobility enabled them effectively to put the city under siege.

Eumenes, however, had stayed in Babylon. As a Greek, he was able to steer a course among the opposing Macedonian factions. Meleager could see that the blockade of the city would quickly undermine his position, and certainly not all the infantry were in favor of civil war. So, a few days later, Meleager agreed to the compromise Eumenes suggested, certainly with Perdiccas's approval: that Arrhidaeus and Rhoxane's child (if it were male) should *both* be kings; that Meleager should become Perdiccas's second-in-command; that Antipater should be retained, with the title "Royal General of Europe"; and that Craterus, who was the troops' favorite as well as a friend of Meleager, should be made "protector of the kingdom," perhaps the new Harpalus, responsible for the imperial exchequer.[6] This compromise calmed things down enough for Perdiccas to return to Babylon, and the agreement was ritually ratified in the presence of Alexander's corpse, "so that his majesty might witness their decisions."[7]

With hindsight, it is easy to see that Perdiccas never intended to honor this agreement.[8] His concession was meant only to defuse the current crisis and buy him time. Perhaps this is how he had persuaded Leonnatus to take a back seat, when the first meeting had offered him equal power with Perdiccas in Asia—by telling him, "Give me a few days, and we should be able to bring you back on to center stage." At any rate, if Meleager felt secure, he was sorely mistaken. Under the guise of continuing the reconciliation process, Perdiccas isolated Meleager from his most important ally by offering Attalus his daughter in marriage.

When Perdiccas struck he did so in a highly dramatic fashion. The reconciliation and the formal acknowledgment of Arrhidaeus as King Philip III were to be marked by a review and lustration of the entire army, and Perdiccas persuaded Meleager that they should also use the occasion to root out the last of the potential mutineers. In the course of the review, then, the troublemakers were called out—and they were all supporters of Meleager. Three hundred were thrown to the elephants, to be trampled to death—the first time this terrible form of punishment had been used in the Greek world—and to intimidate the infantry. Meleager himself survived for a day or two longer, before being summoned to face Perdiccas. He died "resisting arrest." Meleager was the first to try to ride to power on the waves of chaos created by Alexander's death. Those with latent ambitions looked on. Perdiccas's cruelty taught them an important lesson: the only right would be might.

Perdiccas's supremacy was ratified when the Bodyguards and other senior officers met again, this time without interference. At this final conference, Perdiccas was made regent, "Protector of the Kings," one unborn and the other not fully competent; theoretically, all the regional governors of the empire would be subordinate to him. He promoted Seleucus to be his second-in-command, the post left vacant by Meleager's death, and commander of the elite Companion Cavalry, the main strike force of the army.

The clearest sign of Perdiccas's dominance is that he felt he could insult Leonnatus, who had been promised the coregency at the initial conference but was no longer slated for such an elevated role. It is likely that Perdiccas and Leonnatus had quarreled and fallen out; at any rate, Perdiccas hardly saw any need to appease him.

Antipater was confirmed as regent in Macedon; he was not to be recalled, as Alexander had wanted. This was sensible of Perdiccas, because whereas Antipater might have obeyed a summons from Alexander, he was hardly likely to submit to Perdiccas. As for Craterus, there was no further mention of "protector of the kingdom"—a grand, but perhaps empty title, probably accepted by Perdiccas and his followers only temporarily, as part of the process whereby they could eliminate Meleager and bring the infantry to heel. He was fobbed off with the joint generalship of Europe, when under Alexander's orders he would have had this position all to himself. But perhaps he soon would anyway, since Antipater was well advanced in years. In any case, Craterus was far away in Cilicia; what was he going to do about it?

CONSEQUENCES

At the top of the tree, then, the final Babylon conference established an unequal triumvirate of Perdiccas, Antipater, and Craterus. Perdiccas had taken all Asia for himself; Antipater and Craterus had been restricted to Europe, where Perdiccas was content to leave them to find some way to work together, or to wait for Antipater to die. Before long, however, the framework for a reconciliation between Antipater and Perdiccas was in place. As well as reinstating the old viceroy, Perdiccas also offered to marry his daughter Nicaea. And Antipater's son Cassander was given the command of the Shield-bearers, the position left vacant by Seleucus's promotion.

Now that the succession had been settled, provisions had to be made for the maintenance of the empire. Perdiccas kept a number of his supporters by his side, but rewarded others with satrapies. He and his fellow marshals assiduously avoided taking thought for the longer-term administration of the empire. They simply retained the existing structure, for the time being, and took over the old, somewhat laissez-faire Persian system, whereby all the satraps were answerable to the king, but as long as they paid their satrapies' taxes and kept the peace within and on their borders—as long as they did not draw attention to themselves—were left pretty much to their own devices. They could enrich themselves and their favorites and live like kings in their own right. The only difference was that this time they were answerable not to any single king but to the kings' representative, Perdiccas, who was assigned no particular territory, and therefore occupied the position held in the past by the Persian king or by Alexander.

So, in the name of Philip III, Perdiccas made provisions for all the satrapies, with Alexander's satraps replaced or confirmed in their post. The most important measures were these.[9] Leonnatus, demoted from potential regent first by the necessary elevation of Meleager and then by Perdiccas's manipulations, was given the wealthy satrapy of Hellespontine Phrygia, with its critical control over the sea routes between the Black Sea and the Aegean. As if to add insult to injury, the size of his territory was reduced; Paphlagonia, which had been a subordinate part of this satrapy, was given to Eumenes. But then much of Paphlagonia was more or less independent, as was neighboring Bithynia. Eumenes was awarded trouble spots.

Eumenes received an enormous chunk of Asia Minor—not only Paphlagonia, but also Cappadocia. These are rugged regions, and Alexander had chosen not to slow his eastward impetus by fully pacifying them. Leonnatus and Antigonus were instructed to use their satrapal armies to conquer the region for Eumenes; apart from anything else, it would open up the Royal Road, the main route from Sardis to Mesopotamia. Eumenes was not just a bookish man; he had for the past year commanded a unit of the elite Household Cavalry. But he needed help because his forces were insufficient against the huge numbers of enemy troops, and he had never commanded an entire army by himself.

Ptolemy got Egypt; Alexander's satrap, Cleomenes of Naucratis, was to be demoted and become his right-hand man. Ptolemy must have been delighted: Egypt was populous, virtually impregnable, and fabulously wealthy. Apart from anything else, Alexander had left a war chest there, which Cleomenes had shrewdly increased to eight thousand talents (about five billion dollars), with which Ptolemy could immediately begin recruiting. Moreover, Alexander had initiated a military training program there, so that Ptolemy would inherit native troops who were or soon would be battle-ready. It would make a very good power base for an ambitious man.

Antigonus was retained in western Anatolia (Phrygia, Lycia, and Pamphylia, with western Pisidia and Lycaonia as addenda); he was not considered a threat, and so there was no need to promote or demote him. He was an unknown quantity, not having accompanied the others on the eastern campaigns. Menander was retained in Lydia, where he had been satrap since 331. Peucestas was retained in Persis; after all, he had taken the trouble to learn the Persian language, and was doing a good job. Peithon gained wealthy Media.

Lysimachus got Thrace, with instructions to keep the unruly northern tribes at bay. Lysimachus was known not only as a man of great personal courage, but as a general with the skill required to pacify the warlike and fiercely independent Thracians. Though his appointment looks like a snub to Antipater, since it deprived him of some of his territory, it actually helped him; in the short term, Antipater was likely to be fully occupied keeping the unruly southern Greeks under control, and in the longer term Thrace had never been fully tamed anyway.

Despite the challenges, Lysimachus might not have been too displeased. Thrace was a strategically placed buffer between Asia and Europe. Hence, in the years to come, even when unable or unwilling to participate more fully, he was able to broker passage through or past his territory for this or that ally. Although nominally subordinate to Antipater, he never acted in anyone's interest but his own. Even his friendship with Antipater and later his heirs was self-serving: with his western border causing him no alarm, he could focus elsewhere.

Not all these measures served Perdiccas's interests, but an overall pattern emerges of dividing and thereby hoping, presumably, to conquer. When Alexander died, all seven Bodyguards were in Babylon; now only Perdiccas and his yes-man Aristonous remained there in the center. The distribution put ambitious men in close proximity to one another. In any case, several of them had their forces tied up for the foreseeable future by rebellions within their territories or by necessary military ventures. Perdiccas had at least bought himself time to strengthen his position, now that the immediate storm had been weathered.

He also cancelled Alexander's "Last Plans"—or rather, he saw to it that the army voted them into oblivion. They had had enough of world conquest, and Alexander's plans were as ambitious in the west as they had been in the east. As Perdiccas saw it, and as testified by his desire to bring Cappadocia within the imperial domain, the job now was consolidation, not expansion. But consolidation brought risks: the restless energy of the senior officers would now have no external outlet; it would inevitably be turned upon themselves.

The cancellation also left Craterus with nothing to do in Cilicia, and was an unsubtle reminder that his return to Europe was overdue. Nearchus, who had been slated to command the new fleet, was left without a job, and joined the entourage of his friend Antigonus. The "Last Plans" had also promoted intercourse between easterners and westerners; with their cancellation, few of Alexander's senior officers saw any reason to retain the eastern wives that Alexander had arranged for them in the mass wedding at Susa in April 324. The women were mostly cast aside, no doubt to their relief, since these were forced marriages, a demonstration of the superiority of Macedonians over easterners. Alexander's Successors were far more interested in controlling the east than in blending it with the west. Few of them had any intention of sharing power with the locals, except where necessity compelled them.

Finally, arrangements were made for Alexander's funeral cortège and the construction of the bier on which the embalmed corpse was to be trundled slowly but splendidly from Babylon to its resting place in Macedon, in the Argead tombs at Aegae.[10] Since it was Macedonian tradition that the previous king's funeral rites should be overseen by the dead king's heir, since this would be Philip III's job, and since Perdiccas was responsible for Philip, Perdiccas must already have been intending to enter Macedon himself, accompanied by the king and the cortège. It would be an impressive arrival. The moves he had already made to be reconciled with Antipater were doubtless designed in part to alleviate the aged governor's natural concerns about such a threatening and delicate situation.

In August or September 323, not long after that intense week or two in June, Rhoxane gave birth to a boy, who was named after his father. The waiting was over, but now Alexander's heirs were faced with the uncomfortable situation that there were two kings. Perdiccas assumed the regency of the infant Alexander IV, along with the guardianship of Philip III. In the meantime, with Perdiccas's support, Rhoxane had eliminated the last female members of the Persian royal house, including Alexander's two Persian wives. There is no evidence that either of them was pregnant, but Rhoxane was making it clear that the future lay with her lineage, not theirs. In any case, the immediate future was a foregone conclusion: a struggle to control the empire by controlling the two kings. Pity the poor boys and their mothers, knowing they were pawns in such a major power play, and knowing the Macedonian and Persian practices of assassinating unwanted rivals. As historian Elizabeth Carney reminds us, "No Macedonian child-king had ever retained the throne for any length of time."[11]

3

Rebellion

APPADOCIA WAS UP in arms; Thrace was in open rebellion; the Indian provinces were so disturbed that they were scarcely part of the empire at all; Rhodes seized the moment of uncertainty to throw out its Macedonian garrison, and we can imagine that others did too, even if their struggles did not make the historical record. But two of the most formidable rebellions that followed Alexander's death were Greek, and for a while they had the rest of the world holding its breath.

THE GREEK REBELLION IN THE EAST

Alexander had left Afghanistan secured with fortresses and garrisons. While the subjugation of Bactria had proved relatively easy, Sogdiana, on the far bank of the Oxus, was another matter. It took Alexander the best part of two years to fail to subdue it, and he suffered the worst military defeat of his career when a force of two thousand men under one of his generals was wiped out in an ambush in the Zeravshan valley. He could not expect that the region would remain calm; hence the fortresses and their garrisons.

Bactria was a notorious hotbed of dissension. One hundred and fifty years earlier, it was probably the country identified as rebellious by Xerxes I of Persia on the famous Daiva Inscription.[1] It remained so throughout the early Hellenistic period as well, until, around the middle of the third century BCE, it emerged as an independent Greek kingdom, which spread from Afghanistan to bordering regions of modern Pakistan and lasted for 150 years. The legend of the survival of European races in the area endured until relatively recent times, as in Rudyard Kipling's 1888 short story (filmed in 1975), "The Man Who Would Be King."

Alexander's men had every reason to hate the region: in addition to the massacre in the Zeravshan valley, hundreds more had died from severe weather as they crossed the mountains of the Hindu Kush into Bactria in the first place. Much of the protest came from his Greek mercenaries, and as a form of punishment he left thousands of them there on garrison duty while he marched on India. But Bactria was the Wild West of its day, populated by peoples who had never before come into close contact with Greeks, and the new settlers were living in rough-and-ready forts and outposts, with few amenities. Although the land was famous for its fertility (as well as for its astounding mountains) and was a major crossroads for trade routes from China, India, and the west, it is little wonder that they were discontented. In 325, just at the rumor of Alexander's death in India, a few thousands of these Greek settlers, former mercenaries, abandoned their posts and set out for home. If there is any truth in the late report that some of them made it back,[2] their trek would have made the journey recorded by Xenophon in his *Anabasis* look like a stroll in the park.

The uprising of 323, following Alexander's death, was far more serious, and it met with a far more serious response. The mercenaries, "longing for Greek customs and the Greek way of life,"[3] organized themselves, appointed a general, and prepared for the long journey home. There were over twenty thousand of them. They would have set out west beside the Oxus, and then along what later became the Silk Road to Mesopotamia. Footloose mercenaries, on their way home, were at their most dangerous: they had nothing on their minds other than getting home safe and rich.

The former Bodyguard Peithon, newly appointed to the satrapy of Media, was sent east in December 323 with adequate forces to deal with the problem. Perdiccas himself loaned him over three thousand Macedonian troops. He was under strict orders to treat the rebels with no mercy; to Perdiccas's eyes they were no more than deserters. Nevertheless, after defeating them, Peithon dismissed them back to their homes. Later propaganda read this as Peithon's first bid for power: he wanted to remain on good terms with the Greek mercenaries in order to incorporate them into his army and carve himself out an independent kingdom in the east. But Perdiccas had half expected this to happen, and had told the Macedonian troops what to do. They promptly massacred the Greeks in their thousands. Peithon, having been put in his place by Perdiccas, was allowed to return to his satrapy. If he had not entertained dreams of autonomy before, he began to then.

MOBILITY AND THE SPREAD OF HELLENISM

Despite the long hostility between Greeks and Persians, Greeks had also played peaceful parts in the Achaemenid empire. As mercenaries, traders, artists, artisans, physicians, secretaries, engineers, envoys, entertainers, explorers, and translators, they had passed through or been resident in the domains of satraps, and even occasionally in the court of the Great King himself. But the numbers involved in these earlier interactions were nothing compared to the influx of Greek and Macedonian settlers in the wake of Alexander's conquests. As the eastern Greek rebellion shows us, there were already at least twenty thousand Greek immigrants just in far-flung Bactria, before any permanent or large-scale settlements had been built there.[4]

The main wave of immigration lasted no more than three generations after Alexander's conquests.[5] There were two phases. In the first, land needed to be secured in the short term, and so the first settlers were usually men who had been hired as mercenaries and were now detailed to garrison an existing town or a fortress. In the second, these mercenaries were given a grant of land (the price of which was that they or their sons remained available for military duty), and the fortresses, or some of them, grew into or were replaced by Greek-style cities, and attracted further immigrants. Hence Alexander himself founded few cities but many fortresses, and the pace of city foundation gradually increased, peaking in the second generation of kings, by when immigrants with peacetime skills were in as much demand as soldiers. Dozens of these cities were founded in Asia. A magnificent Hellenistic city has been discovered, for instance, in Afghanistan. Its ancient name is unknown, but Ai Khanum was probably founded as a simple fortress by Alexander, and grew into a major Greek city that flourished for a hundred years or more.[6]

One of the most astonishing discoveries at Ai Khanum is an inscription showing that a philosopher transcribed the famous moral maxims from the sanctuary of Apollo at Delphi in central Greece, and brought the copy five thousand kilometers (three thousand miles) east as a kind of foundation document for the new city.[7] The story encapsulates two important points: first, the philosopher's journey epitomizes the general mobility of the period; second, the Delphic maxims, such as "Know yourself" and "Nothing in excess," formed the heart of Greek popular morality, so that Ai Khanum was to be a fully Greek city, even if it lay on the banks of the Oxus. I should say that, in cultural terms, even Macedonians were Greeks, since for about two hundred years Macedonian kings and aristocrats had adopted and patronized the culture of their southern neighbors, and the native Macedonian language was, probably, an obscure dialect of Greek.

The fact that the cities were created as oases of Greek culture means that the mobility of the period was largely Greek mobility. Every city was bound to have a theater, for instance, and so the Guild of Dionysus came into existence (first in Athens) as an organization that supplied actors and the expertise needed to stage plays all over the world.[8] As well as a theater, each new foundation had to have a gymnasium, a stadium, and Greek-style temples and porticoes grouped around an agora (a combination of city square, marketplace, and administrative/religious center). Law codes, civic constitutions, and forms of public entertainment were all recognizably Greek. Tableware, though locally made, reproduced Greek styles, as did jewelry, painting, architecture, and so on. In Ai Khanum alone, archaeologists have unearthed "a Macedonian palace, Rhodian porticoes, Coan funerary monuments, an Athenian propylaea, Delian houses, Megarian bowls, Corinthian tiles, and Mediterranean amphorae."[9] Sophocles was performed in Susa, Homer was read in Herat—but on the other hand a poet like Aristophanes, whose work was largely pegged to a particular time and place (late-fifth-century Athens), was less popular. A great intermingling was taking place of Greeks from different parts of the world. The only aspects of Greek culture to survive such transplantation were those which were sufficiently common to all the new immigrants. A new, more universal Hellenism began to emerge in the time of the Successors.

The uniformity of Greek culture all over the new world is remarkable. On the face of it, one might imagine that literature and art in Afghanistan would have developed in different directions from those they took in Egypt. But this was not so. As art historian Martin Robertson says: "Absorption of or modification by oriental influence . . . is a trivial and marginal element in Hellenistic art."[10] Greeks had a long history of considering their culture superior to that of any other people in the world, and the new cities were regarded by their inhabitants as oases of Hellenism in deserts considered otherwise to be more or less devoid of cultural interest. The separation between rulers and subjects in this respect is particularly striking in Egypt, where the two artistic traditions continued side by side—the Greek in Alexandria and other Greek enclaves, and the Egyptian elsewhere. There was little cultural interchange or hybridity.

In addition to security, the new settlements also facilitated trade, another major form of mobility. Even if primarily for military reasons, they commanded roads and rivers and coastlines, and hence came to play important commercial roles. Ancient trade was limited by a number of factors—chief among them being lack of technological development (due to the cheapness of available labor), too many frontiers, poor roads, and piracy—but the opening of the east enabled it to expand to the extent that it could. Traders traveled farther, established new markets, and dealt in new products (especially luxuries). Alexander undoubtedly saw the potential for this, since he standardized coinage and bullion values throughout the empire. But it took time. In the first years after his death there were only a few regions that were untroubled enough for trade to pick up. In fact, one of the goals of the contending Successors was to control regions that could provide them with the most vital commodities, such as timber, minerals, and grain—to try to corner the markets and deny them to their opponents.

For commercial as well as military reasons, then, frontiers were being pushed back. Both kinds of reason have always encouraged exploration. In the early Hellenistic period, Pytheas of Massalia sailed from southern Spain, circumnavigated the British Isles, and explored the amber coasts of the Baltic; meanwhile, military expeditions pushed farther into unknown parts of Asia than ever before, beyond the official boundaries of the empire.[11] As always, the expansion of the known world created a hunger for information about distant regions. Megasthenes wrote about India, Nearchus of his voyage back from India to Arabia, and utopian writers such as Euhemerus of Messene also set their fantasies in exotic locations. On the coattails of navigation (and of an increasing interest in astrology and calendrical systems), astronomers such as Autolycus of Pitane developed more precise models to account for the apparent movements of the heavenly bodies. Around 300, a former student of Aristotle's called Dicaearchus of Messana drew up the first map of the known world showing a few orientation lines, the precursors of longitude and latitude.

Literal mobility across geographical borders found metaphorical echoes in society. Certain conventions did not survive the transposition to the east, and social mobility increased. Fortunes were made by men from outside the highest social classes, and even by slaves, while the pinnacle of the social ladder was reached by a very few, invariably aristocrats, who became official Friends of a king. The emancipation of slaves became more common, and there was a huge increase in the number of cases in which divine honors were awarded to human beings, as though even the barrier between humanity and divinity had become permeable.

Mobility led to the erosion of old family-based structures, not just in the sense that families themselves were physically broken up as one or more members emigrated in search of opportunities abroad, but also because these emigrants were uprooted from their ancestors and their kinship groups, with all that this implied in terms of family pride and cult. Hence, in part, the importance of gymnasia and social clubs in these far-flung foundations: they were substitutes for extended families. In the era of the Successors, emigrants were usually single men, but there were also a few widows looking for better opportunities for their children, as well as unmarried women. Having left their menfolk behind, they had to be allowed to manage their own assets, which was traditionally the job of the nearest male relative, and so women gradually won greater freedom and responsibility for their own affairs. But they never gained a significant political role.

As well as enhancing security and promoting trade and other forms of mobility, the new foundations also had an accidental result. Since Greeks were the ruling elite, a certain proportion of the native population came to assume at least some of the trappings of Greek culture as a way of gaining a share of the power. The Greeks themselves, however, made little effort to educate the natives, beyond having those who were employed in the administration learn Greek; the official language was everywhere the same, a version of Athenian Greek called *koinē*, introduced by Philip II into his court and then spread around the world by Alexander's army.[12]

The new immigrants were not there to educate but to enrich themselves. They did not see themselves as bearing any ancient equivalent of the White Man's Burden to civilize barbarian races, nor did they pretend they were bringing freedom and free trade (another pretext put forward by more recent European imperialists). Enrichment was the motive for uprooting the family and moving hundreds or thousands of miles from home. The ideal of cosmopolitanism—of a world in which different cultures mingled and met as equals—was a philosophers' fancy, and had little bearing on Greek and Macedonian attitudes or policies. The new immigrants arrived with the assumption that their culture was superior to that of any non-Greek people, and simply wanted to enjoy its benefits themselves, however far they were from home. Immigrants invariably yearn for the homeland and surround themselves with familiar cultural trappings. All the same, it became a sign of prestige for a native to be a member of the local gymnasium or one of the other Greek clubs, or to worship at a Greek temple. Over time, then, Greek culture began to filter out of the compounds of the ruling elite and trickle farther down the social scale. From the start there were a few educated natives who knew Greek—the Egyptian historian Manetho wrote a history of Egypt in Greek around 285 BCE, for instance, and a decade or two later Berossus of Babylon did the same for Babylonian history—but the pace picked up somewhat as the years passed.[13]

Naturally, this trickle-down was limited, in the sense that it was largely restricted to the cities, and to elites within the cities. The 80 or 90 percent of the population who were peasant farmers found their daily lives more or less untouched by regime changes and international markets. They were still selling their products locally, mostly by barter; their ignorance of the Greek language was an uncrossable barrier. If their lives changed at all, it was as a result of different taxes, increased monetization, and the introduction of Greek agricultural stock and methods.

Nevertheless, there was a certain diffusion of Greek culture, even if limited, so that in due course of time, the term "Greek" came to designate not blood but education and mental outlook. And so an unintended result of the foundation of new cities such as Ai Khanum, whose first purpose was to secure the land, was the diffusion of Greek culture all over the world. The enterprise to which all the energy of the forty years following Alexander's death was devoted was, as it turned out, the enterprise of creating the Hellenistic world out of Alexander's inchoate ambitions.

THE GREEK REBELLION IN THE WEST

While their compatriots in the east were being slaughtered on Perdiccas's orders, the Greeks of the Balkan peninsula were also preparing for rebellion. As we have seen, Alexander's Exiles Decree had stirred them up, and especially the Aetolians and Athenians, who had the most to lose. Those who had already suffered most (the Spartans, defeated by Antipater in 331) or profited most (the Boeotians, who had been freed of Theban hegemony by Alexander's destruction of the city in 335), stayed aloof from the Greek cause, but for the rest it was a last push for autonomy. Hence the Greeks referred to the war as the Hellenic War, the war for Greek freedom, but it has come to be known as the Lamian War after the site of its most critical phase.[14] Encouraged by Athens and the Aetolians, and seizing the opportunity created by Alexander's death, a large number of Greek cities joined the rebels. Apart from hostility toward the Exiles Decree, the whole of mainland Greece had been suffering from a severe shortage of grain, and deeply resented the fact that Alexander had denied them supplies while sending tons east to support his campaigns. They were not yet ready to face the economic realities of the new world.

The Athenians employed the skilled mercenary commander Leosthenes as commander in chief of the allied forces. With the help of some of Harpalus's money, opportunistically confiscated by the Athenians, he recruited a substantial force, consisting largely of mercenaries disbanded a few months earlier by Alexander's order from his satraps' private armies. Further major contributions came from Athens and Aetolia, while other cities did what they could. A formidable army of more than twenty-five thousand marched north to confront Antipater. Olympias, meanwhile, did her best to get her fellow Epirotes to aid the rebels by invading Macedon from the west.[15]

Antipater lacked the forces to be at all certain of defeating the Greeks, and some would have to be left behind to defend Macedon itself. So before doing anything else, he summoned Craterus and Leonnatus, sweetening the appeal in both cases with offers of marriage to daughters of his. Military help was supposed to flow both ways between in-laws. The immediate context of the alliance was the Greek rebellion, but all three had reasons to be dissatisfied at their treatment by Perdiccas in the final Babylon settlement, and the alliance was certainly intended to outlast the immediate turmoil in Greece. Recognizing this, Perdiccas approached both the Aetolians and the Athenians for alliances against the Antipatrid coalition that was forming against him. No one was trying to pretend anymore that civil war between Macedonians was not inevitable.

Craterus was an obvious choice for Antipater, since he was in any case due to repatriate the 11,500 Macedonian veterans under his command;

but he still did nothing for months. Was this an Achillean sulk, or appropriate caution? Or, by the time he was ready, was it simply winter, making it difficult to travel across the Taurus Mountains of southeastern Asia Minor?

Craterus finally set out for Greece in the spring of 322—and even then he seems to have been prompted to move only by another factor: Perdiccas was on his way to Asia Minor to install Eumenes in Cappadocia, which meant he would pass through Cilicia. Craterus did not want his troops to be commandeered by Perdiccas in the name of the kings. At the same time, he sent Cleitus with the bulk of the Macedonian fleet to the Aegean; with the Athenians involved, naval warfare was sure to play a part. So Craterus took about six thousand of his men to help Antipater. They were seasoned campaigners, having in many cases served with Alexander ever since the beginning; many of them were in their fifties, some even in their sixties, but they were supreme battlefield warriors. In ancient battles, experience and training often outweighed youth.

Leonnatus came from Phrygia, where he had joined Eumenes in obedience to Perdiccas's orders, prior to their invasion of Cappadocia. In part, Perdiccas's Babylonian manipulations had annoyed him, especially because he did not come off as well as expected; in part, Eumenes had informed him that Alexander's sister Cleopatra was prepared to become his wife. This was undoubtedly Olympias's doing; having sided with the rebels, she needed to have Antipater replaced in Macedon or face his retaliatory wrath. Cleopatra's offer decided Leonnatus, and so he rejected Antipater's daughter and came not so much as an ally of Antipater as a potential usurper of the Macedonian throne; already related to the Argead royal family, he would also be married to Alexander's blood sister and have the backing of Alexander's mother. He had long affected a number of mannerisms and extravagances that spoke of royal pretensions.[16] While preparing to go to Greece, he sounded out Eumenes, suggesting that he should join him in his attempt to seize the Macedonian throne. Eumenes must have been tempted, because he was close to Olympias and Cleopatra, but he remained Perdiccas's man. He not only refused Leonnatus's offer, but personally traveled to Babylon to inform Perdiccas of Leonnatus's designs.

Meanwhile, however, before the arrival of either Leonnatus or Craterus, Antipater had marched south to preempt a Thessalian rebellion. Leosthenes marched steadily northward, easily defeating the Boeotians and occupying the vital pass of Thermopylae, the only feasible entrance into central Greece for a land army from the north. The two armies met not far north of Thermopylae. Leosthenes defeated Antipater in battle—the first defeat of a Macedonian army for thirty years—and bottled him up in the town of Lamia. Success bred success: some Thessalians deserted from Antipater's army and swelled Leosthenes' ranks, while others barred Antipater's escape route to the north. Macedon itself was vulnerable—except that Leosthenes could not afford to leave Antipater behind him in Lamia. Antipater managed to secure the town, but spent the winter of 323/322 in danger of being starved out. Leosthenes, however, died in a skirmish outside the town. The burial of his body and those of other early victims of the war occasioned a magnificent funeral speech in Athens from Hyperides, one of the most famous orators of the day. It was the swan song of Athenian democracy and independence.[17]

The new commander of the Greek forces was not the man Leosthenes had been, and the Aetolians were forced by the threat of invasion to return home. The remaining Greeks were still optimistic, but in the early summer of 322 Leonnatus arrived with massive reinforcements. The Greeks attacked before Leonnatus could join up with Antipater in Lamia. The infantry were evenly matched, but the Thessalian cavalry overwhelmed Leonnatus's cavalry and killed Leonnatus himself. He was not destined after all to become one of the pretenders. But the next day his infantry forced their way into Lamia and Antipater was saved. Given Leonnatus's ambitions, Antipater was saved in another sense too. The Macedonian army promptly pulled back north with the rescued regent. Central and southern Greece were briefly free of Macedonian control. These were heady but anxious times for the champions of Greek freedom.

Meanwhile, at sea, the main theater of war was the Hellespont, where the Athenian fleet planned to defend their grain route from the Black Sea and do what they could to hamper the progress of the reinforcements coming from Asia with Craterus. The Athenians sent a large fleet to destroy Antipater's Hellespontine fleet. But Cleitus arrived from Cilicia, and when his ships joined Antipater's the combined fleet defeated the Athenians twice in short order in June 322, off Abydus in the Hellespont and then off the Aegean island of Amorgos.

The opening of the sea made it possible for Craterus to complete his trek; he diplomatically placed his forces at Antipater's service. The Macedonian veterans had at last come home. In the heat of August the combined Macedonian army, now with enormous numerical superiority, confronted the Greeks at Crannon in Thessaly. Antipater had already bribed some Greek cities into withdrawing their troops from the forces opposing him. It was not a massacre, but the Greeks lost, and the war was over. Antipater rapidly quelled the Thessalian rebellion, and then turned his attention toward punishing and pacifying the Greek states. He marched south toward Athens.

Many Athenians expected their city to be razed, as Alexander had razed rebel Thebes in 335. After intense negotiations, the terms were scarcely less harsh: Athens was to become a second-class city. The Athenians were to dissolve their famous democratic constitution in favor of a limited franchise, accept a Macedonian garrison in Piraeus (which would control the city by controlling its lifeline to the sea), not rebuild their lost warships, and pay a massive indemnity. They also lost some disputed land to their northern neighbors, the Boeotians. Naturally, the most prominent anti-Macedonians were to be killed, including Demosthenes, who in a series of impassioned speeches stretching back almost thirty years had been warning his fellow citizens about the Macedonian menace. Demosthenes fled the city, but there was no escape, and he killed himself rather than fall into Antipater's hands. Some time later, the Athenians erected a bronze statue in his honor, with the following inscription:[18]

> If your strength had matched your wits, Demosthenes,
> Greece would never have fallen to a Macedonian warlord.

Within a few months the Athenians also learned that their petition to make their possession of the island of Samos a special case, exempt from Alexander's Exiles Decree, had failed: Perdiccas ordered the Athenian settlers off the island. Thousands of Athenians were forcibly deported to colonize parts of Thrace for the Macedonians, though many may have been glad to escape the overcrowding generated by the returning Samian Athenians and the poverty resulting from the huge indemnity.

Garrisons could stimulate the local economy to a certain extent in places smaller than Piraeus and Athens, but generally they were a hated burden and a humiliating symbol of subordination to a foreign power. The mercenaries who were employed on garrison duty were often little better than "murderers, mutilators, thieves, and housebreakers."[19] A lead curse tablet has been found in Athens, dating from the end of the fourth or beginning of the third century, that had originally been placed in a grave. The intention was to harness the underworld power of the grave's ghost to make the curse effective, and this particular curse was aimed at the garrison in Piraeus and four named senior Macedonians, who were clearly supposed to be representative. The meaning was "Curse the whole damn lot of those Macedonians!"[20]

Nor was just Athens reduced. Philip II had put the League of Corinth in place as an alliance of nominally free cities. Now, after the end of the Lamian War, the league was dissolved in favor of more direct means of control. Antipater imposed garrisons on all the critical cities and made sure that they were governed by pro-Macedonian oligarchies or tyrannies. One of the principal consequences of the Lamian War, then, was that Macedonian rule of southern Greece became considerably less benign than it had been under Philip or Alexander. Since many Greek states plainly refused to accept Macedonian rule, Antipater had no choice. The Aetolians were the only ones who, recognizing this, refused to negotiate; for their pains, they had to endure a Macedonian invasion. Incredibly, they managed to survive, but only because the invaders, Antipater and Craterus, were called away by more pressing business in Asia.

The marriage of Craterus to Antipater's daughter Phila sealed their new alliance. Ptolemy, who, as we have already seen in Babylon, had no love for Perdiccas, also aligned himself with the emerging coalition, by accepting another of Antipater's daughters, called Eurydice. These were the first of the interdynastic and often polygamous marriages by which the Successors created a complex network of blood relationships among themselves. This served not just as a form of alliance, "bedroom diplomacy," but also to exclude foreigners and ensure that Macedonians remained the ruling class all over the known world (somewhat like early modern Europe, where nearly all the ruling families were closely interrelated). The Macedonian aristocracy had always been predominantly endogamic, and this instinct survived the massive expansion of their territory. It created multiple links, often forged in the first place for some temporary gain, though the marriages usually persisted even when, say, a son-in-law was again at war with his father-in-law. Polygamy was a sign of the instability of the times, and one could almost say that the more wives a king had in the early Hellenistic period, the less stable he felt his position to be. After Alexander's immediate successors, polygamy became much rarer.[21]

Craterus was now in a far stronger position than he had been in Cilicia and, in defiance of his official restriction to Europe, he entertained hopes of getting back to Asia, with Antipater's help. They had more than twenty thousand Macedonian troops between them, and the finances to hire mercenaries, but they may still have been hoping for a peaceful solution. If Antipater kept Europe and Craterus was responsible for Asia, Perdiccas could retain his nongeographical commission as regent for the kings, and the triumvirate originally planned at the Babylon conferences would remain in place, but under terms that were more favorable to Craterus. Fond dreams!

4

Perdiccas, Ptolemy, and Alexander's Corpse

A T THE BABYLON conference, everyone pretended that the settlement they put in place would bring peace and stability to Alexander's empire, once a few rebellions had been put down and some trouble spots pacified. But after three years of tension, intrigue, and civil war, another conference and an entirely new dispensation would be needed. Only the pretence would be the same.

Cracks began immediately to appear in the edifice. It had been agreed in Babylon that Eumenes would take the satrapy of Cappadocia, once Leonnatus and Antigonus had subdued it for him. Much of the region was still in the hands of one of the last Persian holdouts, who had never fully acknowledged Macedonian dominion. But Leonnatus, who had been willing to help Eumenes, had died in Greece, and his forces had been lost to Antipater and Craterus; and Antigonus simply refused to help. Apart from resentment of Perdiccas's highhanded manner, Antigonus may not have relished his chances on his own against the formidable enemy forces in Cappadocia. At any rate, it is clear that sides were already forming, and that Antigonus would not be taking Perdiccas's part. The weakness of Perdiccas's plan to divide and conquer was that some of those he divided might unite against him.

In the spring of 322 Perdiccas himself left Babylon at the head of a substantial army, with all the trappings of the royal court, and traveled to Asia Minor, arriving in the early summer. Since Leonnatus could not and Antigonus would not help Eumenes, he would do the job himself; in any case, he needed a show of force in Asia Minor, to counteract the buildup of troops in Europe. His approach was, as we have already seen, the trigger for Craterus to leave Cilicia and join Antipater in Greece.

Perdiccas and the royal army invaded Cappadocia in the summer. It took two battles, but the Macedonians were finally victorious. The rebel Persian ruler was captured and suffered mutilation and impalement, while his entire family was annihilated. This was the usual penalty for rebels against the Persian throne,[1] which was now represented by Perdiccas, but following his treatment of Meleager's gang and the Bactrian rebels, the act highlighted Perdiccas's cruelty and ruthlessness. His enemies took note.

Eumenes took over the administrative reins in Cappadocia, but there was still plenty of work to be done in the area, and Perdiccas stayed near at hand. First, having opened up the Royal Road by conquering Cappadocia, he did the same for the main southern artery to Syria, which ran through arid Lycaonia, a land more of nomads than settlers. It was another brutal campaign, in which the inhabitants of one town preferred mass suicide to mass execution. Then he moved south to winter quarters in Cilicia, and early the next year continued the work of pacification in eastern Pisidia, another region that Alexander had bypassed. But Armenia remained troubled: the remnants of the rebel Cappadocian army rallied there, and Neoptolemus, the general Perdiccas had sent to the province, began behaving more like a satrap than a general. He was, after all, a proud scion of the Molossian royal house. Perdiccas instructed Eumenes to help Neoptolemus pacify Armenia, and at the same time to check his ambitions. There was no reason for him to doubt the wisdom of such a move, but within a year the personal animosity between his two lieutenants would bear bitter fruit. Nevertheless, Perdiccas could be pleased with his work; by the summer of 321, Asia Minor was a tidier bundle than it had been before.

The tensions between the major players, however, were only getting worse. Perdiccas's breach with Antipater and Craterus was now almost irreparable, with only the prospect of his marriage to Nicaea to redeem the situation. And over the past few months news had been arriving of disturbing events in Egypt. Ptolemy had been instructed to retain the former satrap, Cleomenes, as his second-in-command, but instead he had him killed, on the charge of embezzlement, while presenting the killing to his new subjects as the removal of a harsh and hated administrator. This was sheer propaganda, since Ptolemy kept all the money Cleomenes had raised, and would prove to be just as exploitative of Egypt's resources. More to the point were his suspicions that Cleomenes had been in touch with Perdiccas, hoping to retain Egypt for himself, or at any rate that he was "a friend of Perdiccas and therefore no friend of his."[2]

Moreover, in 322 Ptolemy also annexed the five cities of Cyrenaica (northeast Libya, in modern terms) as a province of Egypt, in order to control the caravan trade from the interior of Africa, and especially the export of silphium, a plant (now extinct), unique to the region, that was widely used around the Mediterranean for culinary and medicinal purposes, especially contraception. The constitution of the cities was changed and a pro-Ptolemaic oligarchy put in place, supported by garrisons and a military governor.[3] This irritated Perdiccas. In the first place, it went against his abandonment of Alexander's "Last Plans" and his general focus on consolidation rather than expansion. In the second place, Ptolemy did not ask anyone's permission before attacking his neighbors; he just went ahead and did it, on the pretext that he had been invited by the oligarchic faction of the cities. Satraps were expected to protect their borders, and if pushed Ptolemy would have argued that that was all he was doing, but still, it rather looked as though he was flexing his muscles, as an equal rather than a subordinate of Perdiccas.

PERDICCAS'S CHOICE

Olympias was still nervous about Antipater. Once he had finished settling affairs in southern Greece, he was bound to punish her for her support of the Greek rebellion. She came up with a bold ploy. Knowing that Nicaea was betrothed to Perdiccas and was even now on her way to Pisidia for the wedding, she simultaneously sent Cleopatra to Sardis, and wrote to Eumenes suggesting that Perdiccas might like to marry her daughter instead. She needed Perdiccas to be Antipater's enemy, not his son-in-law. She needed Antipater to be distracted by war in Asia and unable to turn his attention to Epirus. The plan worked perfectly.

Olympias's overall intention, now and in the following years, was to see her grandson Alexander IV gain the Macedonian throne, even though the chances of his attaining his majority must have appeared very bleak. Offering Cleopatra to Perdiccas was a major plank in the scheme. She wanted to see Perdiccas arrive in Macedon married to Alexander's sister, welcomed by Alexander's mother, with two kings and Alexander's corpse in his train, and at the head of the army with which Alexander had conquered the east. Under such circumstances, Antipater would have had no future. Barring unforeseeable accidents, Perdiccas would have been the sole ruler of the empire until Alexander IV came of age, with Olympias by his side.

Perdiccas was tempted: marriage to Cleopatra would accelerate the fulfillment of his own wishes. While his brother Alcetas insisted on the prudence of marrying Nicaea, Eumenes pointed out the advantages of Cleopatra. The marriage to Nicaea went ahead, with due ceremony and courtesy, but before long Perdiccas sent Eumenes to Cleopatra in Sardis with gifts and an offer of marriage. He seemed prepared to put aside his new bride almost immediately. He obviously felt full of confidence and well able to handle all his rivals. There is no other explanation for his behavior. His marriage to Nicaea was the one chance for peace between himself and Antipater. He cannot have thought that he could be married to both Nicaea and Cleopatra: they were contradictory strategies. Marriage to Nicaea would make him Antipater's equal; marriage to Cleopatra would be a springboard to the throne or regency of Macedon. He would rule not only Asia but Europe as well, all of Alexander's empire. Perdiccas was at last declaring his hand, as if it had not been obvious from the start. Alcetas might argue that his peaceful return to Pella depended on a rapprochement with Antipater, and that Eumenes' course meant war, but Perdiccas no longer cared, or was prepared to take the risk.

A puzzling incident, however, suggests that he had not secured the full loyalty of his army. Two more formidable Macedonian women were involved. Cynnane was the half sister of Alexander the Great and the widow of Amyntas, one of the possible rivals who had been assassinated on Alexander's orders. Cynnane had fallen out with Antipater, and decided to take herself and her daughter off to Perdiccas in Asia Minor. Naturally, Antipater did not want to see Perdiccas's court enhanced by yet another member of the royal family, and he tried, but failed, to use force of arms to stop Cynnane leaving.

So Cynnane arrived in Asia Minor along with her daughter Adea and a strong escort. So far from welcoming her, Perdiccas sent Alcetas to try to dissuade her. Whenever precisely the incident took place—it was not long after his marriage to Nicaea—he must still have been concerned not to anger Antipater. If he already had designs on Cleopatra, he was not yet ready to make them public. But

Cynnane's bodyguards resisted Alcetas, and in the fracas Cynnane was killed.[4]

Perdiccas's Macedonian troops, still loyal to the Argead house, were outraged by the murder and rioted. Cynnane had intended for Adea to marry Philip III, and the only way Perdiccas could calm things down was by letting the marriage go ahead. The situation must have been truly desperate for him to agree. He knew that, even though still a teenager, Adea (who took the name Eurydice on her marriage) was not to be trifled with. Both she and her mother had been trained in the arts of war. This union of "an Amazon and an idiot"[5] was sure to undermine Perdiccas's control of the king, but at least he had restored order, for a while, among his troops.

In the meantime, his marriage to Nicaea afforded the world a breathing space from war. But it proved to be brief. In the autumn of 321, back in Sardis after his campaigns, Perdiccas summoned Antigonus, to question him about his failure to support Eumenes in Cappadocia. But Perdiccas had tactlessly insulted Menander, the satrap of Lydia, the capital city of which was Sardis. Cleopatra was used to wielding power: she had ruled Molossia as queen for a number of years after the death of her husband. In order to flatter her, Perdiccas had put her in charge of the province, and demoted Menander to be her second-in-command, responsible for the military but not for the administration.

Menander explained to Antigonus that Perdiccas's and Antipater's rapprochement was not going to last—that Perdiccas had accepted the inevitability of war and was actively courting Cleopatra. Antigonus had already decided that, if it came to war, he would not side with Perdiccas. He therefore ignored Perdiccas's summons (which would probably have led to his death) and fled to Greece instead, abandoning his satrapy. He found Antipater and Craterus in the middle of their Aetolian campaign.

At the news that Antigonus brought, about the death of Cynnane and Perdiccas's designs on Cleopatra, they immediately came to terms with the Aetolians and returned to Macedon to prepare for war with Perdiccas. The first thing they did was write to Ptolemy, to see where he stood. No doubt the reply they received was encouraging. They would be able to force Perdiccas to fight on two fronts. But many subsequent Macedonian kings would regret that the Aetolians had not been subdued once and for all; their inveterate hostility, combined with their dominance of central Greece, was a perennial problem.

Two factions, then, had emerged, both well equipped militarily. Perdiccas and his staff had the kings and all the resources of the royal treasuries of Asia; on the other side were Antipater and Craterus, along with their allies. Neither Antipater nor Craterus had been present at the Babylon conferences, and both felt that their dignity had not been properly acknowledged. Besides, it seemed that Perdiccas wanted war—the war that Olympias had hinted at when she offered Cleopatra to him. Now it was only a question of what would trigger it.

After Alexander the Great's death, a Macedonian notable called Arrhidaeus had been put in charge of preparing the funeral cortège. The body was in Babylon, due to be transported to Macedon. Ptolemy had other plans, however, and he had already seeded the idea that Alexander had wanted to be buried at the oasis of Siwah, in remote northwestern Egypt (about 450 kilometers, or 280 miles, southwest of Alexandria). This was the location of an oracle of Zeus Ammon that Alexander felt had confirmed that his father was Zeus.[6]

It had taken Arrhidaeus almost two years to prepare the casket and the catafalque, which was as elaborate and expensive as one might expect—and far more gaudy. Within a golden coffin, the embalmed body rested on precious spices, and a pall of gold-embroidered purple covered the casket. Around the coffin a miniature golden temple had been built, whose entrance was guarded by golden lions. Ionic columns, twined with relief sculptures of climbing plants, supported a barrel-vaulted roof of gold scales set with jewels; the roof was topped with a golden olive wreath. At each corner of the roof stood a golden Victory holding a battle trophy. The cornice of the miniature temple was embossed with ibex heads from which hung, on each side, a multicolored garland, looped through gold rings. From the tasseled ends of the garlands hung bells, which tinkled as the catafalque moved. On each side of the temple, under the cornice, were friezes. One showed Alexander in a stately chariot with a scepter in his hand, surrounded by Macedonian and Persian bodyguards; another showed a procession of Indian war elephants; the third portrayed the Macedonian cavalry in battle array, and the fourth a fleet of ships. The open spaces between the columns were hung with golden nets to shade the casket but allow spectators a glimpse inside. The catafalque was pulled by sixty-four mules, each with a gilded headpiece, a golden bell on either cheek, and a collar set with gems.[7]

So in the late spring of 321 Alexander's corpse began its leisurely, glittering, tinkling journey from Babylon, under the command of

Arrhidaeus. A considerable body of cavalry supplied by Perdiccas escorted it, and workmen were sent ahead to repair the roads as necessary, though the carriage was fitted with a new invention: shock absorbers.[8] Thousands lined the route to witness the temple on wheels, the temple of a god. When the cortège reached southern Syria in July, it was met by a troop of Ptolemy's soldiers, who drove off Perdiccas's escort and hijacked the corpse. Ptolemy had decided that Egypt was to be the final resting place of Alexander's body. He understood how important the issue of legitimacy would be to him and his fellow Successors. Whoever buried the dead king made himself, by that very act, the legitimate successor of the king. Besides, one of the aristocrats present at the Babylon conferences is said to have prophesied that "the land that received the corpse would remain for ever blessed and unravaged."[9]

The theft of the body was more or less an act of war. On top of Ptolemy's appropriation of the Egyptian treasury (the contents of which, strictly speaking, belonged to the kings, and were therefore Perdiccas's by right of regency) and annexation of Cyrene, it was extremely provocative. Of course, Perdiccas (still in Pisidia at the time) sent an army to try to recover the body, but it was too late. The theft of the corpse made Ptolemy Perdiccas's prime target; when war broke out, he would attack Egypt first.

Ptolemy probably never intended the corpse to rest in remote Siwah. He wanted it by his side. Alexandria, the projected capital of Egypt, was still a vast building site, and so Ptolemy kept the body first in the old capital of Memphis and moved it some years later, when the palace compound at Alexandria was ready. He celebrated the arrival of the body in Memphis with games, and instigated a cult of Alexander as founder of Alexandria. He also began at much the same time to issue coins with Alexander's head, the first of the Successors to do so.

When the body eventually moved to Alexandria, a new national cult was initiated of the deified Alexander. Close to the palace he constructed a kind of tomb-cum-shrine—a most un-Macedonian miscegenation, an invention of Ptolemy's to emphasize the divine blessing his rule was receiving. Henceforth Alexandria, not Memphis, would be not only Ptolemy's capital, but also implicitly the center of the empire Alexander had created.

In due course of time, Alexandria became famous for four prominent statues of Alexander, as well as a number of paintings: the cult statue; an equestrian statue of Alexander as founder; a nude (the most common form of statue for Hellenistic kings); and an ensemble, housed in the sanctuary of Fortune, showing Alexander being crowned by Earth, who was in turn being crowned by Fortune, who was flanked by two statues of Victory.[10] The Greek and Macedonian communities of Alexandria were not to forget that the Ptolemies were Alexander's heirs. Fortune had blessed Alexander, and now Alexander's Fortune blessed the Ptolemies. Their possession of the body let the world know that they and Alexander were inseparable.

LEGITIMATION

Each of the Successors exploited the image and memory of Alexander to legitimate his bid for power. Ptolemy's hijacking of the corpse and subsequent adornment of Alexander's city with statues of its dead founder were simply the most blatant and outrageous.[11] Perdiccas, as we have seen, preferred not to manage the Babylon conferences in his own name, but in the presence of Alexander's throne. Before long, we will find Eumenes doing much the same, in response, he said, to instructions received from Alexander himself in a dream. Seleucus too claimed that Alexander had appeared to him in a dream and predicted future greatness. Just as it was well known that Olympias claimed to have conceived Alexander by Zeus, so Seleucus let it be known that his true father was Apollo.[12]

All the Successors did their best to ally themselves as closely as possible with members of the Argead house; all of them, if they could, made sure that everyone knew how important a role they had played in the eastern campaigns. Ptolemy even wrote an account of the campaigns, which emphasized his own role, of course,[13] and he or someone in his court later spread the story that he was actually an illegitimate child of Philip II, and so Alexander's half brother. Craterus marked the end of the Lamian War with a large monument at Delphi, sculpted by the best artists of the day, that showed him saving Alexander's life during a hunt, and he dressed in Alexander's style. Leonnatus too dressed and wore his hair like Alexander. Cassander commissioned a huge picture showing Alexander and Darius in battle, which may have been the original of the famous Alexander Mosaic in the Naples Archaeological Museum. Alcetas's tomb was adorned with Alexander motifs.[14] All those who came to establish kingdoms founded cities bearing Alexander's name and minted coins with Alexander's head in the place of divinity (the obverse, or "heads" side), to announce to their subjects and to the world at large their allegiance to his memory and protection by his ghost. When they portrayed themselves on their coins, there were still significant echoes of Alexander—his distinctive clean-shaven face, the tilt of his head, the longer hair that helped to mark him out as superhuman.

It is easy to see the motive behind these moves: to win the support of actual or potential subjects. In much the same way, American presidential candidates from time to time subtly model themselves on the talismanic John F. Kennedy or Ronald Reagan. Alexander was talismanic in the first instance simply because of the enormous pride that everyone involved felt at having been associated with a man who had achieved so much. The particular magic of his name and image was due to the fact that, for his achievements, he was recognized after his death as a god. The Successors did not invent the use of propaganda, but they made more extensive use of it than anyone in western history had before. The evocation of Alexander's spirit was an important element.[15]

THE ETHOS OF INDIVIDUALISM

Another aspect of Alexander's postmortem influence was less subtle. It did not stem so much from what one might call his "ghost"—all the ways in which he was evoked as an archetype (a practice that continued for centuries among holders of power in Rome and Byzantium)—but was a consequence of the changes he brought about in the world. One of the most striking aspects of the Hellenistic period, by comparison with what came earlier, is its focus on the human individual. Social historians agree with historians of philosophy, art, and literature that this phenomenon is characteristic of the age. Quite why it happened, however, is less commonly observed. It was a consequence of the era of absolute rulership that was ushered in by Philip II's conquest of Greece and confirmed by Alexander's conquest of the east and incorporation of all the Greek poleis (cities) of Asia Minor into his empire.

Strange though it may seem, a citizen of a Greek polis of the Classical period—the period that Alexander's conquests brought to an end—would have struggled to understand the value of individualism. We use the term to describe part of a spectrum of political possibility, ranging from absolute individualism (or anarchy) at one end to absolute collectivism (communism, perhaps) at the other. We think of ourselves as individuals by contrast with the soulless, faceless apparatus of state control. But the Classical Greek polis was not soulless and faceless; it was animated by and wore the faces of each generation of its citizens.

The most accurate, but somewhat awkward, translation of the ancient Greek word *polis* is "citizen-state," because the citizens of a polis were, by direct participation, responsible for the running of the state. And this was true whatever the state's constitution; in a democracy such as Athens more men were involved in the running of the state than in an oligarchy like Sparta, but in both cases, and in all intermediate cases, citizens were by definition those who ran the state. It was just that there were more enfranchised citizens in Athens than there were in Sparta. There was no power set over the citizens that one could call "the state"; the citizens were the state. By directing citizens' energies toward the good of the state, the system allowed poleis to flourish, but the price was a higher degree of collectivism than most of us would find acceptable today.[16] By contrast, we consider ourselves free the more we are able to avoid or ignore the state apparatus and remain within our private lives. A citizen of a Classical Greek polis had a far more restricted sense of privacy. Almost everything he did, even fathering sons and worshipping gods, was done for the good of the state—that is, for the good of his fellow citizens.

The Macedonian empire, however, changed the rules. Although poleis retained a great deal of their vitality, the inescapable fact was that they had become greater or lesser cogs in a larger system. Cities were still ruled by democracies or oligarchies made up of their own citizens—to that extent nothing had changed—but these local administrations had relatively little power. All major foreign-policy decisions were out of their hands, for instance. And a great deal of the apparently political maneuverings of the cities were merely "ceremonial and repetitive."[17] They still clung to the ideal of autonomy, and some cities tried to regain their freedom by armed rebellion, but as the years passed and successive rebellions were crushed, the ideal came to be seen as no longer feasible. A pancake model, in which all citizens of a polis were theoretically equal, was inevitably replaced by a pyramidal model, with kings at the top and local magnates ruling the civic roosts.

The relative disempowerment of citizens as political agents made it possible for them to see themselves, to a greater extent, as individuals, rather than just as contributors to the greater good. Of course, people had chosen not to play a part in the public life of their cities before— they were known as *idiōtai*, the remote origin of our word "idiot"—but as the Hellenistic period progressed, fewer citizens played a significant part in the political life of the city and larger numbers gained more of a private life, and hence the context within which the value of the individual might be recognized.

It is not surprising, then, that the ultimate *idiōtai*, Cynic philosophers, flourished in the period. Believing that human happiness lay in shedding conventions and possessions, they lived as tramps and preached asceticism as the road to moral integrity. As wandering beggar preachers, they could be found all over the empire, an integral part of the mobility of the period. There was a long tradition of Greek praise of poverty, but the first true Cynics began to appear in the middle of the fourth century; the most famous of them, Diogenes of Sinope (who was said to live in a large jar), was admired by Alexander the Great.[18] Crates of Thebes, contemporary with the Successors, wrote of a Cynic utopia, where there was no need for work or politics because the soil itself produced all that was necessary for a simple life.[19] The first Epicureans were scarcely less "idiotic," since they lived apart from society in a commune, and Epicurus recommended avoiding the hurly-burly of public life as detrimental to the goal of inner tranquility.[20]

The most popular philosophers of the period were precisely those who appealed to the new sense of individual worth. The same goes for religion, too: there was a surge of interest in the mystery cults. These were not new; they had been around for centuries. But larger numbers than ever before turned to them, because initiation into these cults, a profoundly emotional experience, was supposed to bring individual salvation. By the same token, small-scale, more personal forms of worship flourished in increasing numbers alongside the great civic cults.

In terms of factual history, scholars are justified in looking back and finding a pretty clean break between the Classical and Hellenistic periods, marked by Alexander's conquest of the east and the Successors' struggles. But it would be a distortion to try to find the same kind of break in literature or art or religion or philosophy. There was no sudden revolution; we are talking about a trend that became markedly more prominent in the Hellenistic period.

The trend is as apparent in art as in philosophy and religion. Sculptors earlier in the fourth century had already begun to lose interest in representing only famous men or in portraying them merely as bearers of civic virtues, but this trend rapidly accelerated. Its most striking fruit lay in portraiture, where artists—catering now for the private market that developed quite early in the Hellenistic period—soon excelled at expressing their subjects' characters and feelings, and found ordinary people of interest for their individuality. Every such portrait is a minibiography, and it is not surprising that the literary genre of biography also gained momentum in this period. This focus on the accurate depiction of individuals is modern enough to invite the thought that the hundred years from the middle of the fourth century to the middle of the third was the period when art as we understand it was born.

Portraiture shaded into more baroque forms of expression. Having discovered the beauty of the particular, artists also became fascinated by more outré experiences and states of consciousness, such as fear, sexual arousal, and drunkenness. Statues large and small struck theatrical poses expressive of emotional intensity. An epigram of Posidippus of Pella (first half of the third century BCE) explicitly draws a parallel between sculpture and the poems of Philitas of Cos, the teacher of Ptolemy II, on the grounds that both depict character with equal precision.[21] Commemorative epigrams, a genre of poetry perfected in the Hellenistic period, focused poignantly on ordinary folk and their sentiments:

> All Nicomache's favorite things, her trinkets and her Sapphic
> conversations with other girls beside the shuttle at dawn,
> fate took away prematurely. The city of the Argives
> cried aloud in lament for that poor maiden,
> a young shoot reared in Hera's arms. Cold, alas, remain
> the beds of the youths who courted her.[22]

Epigrammatists also used the form to express the same kinds of emotions as are found on sculptures. In this poem, Asclepiades of Samos (late fourth century) addresses the Erotes (gods of love) as his personified lust:

> I'm not yet twenty-two and I'm sick of living. Erotes,
> why this mistreatment? Why do you burn me?
> For if I die, what will you do then? Clearly, Erotes,
> you'll go on heedlessly playing dice as before.[23]

The emphasis on ordinary people and ordinary emotions stands in striking contrast with the grandeur typical of Greek poetry, painting, and sculpture of earlier eras. It is hard to conceive that classical artists would have dedicated their skills to portraying social inferiors such as laborers and slaves, women and children, and even animals; but all of these subjects feature prominently in the early and later Hellenistic periods. It is equally hard to imagine that Jason, the heroic collector of the Golden Fleece, could have been portrayed as he was in the often tongue-in-cheek *Argonautica* of Apollonius of Rhodes (born ca. 295)—not as a mighty warrior, but as a team builder. Both heroes and gods tend to become reduced in Hellenistic poetry to the level of ordinary human individuals.

A stronger sense of the worth of the individual had social repercussions as well. It led, above all, to a less repressive regime for women. As reflected in the light comedies of Menander (342–291), men were exploring the possibility of marrying for love, not just for practical reasons. An appreciation of wives as individuals, rather than merely as bearers and rearers of the next generation of citizens, led to a greater appreciation of women in general as at least marginally more rational than they had previously been supposed or allowed to be. And so schools began to cater for the education of girls as well as boys, and we begin to meet more female writers.

The poems of Theocritus (first half of the third century BCE) and Herodas (a decade or two later), both of whom lived and worked in Ptolemaic Alexandria, include charming depictions of everyday life. They show women attending a festival, setting up a commemorative plaque in a temple, pushing their way through crowded streets, shopping, visiting friends—in short, living ordinary lives that were less restricted to the home. The goods that accompanied dead women in their graves began to be more nearly equal in value and kind to those found in male graves, suggesting greater equality.[24] In due course of time, we find women being allowed privileges that would have been unthinkable in the Classical period, such as being benefactors of their cities in their own names, holding public office, and being signatories of their own marriage contracts (which had previously been contracts between her husband and her father or guardian).[25] This is not to say that most women did not still live confined lives, in legal dependency on the male head of the household. But there could be exceptions, and there was overall improvement.

Every government has to find a balance between the demands of individual citizens and the demands of the state as a whole, for the greatest good of the greatest number. Otherwise individuals might express their sense of their own worth in ways that are neither attractive nor constructive. The Successors were untrammeled by any state apparatus, because they were the state apparatus. The Greeks had a word, *pleonexia*, which meant precisely "wanting more than one's share" or "self-seeking." In the Classical period, this individualist form of greed was invariably regarded as a particularly destructive and antisocial vice, and it was expected that the gods would punish it or that it would arouse fierce opposition from other humans. The historian Thucydides, for example, thought that Athenian overreaching was one of the main reasons that they were defeated in the Peloponnesian War.[26] The Successors trampled on such views. For them, and for all the Hellenistic kings who came after them, greed was good. Individualism and egoism are close cousins.

The First War of the Successors

WAR WAS ABOUT to break out among the Successors. No one can have been surprised. There had never been much of a chance that this particular succession crisis would pass without bloodshed. But perhaps no one can have foreseen quite how much blood would have to be shed before the dismemberment of Alexander's empire was complete. The two decades from 321 to 301 saw four brutal wars—or rather, a more or less unbroken period of warfare, with each phase triggered by the concluding event of the previous one. It was civil war, Macedonian against Macedonian, but on such a scale that it truly deserves to be called a world war. First, the action took place all over the known world, shifting between the Greek mainland and islands, North Africa, Asia Minor, the Middle East, and Iran. Only the western Mediterranean was spared the Successors' attentions, but it was no less disturbed.[1] Second, the objective of a number of the participants was world domination. Thousands upon thousands of lives were lost on battlefields; our sources leave us merely to imagine the suffering and loss of life among civilians. One of the most savage periods of human history was ushered in by the ruthless ambitions of the Successors.

ASIA MINOR

The causes of the first phase of this war, then, were Olympias's scheming, Perdiccas's manipulation of the Babylon conference and desire for supreme rule, and Ptolemy's boldness. Having decided to attack Egypt, Perdiccas knew that Antipater and Craterus would try to invade Asia. They had approached Lysimachus and would be allowed safe passage through Thrace so that they could cross at the easiest point, the Hellespont. Perdiccas sent Cleitus with a fleet to the Hellespont to block their passage and control the Hellespontine cities, and gave Eumenes a land army of twenty thousand to protect Asia Minor. He also ordered Alcetas and Neoptolemus to place themselves and their forces at Eumenes' disposal.

Things started badly for the loyalist cause. Antigonus, long familiar with Asia Minor, was sent ahead to test the loyalty of some of the satraps, and he won the immediate defection of Caria and Lydia. The satrap of Caria, Asander, was an old ally, and in Lydia Menander, as we have seen, felt himself to have been slighted by Perdiccas. These defections happened so quickly that Antigonus was almost able to catch Eumenes in a trap near Sardis, but Cleopatra warned her friend, and he escaped.

The rebels thus gained an enormous bridgehead in western Asia Minor. If they could not make the easier crossing from Thrace, they could land an army there. At the same time, Antipater continued a very successful campaign of subornation among Perdiccas's senior officers. Eumenes stayed loyal, but Cleitus changed sides immediately, and Neoptolemus was drawn into secret negotiations. Moreover, Alcetas declared that he would not support Eumenes—that he would not lead his men into battle against Craterus. This was due not so much to any affection Alcetas might have had for Craterus as to his fears that, given Craterus's popularity among the Macedonian troops, his men would simply refuse to fight. Alcetas stayed in Pisidia and waited to see what would happen. The loyalist defense of Asia Minor was falling apart before it had started. A lot would depend on the relatively untried Eumenes.

With western Asia Minor lying open, Eumenes fell back toward the borders of Cappadocia. Meanwhile, Perdiccas had marched south, taking the whole court with him, because there was no entirely trustworthy place to leave the kings and their presence legitimated his venture. He made Cilicia his first stop, where he deposed the satrap, who was known to be a friend of Craterus. Meanwhile, one of his senior officers was sent to do the same in Babylonia. The satrap there was close to Ptolemy and was suspected of collusion in the hijacking of Alexander's corpse; in any case, Perdiccas did not want him on his left flank as he marched south toward Egypt.

Perdiccas assembled a fleet in Cilicia, and divided it into two. One section, commanded by Attalus, was to accompany the land army to

Egypt; the other, under Aristonous, was sent to Cyprus. The island was important for its strategic location (its fortified ports made excellent bases), its naval expertise, and its natural resources (minerals and timber, especially), but it was ruled by princelings who, if they owed allegiance to anyone, had treaties in place with Ptolemy.

Meanwhile, thanks to Cleitus's defection, Antipater and Craterus crossed the Hellespont unopposed. They divided their forces: Antipater headed for Cilicia, while Craterus marched to face Eumenes. The plan was for Craterus to annihilate Eumenes, while Antipater occupied Cilicia with all its resources of money and men. Then Craterus would link up again with Antipater, and together they would march south. Perdiccas would be trapped between their forces and those of Ptolemy. Antigonus was dispatched to deal with Aristonous in Cyprus.

As Craterus advanced, Neoptolemus set out to meet him—not as a foe but as a friend. He too had finally decided to change sides. But Eumenes found out what was going on and confronted him. This battle between the armies of supposed friends, late in May 320, was the first action in the civil wars that were to continue for the next forty years. Neoptolemus lost and fled to the enemy with a small cavalry force. Eumenes captured Neoptolemus's baggage train and used this as a bargaining counter to persuade the rest of Neoptolemus's men to join his camp. He had sufficient men to face Craterus, but their mood was uncertain.

The precise location of the battle on the borders of Cappadocia is unknown, but its outcome was a brilliant victory for Eumenes. As he advanced toward Craterus, he took pains to conceal from his men, especially the Macedonian troops, just whom they were going to face. He made out that Neoptolemus, a Molossian, was the enemy commander—and added that Alexander had appeared to him in a dream and promised him victory.

He was doing his best to raise his men's morale, because he knew that he was at a disadvantage. The chances were that, if it came to a battle between the two infantry phalanxes, his Macedonians, most of whom had been on his side only since his defeat of Neoptolemus, would desert. But Eumenes had considerable cavalry superiority. He sent his Cappadocian horsemen into the attack before the phalanxes were fully deployed for battle, and they swept the enemy cavalry off the field. In the mêlée, Craterus's horse stumbled and the would-be ruler of Asia was trampled to death. On the other wing, Neoptolemus was killed in hand-to-hand combat by Eumenes himself. Plutarch tells a story of mutual loathing, in which the two grappled on horseback before tumbling to the ground, where Eumenes dispatched his adversary. Even while he was stripping the supposed corpse of its armor, however, Neoptolemus managed one more feeble strike before expiring.[2]

The death of the two enemy commanders gave Eumenes the opportunity to wrap up the battle. He sent one of his staff officers to address Craterus's phalangites. The message was "We won't fight if you don't," and the enemy infantry surrendered and agreed to swell Eumenes' ranks. But they slipped away by night a short time later and went to join Antipater. Despite his success, Eumenes was still a long way from securing Asia Minor. Now that Craterus was dead, however, Alcetas had little reason to withhold his support, and Eumenes probably planned, with Alcetas's help, to contain the trouble spots until Perdiccas had defeated Ptolemy in Egypt. After that, he could expect his remaining opponents to surrender, or he could bring massive forces against them by land and sea.

LAND BATTLE

In the early Hellenistic period, land armies consisted of two arms, cavalry and infantry, both of which came in heavy and light forms. Elephants were extra. The heart of the army was the heavy infantry phalanx, which would expect to bear the brunt of the fighting in any pitched battle. And at the heart of the phalanx were the Macedonian troops (either genuine Macedonians or soldiers trained and armed in the Macedonian fashion), as reformed by Philip II.[3] Piled many ranks deep, and with its front a bristling line of sturdy pikes, each five meters long (over sixteen feet), it was, until the advent of the Roman legion, virtually impregnable in defense and terrifying in attack. Butt-spikes on the ends of the pikes fixed them firmly in the ground for defense, and could also be used as an offensive weapon should the need arise. For hand-to-hand fighting, phalangites also carried a short sword and a light shield. Next to the Macedonian phalanx fought an even larger phalanx of Greek hoplite mercenaries, armed with a heavier shield, a stabbing spear, and a sword.

As long as a phalanx remained solid, it was almost invulnerable. A direct assault even by heavy cavalry was rarely effective; the men knew how reluctant horses are to hurl themselves at a mass of men, and stayed firm. Elephants occasionally achieved some success, but they were a risky resource: when wounded they were as likely to run amok among their own lines as they were to trample enemy soldiers. A more consistent tactic was to try to outflank the phalanx, and for battle the cavalry were therefore invariably deployed on the wings.

Typically, then, the cavalry's work was divided between attempting to outflank the enemy and defending against the enemy cavalry's attempts to outflank their own phalanx. The phalangites normally faced forward, though in case of encirclement they could rapidly form a square. Given the enormous numbers of men in a phalanx, it consisted of smaller tactical units, each with its own officer, which were capable of independent action in an emergency and of rapid response to emerging situations. The main weakness of the phalanx was that it became very vulnerable if its formation was lost as a result of lax discipline, failure of nerve, or uneven terrain. It was rightly considered a sign of fine generalship to force a confrontation on terrain that gave his men the advantage.

The light infantry, typically mercenaries and native troops, were usually posted (along with the elephants, if the army had them) in front of the entire line of infantry and cavalry at the start of the battle. Their job was to screen the deployment of the main army and do as much damage as possible before slipping back through their lines to take up a position in the rear. If they still had some missiles left, they could act as a reserve in case of an encircling or outflanking movement by the enemy; otherwise, their work was done. They were also useful as marauders, or to run down heavier armed fugitives. Only in rough terrain did they become a strike force. If elephants were involved, it was the job of the mobile troops in the opening stages of the battle to try to cripple the creatures, while protecting their own.

Light cavalry, archers and javelineers, were used mainly as scouts, skirmishers, and scavengers. A heavy cavalryman was typically well armored from head to foot and wielded a long lance. Macedonian and Thessalian horsemen were particularly highly regarded as shock troops, but by the time of the Successors they had been joined by formidable native contingents. On parade, or sometimes for formal battle, the heavy cavalry made a gorgeous display, worthy of their wealth and social standing. As in all eras (think of the *hippeis* of classical Athens, the *equites* of Rome, the *chevaliers* of medieval Europe), the cavalry contingents tended to consist of members of the social elite, because by tradition a cavalryman was expected to provide and look after his own horse, and horse rearing was expensive. Only the wealthy had spare pasturage and the time to acquire equestrian skills, especially in the days before stirrups and saddle. The cavalry usually went into battle in waves of squadrons consisting of perhaps fifty or a hundred horse, operating as semi-independent units.

Every army was followed by a host of noncombatants: slaves, wives, prostitutes, doctors, translators, priests, philosophers (the founder of Scepticism, Pyrrho of Elis, accompanied Alexander, for instance), dignitaries, diplomats, coiners, merchants, slave traders, bankers, entertainers, various artisans such as carpenters and blacksmiths, diviners, scribes and other civil servants, engineers, and sappers. Then there were the carts for the transport of food and drink, fodder, artillery and siege equipment, arms and armor, the wounded and sick, swathes of canvas for tents, cooking equipment and countless other utensils, spare timber, leather straps, and everything else that an early Hellenistic army might need by way of support.

One of Philip's most important military innovations had been to slash the number of noncombatants and wagons and to decrease the individual soldier's burden, to allow for greater mobility, but there was still a multitude of men and animals—horses, mules for the carts, elephants, plundered livestock—and the logistical problems were enormous. Every person required about 1.25 kgs (2.75 lbs) of food per day; every mule or horse about 9 kgs (20 lbs) of chaff and grain; every elephant up to 200 kgs (440 lbs) of fodder. Generally speaking, little water was carried (though plenty of wine was), and campsites were chosen for the availability of good water and fodder.

The baggage train would typically be parked some distance from the battlefield. The word "baggage" may give an inadequate idea of what was involved. For professional soldiers such as the Macedonians and mercenaries, their baggage was everything: their womenfolk, families, and all their possessions. Some of the Macedonians in both Eumenes' and other armies had been continuously campaigning away from home for twenty years; their whole lives were bound up in their "baggage." And so it was a common tactic in ancient warfare to try to seize the enemy baggage, which could then be used as a bargaining counter. We have already seen Eumenes do this to Neoptolemus.

For a pitched battle, the troops were typically deployed in a long line. The phalanxes occupied the center, the cavalry was divided between the wings, and the light infantry and elephants were posted out in front. If there was broken terrain on one of the wings, mobile infantry might be posted there instead of cavalry. After the light infantry had expended their missiles, one side or both would make a general advance, either in a straight line or obliquely, favoring one wing or the other. Typically, it would be the right wing that was weighted with more shock troops than the other and would lead the attack. For Greeks and Macedonians, the right wing was the place of honor, and this was where the king or commander tended to take up his position. Ancient generals still fought from the front.

The formulaic layout of the troops meant that, provided numbers were more or less equal, each type of contingent was most likely to clash first with its opposite number: cavalry fought cavalry, phalanx clashed with phalanx. Normally, it was only in the event of success or failure, or of ambush, that they would find themselves fighting dissimilar troop types. Commanders usually committed all or the vast majority of their troops at once, rarely holding any in reserve. One fundamental tactic, then, was for the winners of the cavalry engagement to try not to race so far off the battlefield that they were unable to return and support the central phalanx.

Elephants were newcomers to Greek or Macedonian battlefields in the early Hellenistic period. Alexander's eastern conquests had first brought them to western attention, as he met them in battle against both the Persians and the Indians. They were as important and unreliable as the new armored tanks of World War I. Apart from serving as a potent symbol of a war leader's might and raising the morale of men who felt secure that they had these awesome beasts on their side, they had two main military purposes. Their defensive purpose depended chiefly on the fact that their smell and sight upset horses, so that they could blunt a cavalry assault. Their aggressive purpose was to disrupt the enemy lines, either by trampling them or simply by terrifying them into falling back, while archers riding behind the mahouts fired down on their foes. If both sides had elephants, a terrifying spectacle followed, which was witnessed by one ancient historian: "Elephants fight by tangling and locking their tusks together, and then pushing hard while leaning into each other, trying to gain ground, until one overpowers the other and pushes its trunk aside, thereby exposing its opponent's flank. The stronger elephant then gores its opponent, using its tusks as a bull does his horns."[4]

Pitched battles were often decisive, and sometimes armies would maneuver for days or weeks before meeting in full battle, knowing that the outcome of the war, and the future of their state, might well depend on it. Battles were generally over within a few hours. In the event of a rout, casualties could be appalling, but in the era of the Successors mass surrender was common; defeated troops were likely simply to join the enemy army. After all, the opposing commander had just proved himself potentially a better paymaster than their previous commander had been.

THE INVASION OF EGYPT

Eumenes had won a notable victory—but the news did not reach Egypt in time to make a difference. Perdiccas was having a hard time of it. He had never managed to win the confidence of his men, and the expedition was plagued by desertion. Ptolemy undoubtedly had a very active fifth column within Perdiccas's camp, and many of the officers as well as the rank-and-file troops were not convinced of the wisdom of attacking Ptolemy, or of the necessity for civil war. But Perdiccas stuck at the task and by May or June 320 was not far from the capital, Memphis. Then disaster struck.

Memphis was on the farther, western side of the Nile, but Perdiccas managed to find a place where he could cross the river unopposed. As it turned out, there was a good reason for its being undefended: it was not a true crossing. Many men forded the chest-high waters, with Perdiccas cleverly deploying his elephants upstream to lessen the force of the current. But their passage disturbed the sandy bed of the river and increased its depth, so that the rest were unable to cross. Those who had made it were too few to risk an attack on Memphis, and Perdiccas recalled them. Hundreds were swept away by the river and drowned.

The Nile has been forced only about a dozen times in history; even so, Perdiccas seems to have chosen an inept way to make the attempt. The ghastly episode added considerably to the disgruntlement in his camp. A failing Macedonian war-leader was always at risk, and a group of senior officers, led by Peithon and Antigenes (the commander of a regiment of Alexander's veterans that Perdiccas had recruited in Cilicia), now took advantage of the troops' despair. They entered Perdiccas's tent under the pretext of official business and killed him. Given that Perdiccas represented legitimate authority and direct succession from Alexander, it was a momentous step.

The murder was certainly carried out with Ptolemy's prior knowledge and encouragement, because within a few hours he had ridden into the enemy camp for a meeting with the senior officers. He was made welcome. They decided to convene the army and explain the situation to them. The assembly was in effect a kind of show trial of Ptolemy. He was found innocent of any crime, which meant that

Perdiccas had no cause for invasion and therefore his murder was justified. Ptolemy also endeared himself to the troops by promising to supply them and send them on their way.

Who would now be regent of the kings? The post was offered to Ptolemy. He was a senior man, who had the necessary cachet of having served Alexander long and well, and the added prestige of having been a boyhood friend. But, in a momentous decision, he refused. Why? Subsequent events showed that he was not short of ambition, so perhaps he felt the time was not yet right, that matters were too fluid and unstable. Most probably, he did not want to fall out with Antipater and Craterus (not yet knowing that Craterus was dead), and wanted more than anything to be left alone. He did not want to become a target, and thought he could build Egypt into a powerful stronghold for himself and his heirs. He was right, but there was a long way to go yet before such visions could be fulfilled. But at least he had gained a powerful argument to wield against anyone who challenged his rule of Egypt: he had not just been granted it by a committee but had won it by conquest. It was now his "spear-won land." But, since there had been little actual fighting, apart from the defense of a fortress, this was close to an admission from Ptolemy that he had been behind Perdiccas's death.[5]

Instead of Ptolemy, then, Peithon and Arrhidaeus were made temporary guardians, tasked with protecting the kings and the court until a new settlement could be reached. A few days later, when the army heard about the popular Craterus's death, the officers conducted another show trial, at which Eumenes, Alcetas, Attalus, and about fifty others were condemned to death as traitors. This signaled a commitment to war, not reconciliation. Perdiccas's court was purged of his most loyal friends, and even his sister, Attalus's wife, was slaughtered. A minor incident, but a foretaste of a brutal future.

A week earlier, Eumenes and the rest had been on the side of the angels, protected by Perdiccas's legitimate regency; now the loyalists were the outlaws. Attalus took the fleet back to the Phoenician city of Tyre, where Perdiccas had left a war chest of eight hundred talents, and made it a haven for loyalist survivors. Thousands gathered there; with Eumenes and Alcetas in Asia Minor, the Perdiccans were still a force to be reckoned with. On Cyprus, however, Aristonous made peace and was allowed to live. He returned to Macedon, on the understanding that he would retire quietly to his baronial estates— or so I interpret his temporary disappearance from the historical record.

THE TRIPARADEISUS CONFERENCE

Within three years of Alexander's death, two members of the triumvirate that succeeded him were dead. The Babylon settlement had plainly already been superseded, and a new dispensation was now needed. The anti-Perdiccan allies arranged a conference for the late summer of 320 at Triparadeisus in Syria (perhaps modern Baalbek).[6] A *paradeisos* was a playground for the Persian rich, a large, enclosed area combining parkland, orchards, and hunting grounds—a "paradise" indeed. Triparadeisus, as the name implies, was extra special, a suitable location for such a summit meeting. Under the command of Seleucus, Perdiccas's former army, with two kings, two queens, and two regents, moved north from Memphis through Palestine and Phoenicia to the triple *paradeisos*. In due course, Antipater arrived from Cilicia, and Antigonus from Cyprus.

Sixteen-year-old Adea Eurydice clearly felt that Perdiccas's death was an opportunity to agitate for greater power for herself. She accepted that there had to be a regency, but wanted the regent or regents to consult her as an equal, since she could speak for the only adult king. She achieved half her objective relatively easily: Peithon and Arrhidaeus could not handle her and resigned the regency in favor of the still absent Antipater. For a few days, before Antipater's arrival, the field was clear for Adea. The young warrior queen was popular with the troops, and she exploited the fact that some of Alexander's veterans were pushing for a generous bonus that had been promised them. These were the three thousand veterans commanded by Antigenes, who had been incorporated into Perdiccas's army as he passed through Cilicia. Craterus had paid the rest of the veterans when he took them back to Macedon and joined Antipater, and Antigenes' men were resentful at the delay in their case. Perdiccas had perhaps promised to pay them as a peaceable way of persuading them to join his Egyptian campaign.

Adea's next action showed how far she was prepared to go: she invited Attalus, officially an outlaw, to come and address the troops. Since Attalus's presence would have been intolerable to many if not most of the officers and men, the fact that he came and went with impunity demonstrates the extent of the disarray in the camp, with different units acting independently of any central command. His control of the treasury at Tyre made him a powerful ally. He and Adea presumably tried to induce the veterans to change sides. Adea seems to have been prepared to take her husband Philip III back over to the Perdiccans. They would regain the legitimacy they urgently needed, and she would gain the power she desired.[7]

When Antipater arrived empty-handed, then, he was greeted by simmering unrest. But with Attalus occupying Tyre and its treasury, no money was immediately foreseeable, and all Antipater could do was prevaricate. The veterans became angry, and Adea continued to inflame their anger, until they came close at one point to lynching the old viceroy. Antigonus and Seleucus, however, managed to calm the situation down. They must have promised money, but there was also the implied threat of conflict, with the rest of the army lined up against the veterans. Adea backed down to avoid bloodshed and her own certain death, and peace was restored.

Antipater was duly acclaimed regent. He ran the conference that followed with the expected new broom.[8] Vacant positions were filled, loyalty was rewarded, and his marriageable daughters passed around. Ptolemy finally married Eurydice, Lysimachus was given newly widowed Nicaea, and Antigonus's seventeen-year-old son Demetrius received Phila, at least ten years his senior, who had been widowed by the death of Craterus.

Naturally, Ptolemy retained Egypt, but he was the hero of the hour, and he was also granted "any lands further west from Egypt that he may acquire with his spear."[9] This was both an acknowledgment that he had made Cyrenaica his and an invitation to expend his considerable energy on Carthage and the western Mediterranean rather than looking eastward. It was well known that he saw Palestine and Phoenicia as logical extensions of what he already had. And he had history on his side: Phoenicia had been under Egyptian control two centuries earlier, before the coming of the Achaemenids.

For their prominent roles in the assassination plot, Peithon was confirmed in Media and given general oversight of the eastern provinces, and Antigenes got Susiana. Seleucus was given Babylonia, though he first had to oust the Perdiccan incumbent by force of arms. Arrhidaeus was awarded critical Hellespontine Phrygia, the crossover point between Europe and Asia. Asander retained troubled Caria, but, oddly, Menander, who had been just as disloyal to Perdiccas, was replaced in Lydia by Cleitus, whose defection had eased the invasion of Asia. Menander himself was attached to Antigonus's staff; perhaps he felt more comfortable there. Eumenes was replaced in Cappadocia by one of Antipater's sons, called Nicanor. Others were rewarded by being made Bodyguards for the two kings. There were the traditional seven of them, but now they were divided between the kings: four for Philip III, and three for Alexander IV.

The greatest winners were the two oldest men present: Antipater, of course, and Antigonus the One-Eyed. Antipater did not really want anything to do with Asia, and had been happy with the prospect of Craterus's taking Asia while he retained Europe. Now, with Craterus dead, Antipater effectively replaced him with Antigonus. Apart from retaining his long-held satrapy of Phrygia and subordinate territories (though at the time they were in Eumenes' hands), he was also, at his own request, made "Royal General of Asia," in the same way that Antipater was "Royal General of Europe." Perhaps this was meant to be a temporary position, because the conference also gave him the job of dealing with the remnants of the enemy forces.

The spontaneous condemnation of the surviving Perdiccan leaders by the army in Egypt was now confirmed and ratified. Antigonus would have right on his side, even though right, as granted by possession of the kings, had been on the other side a few weeks earlier. Antigonus, then, for so long just outside the very center, had found his way right to the heart of matters. At an age when many of us are thinking of retirement, he was entertaining dreams of world dominion. His commission to mop up the remaining Perdiccans was just the instrument he needed.

Antigonus gained the bulk of Perdiccas's former army, but not the three thousand unruly veterans. In what looks very much like a punishment for their near lynching of Antipater, they were sent off, under Antigenes' command as usual, to Susa, to escort the bullion stored there west to Cyinda in Cilicia. Antipater's son, Cassander, became Antigonus's second-in-command. Cassander had argued against the appointment, on the grounds that he and Antigonus did not get on. Besides, with his father's health beginning to fail, he did not want to be away from the center. But Antipater overrode his objections. He had taken the precaution of surrounding Antigonus in Phrygia with satraps who were loyal to himself, but he still felt he needed someone reliable on Antigonus's staff. The relationship between the two most powerful men in the world was based on mutual distrust.

For the present, both the kings were alive and safe. The summit meeting at Triparadeisus carefully preserved the pretense that there was a single empire, the empire of Philip III and Alexander IV. But under the surface, the meeting had also come close to recognizing Ptolemy as a wholly independent agent in Egypt, and had, at least temporarily, abandoned all Asia to Antigonus. The broad outcome of the conference at the triple *paradeisos* was a foreshadowing of the future triple division of the empire.

Polyperchon's Moment

CIVIL WAR HAD followed hard on the heels of the Babylon compromise. The Triparadeisus settlement was not destined to bring peace either. Even in the short term, there was a lot for the new authorities to do. In the summer of 320, Eumenes held central and eastern Asia Minor with a formidable and experienced army. Alcetas was entrenched on the other side of the Taurus Mountains in southern Pisidia. Attalus had a sizable fleet and thousands more troops at Tyre. If the Perdiccans united, they might prove unstoppable. Eumenes wrote to the others, urging them to make a joint effort against the new regime and insisting that legitimate authority was still theirs, not Antipater's. But the logical conclusion of this way of thinking was that they would have to fight to regain the kings, even if it meant taking the war to Macedon itself.

Perhaps in response to his pleas, but more probably in response to Ptolemy's imminent invasion of the region, Attalus left Tyre in the late summer with all his forces and tried to take the strategic island of Rhodes, which commands the sea routes between the Aegean and the eastern Mediterranean. The plan may have been to make this a stronghold for all the Perdiccans and a base from which to carve out and maintain their own corner of the still plastic empire. But Attalus was defeated at sea by the experienced Rhodian navy. He withdrew to Pisidia and joined Alcetas.

Alcetas would be hard to dislodge from Pisidia, especially after he was joined by other Perdiccans, though not all of them brought reinforcements as valuable as Attalus's men and ships. One was Laomedon, the satrap of Syria, who had been sheltering Attalus. In the autumn of 320, Ptolemy took advantage of the fluid situation, and the virtual immunity granted him by his part in Perdiccas's death, to take over the coastal towns of Palestine and Phoenicia. Ptolemy's intention was, as always, to create a Greater Egypt, in which the heartland was protected by buffer zones. Moreover, his possession of the Phoenician ports, which he garrisoned, gained him the raw materials and the expertise with which he could develop a modern fleet. He also recruited mercenaries in the region, as well as settlers for Alexandria, especially among the Jews of Palestine.

The takeover was an act of blatant aggression, in contravention of the Triparadeisus summit, which had warned Ptolemy off such action. Laomedon had been appointed at Babylon and confirmed at Triparadeisus. There was no justification for Ptolemy's invasion, but he clearly felt that the advantages it brought him outweighed the possibility that he might attract the antagonism of his erstwhile allies. As it turned out, his occupation was more or less overlooked for five long years.

Of the two Perdiccan strongholds, Pisidia seemed the more formidable. As Antipater prepared to leave Syria for Asia Minor in the late summer of 320, after the conclusion of the Triparadeisus conference, he had Asander probe Alcetas's position on his way to taking up his governorship of Caria. The attack was repulsed. But could the Perdiccans build on this first success?

Eumenes had been taking steps to win the loyalty of his men, a task that his killing of the popular Craterus had made particularly urgent. First, he made no attempt to disguise the fact that, as a result of the new dispensation, they were no longer the loyalists but the rebels. He even went so far as to give any man who felt impelled to leave permission to do so. Second, he treated Craterus's body with respect, and in due course of time returned the bones to Phila. Third, he tried to get his friend Cleopatra to give her Argead blessing to his ventures. But Sardis, where Cleopatra resided, was within enemy territory, and there was little she could do. When Antipater reached Sardis, he told her off most severely for her inappropriate friends. Cleopatra appears to have taken little notice.

Most importantly, however, Eumenes continued to demonstrate his prowess as a military commander. Ancient generals were expected to enrich the men under their command, and they made it one of their priorities, since it was, naturally, the best way to win loyalty. He even divided Antigonus's satrapy of Phrygia into lots, which he auctioned to his senior officers as fields for plunder. His position became so secure that, despite the enormous price his enemies put on his head, none of his men betrayed him—though he also took the precaution of strengthening his bodyguard. He might be able to enrich his officers, but there were always those who could offer them more.

Attempting to defeat Eumenes by treachery was the main thrust of the new authorities' efforts during the opening months of this phase of the war. Apart from Asander's failed attempt against Alcetas, no concerted military action was taken. This was partly due to Eumenes' strategy of sudden raids from a secure base, but the royal army was also suffering from internal troubles. At one point a considerable number of them, mainly Macedonian veterans, set themselves up as brigands in Lycaonia until they were brought to heel and repatriated to Macedon.

Action against the Perdiccans was Antigonus's job. Antipater returned to Macedon with the kings in the spring of 319. His health was failing, and he still felt that Macedon was the center, where the kings belonged. He probably also incorporated Barsine and Heracles into his court at this time; Cassander was warning him against leaving the kings and other Argeads too long within Antigonus's reach. It was clear that the relationship between Cassander and Antigonus was never going to work, so Antipater withdrew his son from Antigonus's staff and took him back to Macedon as well. In his last illness, he wanted his son by his side. If that seemed to Cassander to be an indication that he was the heir apparent, he was soon to be disabused of the notion.

THE DEFEAT OF THE PERDICCANS

Antipater left the bulk of his army with Antigonus, taking home mainly men who were due for repatriation. Antigonus was adequately equipped and funded for the coming conflict—and hugely helped by the failure of the two rebel camps to unite. The issue was one that was to plague Eumenes on every campaign: challenges to his leadership. It may not have helped that he was a Greek among Macedonians. Alcetas felt himself to be the natural heir of his brother's mantle and had more troops in his camp (though his position too was disputed by other senior Macedonians on his staff), but Perdiccas had entrusted the defense of Asia Minor to Eumenes and had expressly made his brother subordinate to him. Neither was prepared to yield overall command of the rebel forces to the other. Antigonus could deal with them separately.

He decided to start with Eumenes, who had withdrawn to Cappadocia. This was not a difficult decision, since Eumenes was vulnerable, thanks once again to the leadership issue. One of his senior commanders, a Macedonian, had taken three thousand men and set up on his own. Eumenes had put down the mutiny and punished the ringleaders, but Antigonus was aware of his difficulties. His preparations for battle therefore included approaches to more of Eumenes' senior officers, and he did not contemplate giving battle until one of the cavalry commanders agreed to defect. Since Eumenes relied heavily on his cavalry and chose the battlefield with that in mind, the mid-battle defection gave Antigonus an easy victory.

Eumenes retreated toward Armenia, where he could find friends and forces, but Antigonus's cavalry made it impossible for him to get through. For a while, Eumenes tried to survive by guerrilla tactics in the mountains of Cappadocia, but he found that his troops were drifting away. He dismissed the majority of his men, and late in the spring of 319 took refuge with just a few hundred of his officers and Companion Cavalry in the impregnable mountaintop fortress of Nora (in Cappadocia, but no one knows where). The dismissal of his men kept at least some of them loyal for the future, and relieved the pressure on Nora's very limited space and resources. Space was so limited that Eumenes enforced a regime of vigorous walking for his men, and had the horses half suspended off the ground and goaded into thrashing around with their legs to keep them fit.[1]

Antigonus left a force to besiege Nora and turned his attention to Alcetas. He stormed into Pisidia, but found Alcetas waiting for him, occupying the valley through which he had to pass, near a town called Cretopolis. The rebels suffered a resounding defeat. Alcetas fled from the battlefield and committed suicide. The remainder of the senior former Perdiccans were imprisoned. A couple of years later, they managed to take control of their prison fortress, in a manner that would satisfy a scriptwriter of a Hollywood prison-breakout scene: bribed guards, weapons grabbed from the armory, the brutal warder hurled from the parapet to his death, burning buildings. But they still could not escape, and in the end they were betrayed by one of their number and died defending their former prison.[2]

So ended the First War of the Successors. By the autumn of 319, Antigonus was in a hugely powerful position. Much of Asia Minor was under his control. His army, swelled by the remnants of both Eumenes' and Alcetas's forces, now numbered seventy thousand, and was strong in every division. And he could keep his troops because, as the official representative of the kings, he could draw on the otherwise impregnable royal treasuries to pay them. In a few months, he had leapt from being one satrap among many to a contender for Alexandrine supremacy, and doubtless that, or something like it, was exactly what was on his mind.

THE REGENCY OF POLYPERCHON

By the time eighty-year-old Antipater got back to Macedon, he had only a few months to live and was too ill even to avenge himself on Olympias for her support of his enemies and for spreading the rumor that he had been responsible for Alexander's death. His death, in the late summer of 319, threw everything once more into chaos. On his deathbed, he decreed that he should be succeeded as European regent by Polyperchon, and that his son Cassander should be Polyperchon's second-in-command.

On the face of it, this pair of decisions is puzzling. Why was Cassander, who had so often been his father's aide, passed over? But when Alexander sent Craterus west to replace Antipater, he sent Polyperchon too, as Antipater's replacement in the event of Craterus's death. And indeed Craterus had died, even if not in a way that Alexander could have foreseen. So in appointing Polyperchon, Antipater was carrying out Alexander's orders, and attempting thereby to legitimate Polyperchon's regime in these troubled times. In any case, Polyperchon had an impeccable pedigree: he was a member of one of the old royal houses of Upper Macedon, he had been a competent general under both Philip and Alexander, and he had been left in charge of Europe while Antipater was campaigning and negotiating in Asia the previous year. He had risen to the challenge by crushing an uprising in Thessaly, the only outcome of Perdiccas's attempts to create a second front in Greece.

Cassander was passed over because Antipater wanted to avoid giving the impression that he was trying to set up an Antipatrid dynasty. That would not have gone down well with the Macedonian barons. At any rate, Cassander, consumed by resentment, spent the first few weeks of Polyperchon's rule trying and failing to drum up sufficient internal support for a coup. He also looked for help from abroad, and naturally first approached those who had shown themselves to be his father's allies by marrying into the family. But both his in-laws, Ptolemy and Lysimachus, were otherwise engaged, and could do no more than give him their tacit blessing; they did not want to commit themselves militarily. Antigonus, however, was more forthcoming, and when Cassander left Macedon in the autumn of 319, he went to join Antigonus's court at Celaenae. They put aside their former differences and began a propaganda campaign against Polyperchon, claiming that Antipater had no right to appoint a successor on his own.

After just a few months of "peace," war was about to break out again. Antigonus set about securing his position in Asia Minor by eliminating potential enemies, particularly the satraps put in place by Antipater the year before at the Triparadeisus conference, who effectively ringed his domain. In Hellespontine Phrygia, Arrhidaeus got wind of his plans and tried by force of arms to take over the independent city of Cyzicus as a bolt-hole. He failed in this, and also in an attempt to rescue Eumenes from Nora, but he provided Antigonus with the pretext he needed to send an army against him. Once Antigonus had pinned Arrhidaeus inside the city of Cius, a city under independent rulership, east of Cyzicus on the Propontis, he marched against Cleitus in Lydia. Cleitus secured his most important towns with garrisons and fled to Macedon. The news he brought left Polyperchon in no doubt about Antigonus's intentions.

Nicanor, the son of Antipater, fled to Macedon at much the same time. He knew his days were numbered as satrap of Cappadocia. The ongoing negotiations between Antigonus and Eumenes came to a conclusion in the spring of 318. The deal was that if Eumenes would agree to serve him, Antigonus would end the siege of Nora and restore Eumenes to his satrapy, with some additional territories. Nicanor was therefore redundant, in Antigonus's Asia Minor. Antigonus could afford to be generous with his old friend Eumenes, because now that his breach with Polyperchon was public knowledge, he was doing his best to limit the number of allies his opponent could call on. Eumenes agreed to work with Antigonus, and swore an oath to that effect. Antigonus left him in Cappadocia, where he rounded up the remnants of his former army and held them in readiness for Antigonus's orders.

In Lydia, Antigonus managed to capture Ephesus, and a short while later a flotilla sailed into the harbor carrying six hundred talents of bullion from Cilicia to Macedon for Polyperchon. Antigonus kept the money, worth hundreds of millions of dollars in today's terms, for himself. On top of his other actions, it was a declaration of war. When Cassander joined Antigonus, then, there was no doubt of his intentions: to oust Polyperchon from Pella, with the help of Antigonus's wealth and forces, and rule Macedon himself, as regent to the kings. And so, in 318, began the Second War of the Successors, with hardly an interval between it and the first.

POLYPERCHON'S RESPONSE

Antigonus, Cassander, and Eumenes were formidable enemies for Polyperchon, and he could not be certain of either Lysimachus or Ptolemy. He gained the support of the displaced satraps, and Aristonous, ever loyal to the kings or whoever controlled them, came out of his enforced retirement to offer help, but he was still far weaker than his enemies.

Polyperchon's strategy for Macedon went straight to the heart of the matter: he wrote to Olympias in Epirus, inviting her to return to Macedon and take over the regency of her grandson, Alexander IV. Her presence by his side would enormously strengthen his hand. Olympias had been wanting to return for years, but she hesitated. She wrote to Eumenes ("my truest friend"), and he advised her to wait and see what opportunities for a safe return the war might throw her way. At the moment, Macedon was hardly a secure haven.[3]

Polyperchon's other pressing need was an ally to distract Antigonus in Asia—to stop him from marching on Macedon and installing Cassander as regent. Knowing Eumenes' past as a loyalist, and suspecting that his deal with Antigonus might have been opportunistic, Polyperchon approached him with the offer of making him the official Royal General of Asia instead of Antigonus. He would be entitled to withdraw five hundred talents from the treasury at Cyinda in Cilicia immediately, and more as necessary. In theory, all the satraps of Asia would be under his command. And Polyperchon also ordered Antigenes to place his three thousand veterans at Eumenes' disposal. These were the veterans who had been sent by Antipater to Susa to guard the transport of a large quantity of bullion from there to Cilicia. So, along with sufficient cash, Eumenes would already have the making of a powerful army. He promptly reneged on his pact with Antigonus and accepted Polyperchon's offer. Word got out and Antigonus sent an army after him, but Eumenes had already crossed the Taurus Mountains to link up with Antigenes in Cilicia.

Polyperchon's diplomatic skills were serving him well, but he still needed to secure the Greek mainland. Many of the cities there had administrations and garrisons installed by Antipater, who were likely to be loyal to Cassander. And Cassander had in fact written to all his father's garrisons, ordering them to place their forces at his disposal, since he, not Polyperchon, was his father's legitimate heir. The most significant early gain was Piraeus, the port of Athens, where the garrison, imposed by Antipater at the end of the Lamian War, entrusted itself to the command of a personal friend of Cassander, another Nicanor (not the son of Antipater).

Polyperchon's response to Cassander's initiative was as bold as his approach to Eumenes. He wrote an open letter to all the Greek cities, in the names of the kings. In this letter, he urged the Greeks to reopen their battle for freedom by overthrowing the oligarchic administrations installed by Antipater and expelling the garrisons that supported them. In order to help the democratic factions within the cities, Polyperchon ordered that all those who had been exiled at the end of the Lamian War were to be restored under a full amnesty. The Greeks were urged to live at peace with one another—so that they could unite behind Polyperchon against an enemy portrayed as tyrannical—and the letter, or decree, ended with the usual threat: "We shall not tolerate any failure to carry out these instructions."[4]

This was a masterful stroke, but risky: in the past it had been precisely the democratic elements of the Greek cities that had tended to oppose Macedonian rule. The principal difficulty was the unlikelihood that many of the Antipatrid oligarchies would simply dissolve themselves in favor of more democratic constitutions. They would wait and see whether Cassander could keep them in power. There was a good chance that Greece would become a theater of war.

THE FREEDOM OF THE GREEK CITIES

Polyperchon's letter was the first of several such proclamations from the Successors, who from time to time felt the need to profess their support for Greek freedom. The Greek cities were always in an anomalous situation within the Successors' realms. On the one hand, they were, in countless ways, clearly subject to their rulers; on the other hand, they were not organic parts of the realm, but, in theory, distinct and independent entities.[5]

In Polyperchon's case, "freedom" meant "democracy," but the more radical version, which Antigonus was to offer, was general autonomy—the right to be ungarrisoned and free to pursue their own political paths. Each time, these proclamations were no more than cynical propaganda. Every promise of freedom or autonomy for the Greek cities could realistically be read as a veiled threat from a Macedonian ruler, a reminder that their freedom was in his hands. The cities simply lacked the resources to mount a serious challenge against their overlords. This was the nightmare that Demosthenes had long predicted for Athens: Macedonian control of its fortunes. And so we find proclamations such as Polyperchon's made precisely at times when some Macedonian strongman needed to quell unrest in the Greek cities within his domain, or needed them at least to stay quiet and on the sidelines.

The Successors' promises to the cities were often hollow. A couple of hundred years later, the clear-sighted historian Polybius wrote: "All kings mouth platitudes about freedom at the beginning of their reigns, and describe as their friends and allies those who support their cause, but once they have gained their ends they soon treat those who believed them as slaves, not as allies."[6] Even apart from such cynical reasons, it was unrealistic to guarantee that cities in critical locations would remain ungarrisoned. And while cities might be formally exempt from paying a regular tribute, they were in no position to refuse a request from above for a special contribution to the war chest. Efficient income generation and security were the ruler's aims, and if it came down to it he would tolerate any political regime within a city, as long as it supported these aims.

But the promises did make good propaganda, and to the extent that they could be carried out, they made life easier for the authorities. It was expensive to maintain garrisons, and the goodwill of the cities smoothed the extraction of money and of military, administrative, and technical expertise. Hence the Successors, and then their successors, the Hellenistic kings, generally took care to maintain the fiction that the cities were autonomous by phrasing their commands courteously as requests, or politely suggesting "It seems to us desirable that . . ."[7] For their part the cities played the game by acting as if they voluntarily granted the king's requests, and by flattering him. In return for a king's granting of certain privileges or immunities, a city might hail him as its savior and benefactor and grant him civic honors, up to and including cult status as a god.

These are generalizations, and they need to be offset by the reminder that every city was different, and was differently treated by its rulers. A number of factors, such as location and prestige, might determine how bluntly or diplomatically a king intervened in a city's affairs. But one consequence of the new situation was almost universal: nearly all the cities found themselves worse off financially than before. This was a consequence above all of the continuous warfare of the period. Farming, trade, mining—all the usual sources of income were likely to be interrupted. Food shortages were frequent, with the price of grain fluctuating accordingly. At the same time, the kings' demands for money and men were insistent. Even a relatively prosperous city such as Miletus could find itself unable to meet such demands.[8]

Above all, though, there was the sheer cost of modern warfare. With siege warfare increasing in sophistication, the first thing a city needed was good defensive walls and towers. Some cities, such as Ephesus, had to be relocated because their old site could not easily be defended against current siege techniques. Naturally, the costs involved were enormous, especially for port towns. It has been estimated[9] that the cost of building just one tower was enough to maintain over fifty mercenary soldiers for a year; and even a small city needed several towers, with lofty and well-fitted walls between.

When Ephesus was relocated and fortified by Lysimachus in the late 290s (and renamed Arsinoeia after his wife), it had perhaps as many as sixty towers—but then Lysimachus spared no expense. The city was a showpiece, "strong to the point of brutality."[10] The drystone walls with their substantial, quarried limestone blocks were carefully fitted onto the bedrock and followed the contours of the countryside wherever they led for about ten kilometers (over five miles), protecting the harbor and surrounding the city at some distance, to allow for expansion and the emergency evacuation of the rural population. The entire length of the wall consisted of two faces, inner and outer, with rubble and soil infill between, and an average width of almost three meters (ten feet). The walls were crenellated, and relieved not just by irregularly placed towers and occasional zigzag stretches but by a number of postern gates, at least two main gates, windows for defensive artillery, and embrasures for archers.

Defensive walls were so expensive, and so important, that they came to symbolize civic pride, and statues representing the city, or its Fortune, were often crowned with battlements. Important cities would need defensive artillery and countersiege ability, as well as maintaining a limited citizen militia or mercenary force. Then, in time of war, fortresses needed to be manned in the countryside, to protect farmers and land; prisoners might need to be ransomed, and ships to be made ready. If the exigencies of war meant that a friendly army was billeted on the town, the expenses were enormous; if it was an enemy army, the cost was even higher. An enemy would take not just livestock and crops, but next year's seed and probably all the slaves as well; the garrison would defect, the walls would be demolished. In short, the entire economy of the city would be destroyed.

Naturally, cities petitioned their rulers and other states to defray at least some of the costs. Kings were glad to oblige if, as in the case of

Ephesus, the city was critical to the defense of the realm, but lesser cities never received enough.[11] The main upshot of this civic impoverishment was a vast increase in the importance to the Greek cities of citizen benefactors. A small number of people were getting very rich in the new world. If a city could not afford to pay for something out of public funds, such individuals wanted and were expected to bear the cost.

These people were important to cities not just for their wealth but for the circles to which their wealth could gain them entrance. Diplomacy was critical in a world where distant kings pulled the strings, and the wealthy and well-placed men who could gain the ear of the king or one of his advisers became vital to their cities. Some—a very few, and only men—actually joined the charmed circle as an official Friend of some king or other. Hence, as the Hellenistic era progressed, these men came to dominate the affairs of the Greek cities, even those that theoretically had democratic constitutions. From about 300 to the middle of the 280s, for instance, the wealthy Athenian Philippides (who had enjoyed a moderately successful career as a writer of comedies) used his influence with Lysimachus to gain a number of important benefits for the city, including grants of grain and the ransoming of Athenian prisoners.[12]

Cities, then, were expected to prioritize the king's business on their agendas and to align their policies with the king's wishes and whims. But, despite this necessary obsequiousness, the Greek cities retained a great deal of their past vitality, and many of their old structures remained in place. They still strove for economic self-sufficiency; they still had to make day-to-day decisions about the running of their community; they still had to generate an income, mint coins, and set local taxation levels; they still had to maintain a fighting force for local conflicts; they still needed to construct or repair public buildings and monuments and roads, run festivals, pay for public slaves and sacrifices, and relieve the poverty of their worse-off citizens. The basic social fabric remained in place too—the fundamental triad of citizens, slaves, and resident foreigners—with the vast majority of the citizens still being peasant farmers; the phenomenon of massive estates and extensive tenant farming was a later Hellenistic development.

In the greater scheme of things, cities were bound to have a reduced role, but this made little impact on civic pride. Most citizens still felt that their primary loyalty was toward the city of their birth, and were prepared to work to maintain or enhance its importance. And through their citizens cities even came to take on new roles. Precisely because there was now a greater scheme of things, there was more possibility of impartial interaction, so that cities began to send out respected men to act as judges, or even to arbitrate in disputes between neighboring cities. These were occasions for civic pride no less than, say, the successful staging of a major international festival. And such diplomatic links might lead in due course to more formal alliances, or even some form of confederacy, on the principle that union was strength. The Greek city was alive and well in the early Hellenistic period, and learning to adjust to new circumstances.

The Triumph of Cassander

THE LIKELIHOOD THAT Greece would become a theater of war rapidly became a certainty, as Cassander and Polyperchon vied for control of the mainland cities. Political lines became clearly drawn, the only relevant issue being whether any given city would throw in its lot with the legitimate regent or the pretender. By and large, the poorer members of the cities and their champions lined up behind Polyperchon, while the wealthier classes found their interests best served by Cassander. But whichever side was in the ascendant, we can imagine the stress and the bustle as cities tried to determine how close they would be to the front line of the impending war and made their preparations accordingly, and as rival political factions, encouraged by one or the other of the contenders for supremacy in Greece, tried to gain or confirm their power.

THE OPENING CAMPAIGNS OF THE SECOND WAR OF THE SUCCESSORS

In his proclamation, Polyperchon singled out Athens for favorable treatment: not only would the democratic exiles return, as everywhere, but the island of Samos would be restored to the city. It had been removed by Perdiccas just a few years earlier as a consequence of Alexander's Exiles Decree. Somehow, Polyperchon's promise of freedom for the Greeks did not include the Greeks of Samos, who were to be expelled once more from their farmland in favor of Athenian settlers.

But the glittering jewel of Athens in his crown was worth a little inconsistency.

The Athenian democrats contacted Polyperchon early in 318 and requested help in changing the regime that had been imposed by Antipater after the Lamian War. Polyperchon sent his son Alexander south. With an army encamped just outside the city walls, the leaders of the oligarchy were deposed and executed in May 318. Athens thus became a protectorate of the official regime in Macedon, and democracy was restored. Jubilation was muted, however, by the continued presence of Nicanor and the garrison in Piraeus, which could still make a considerable difference to Athenian fortunes. Before long Cassander himself arrived, with men and ships loaned to him by Antigonus, to make Piraeus the launch point for his attempt on Macedon.

Polyperchon responded by coming south in force to join his son for the blockade of Piraeus, but they achieved very little, since they could not control the sea. The Athenians were also finding it hard to feed the army of twenty-five thousand that was encamped on their land. Polyperchon therefore left Alexander with enough men to dissuade Cassander from venturing out of Piraeus by land, and marched into the Peloponnese.

Most of the Peloponnesian cities bloodily evicted the Antipatrid oligarchs on Polyperchon's orders. The most important exception was Megalopolis in Arcadia, and Polyperchon put it under siege. The battle was protracted and closely fought, but in the end the defenders were successful. They even foiled a final push by Polyperchon's elephants through the collapsed wall by laying spikes in the breach.[1] In frustration, Polyperchon left Megalopolis under siege (which was eventually broken off months later without having achieved its objective) and withdrew back to Macedon. Polyperchon's failures at Piraeus and Megalopolis, despite the size of his army, drastically slowed the rate at which the cities threw in their lot with him. It now seemed more sensible for them to wait and see who would win the war in Greece.

With many of his troops tied up in the sieges of Piraeus and Megalopolis, Polyperchon turned his attention elsewhere. Still desperate for allies, he sent the naval expert Cleitus to relieve Arrhidaeus, under siege in Cius, and at the same time to guard against a possible crossing of the Hellespont by Antigonus, who was encamped not far from Byzantium. The expedition went well at first; Cleitus relieved Arrhidaeus and joined forces with him. And when Nicanor arrived from Piraeus with over a hundred ships to help Antigonus, Cleitus inflicted a severe defeat on him off Byzantium. But that very night Antigonus arranged an unexpected counterattack: while he set about Cleitus's camp on land, Nicanor returned with the remnants of the fleet to disable the enemy ships as they lay beached or tried to escape. It was a complete victory. Arrhidaeus either died or surrendered. Cleitus's flagship alone escaped, but when he landed in Thrace, he ran into a detachment of Lysimachus's troops and was killed. It was a wretched end for the man who, after his earlier successes, had styled himself as Poseidon, the god of the sea, and had insisted on being treated as a god.[2] Nicanor fared little better, since soon after returning to Piraeus he was killed on Cassander's orders for being overambitious.

The loss of the fleet meant not just that Polyperchon was now cut off from Eumenes, but also that there was little to stop Antigonus crossing the Bosporus and coming at Macedon that way. But the deal the two allies had made assigned all Europe to Cassander, and Antigonus was not yet ready to leave Asia Minor. It was all under his control now—his personal control or that of allies such as Asander in Caria—from the Hellespont to the Taurus Mountains, but there was the matter of Eumenes just beyond the Taurus. He left most of his forces to protect Asia Minor, entrusted the war in Greece to Cassander, and marched southeast after the renegade Eumenes.

SEA BATTLE

Naval warfare had not changed much since the Classical period. The methods were still the same: skillful maneuvering so that you were in a position to disable an enemy ship by ramming (with or without subsequent boarding by marines) or by breaking its oars and oarsmen. The main innovations or developments in the early Hellenistic period stemmed from the same love of gigantism that produced—to name just a few outstanding examples—enormous armies, the Colossus of Rhodes, the Lighthouse at Alexandria, and the temple of Apollo at Didyma. Ever-larger vessels were being built. Unlike the sleek triremes of the Classical era, larger ships could deploy artillery on their decks—joined together catamaran-style, they might even carry massive siege towers with which to assault a port from the sea—and they could also carry more men. So the two chief developments in the early Hellenistic period were a greater reliance on long-range offensive weaponry, and more direct action. Instead of maneuvering to take an enemy ship from the side, the primary objective of Hellenistic naval warfare became frontal ramming, followed by boarding.[3]

The increased sizes of Hellenistic warships hugely increased the expense of navies. A fleet of a hundred warships of varying sizes, from triremes upward, might employ around thirty thousand men as crew and marines. A single, enormous ship built toward the end of the third century BCE by Ptolemy IV had a crew of almost 7,500 men, including three thousand marines. This vessel was largely for show, but already in our period Demetrius the Besieger was building some lesser, seaworthy monsters.

But even before the crews had embarked, ships were very expensive to produce. It was essential also to control the raw materials, or to have good trading relations with places that controlled them: wood for the hull, mast, and deck (preferably fir, cedar, or pine), for the keel (oak for warships), and for the oars (preferably fir); pitch for caulking and bitumen for coating the hull; hemp, esparto, or papyrus for the cordage; flax to make linen for the sailcloth. The cost of ships was such that enemy ships were extremely valuable booty for the enemy. Being made of wood, holed ships tended to founder rather than sink, and could then be captured and taken in tow.

It was essential also to have access to as many ports as possible, not just as dockyards but as havens. Ancient ships were very vulnerable to bad weather, did not ride comfortably at anchor in the open sea, and, given the sizes of their crews, needed to restock their provisions regularly. They also had a tendency to become waterlogged. This weakness of ancient warships—that they often needed to make land—made it desirable to control not just ports but whole stretches of coastline, as well as islands. Ships that were temporarily beached, away from the safety of a good harbor, were also vulnerable to attack from either land or sea, as Cleitus found to his cost.

ATHENS AND EARLY HELLENISTIC CULTURE

In Athens, constant military and diplomatic pressure from Cassander took its toll. Despairing of any effective action from Polyperchon, the Athenians decided to surrender and opened negotiations. After only a few months, in the summer of 317, the restored democracy fell again, this time in favor of dictatorship by a puppet ruler of Cassander's choice. Cassander gave the job to the Aristotelian philosopher Demetrius of Phalerum, highly regarded, but still aged under forty. Demetrius ruled Athens for the next ten years, with the backing of the

Macedonian garrison, of course. Piraeus and Athens were reunited, and gave Cassander a secure base in southern Greece.

Demetrius of Phalerum's rule, though benign, sealed the end of Athens's world-famous experiment in democracy. Although in later years from time to time the term was used for the constitution, the democratic organs of the state were actually dominated by a narrow group of wealthy families. This, as I have already remarked, is the pattern that came to exist within all the great cities of the Hellenistic world: power devolved upon those citizens who were wealthy enough to support the city both materially and through their channels of communication with distant kings.

Cassander's protection ushered in a decade of relative peace for Athens. No wars were fought on Athenian soil, though of course the city took a keen interest in events elsewhere. Theophrastus (Demetrius of Phalerum's teacher) wrote his *Characters*, light-hearted vignettes of different kinds of people, around this time, and his sketch of a rumor-monger shows him spreading the alarming (and untrue) report that "Polyperchon and King Philip have won a battle and Cassander has been taken prisoner"[4]—a situation that would certainly have spelled trouble for Demetrius of Phalerum's pro-Cassandrian Athens. But Athenians watched from the sidelines rather than being involved in the action, and this was a major change for a city that had been at the center of Greek affairs for almost two hundred years, until the Lamian War.

The relative disempowerment of Athens in the Hellenistic period shows, above all, in the fact that it never again built monumental buildings out of its own resources, without the help of kings and wealthy individuals. It also shows in its literature and art, and most clearly in the comedy that was popular at the time. In the days when Athens had been a major power in the Aegean, comedy had blended farcical fantasy with satire, or even direct criticism, of contemporary figures, especially political figures and their policies. Aristophanes, the main comic playwright at the end of the fifth century, assumed that his job was to instruct his audiences as well as entertain them.[5] By contrast, it is clear that Menander of Athens, the chief surviving representative of the kind of comic plays that were being shown at the end of the fourth century (conventionally called "New Comedy"), was concerned more or less entirely with entertainment. The rural setting of most of his comedies contrasts with the way Aristophanes set his plays in the heart of the city, where the political action was.

Menander's plays are delightful, but they are light, soap-operatic situation comedies. The protagonists are recognizable types, but not political types; they are, for instance, clever slaves, young women with illegitimate children, grumpy old men, braggart soldiers, and worthless young men-about-town, all depicted with great skill and psychological insight. The plots invariably center on a thwarted love affair, which comes out well for the young lovers in the end. Where Aristophanes was engaged in contemporary events, Menander (who was a friend of Demetrius of Phalerum) and his peers do no more than refer to them as a kind of backdrop. Women might be abducted by pirates, or sold into slavery, or captured in war, or have children by foreign soldiers. Men contemplate enlisting as mercenaries, or are assumed to have died abroad on service, or return with a "spear-won" concubine. Menander was writing at a time when thousands of lives were being lost on the battlefields of Asia and Europe, but, not surprisingly, he felt it was his job to distract his audience's attention from such harsh realities, not to comment directly on them. He was writing escapist literature. He drew attention not to large-scale events but to the personal problems of individuals and their families. And so he kept step with the emphasis on the individual that we have already found to be a dominant feature of early Hellenistic culture.

Escapism is apparent too in the new craze among rich town-dwellers for commissioning pastoral paintings to adorn their domestic quarters—the first manifestation of the long European tradition of landscape painting. None of these paintings has survived from the Hellenistic period, but they are known through later imitations, especially those preserved in the ruins of Pompeii and Herculaneum in southern Italy (though of course Roman artists were never merely imitative). Vitruvius, writing in Rome in the first century BCE, described typical scenes as "harbors, headlands, woods, hills, and the wanderings of Odysseus."[6] Such scenes were considered relaxing—which is to say that they took one's mind off current affairs. The men who commissioned these paintings were increasingly cut off from the countryside, and so they idealized it. It is telling that the Greek word *boukolikos*, meaning "bucolic" or "pastoral," also came to mean "soothing," "distracting."

Of course, it is somewhat facile to describe any works of art or literature just as "escapist." They are works of art in their own right, and many of the productions of the Hellenistic era have stood the test of time well. The degree of skill and the quality of the attention paid to works of art make it clear that both the artists themselves and their patrons shared the concept of art for art's sake. The fact that they may have served escapist purposes is important from a social-historical point of view, but it falls far short of any kind of assessment of their worth as artistic productions.

These pastoral paintings quite often occupied panels that were displayed in a room in such a way that they could be read as a continuous narrative. Around the middle of the third century, poets such as Theocritus began to echo the trend by writing pastoral or bucolic vignettes. Not all of Theocritus's *Idylls* are on pastoral themes, but all of them display the typical Hellenistic focus on everyday men and women rather than heroes. In *Idyll* I, the most famous of the pastoral idylls, a shepherd and a goatherd pipe and sing for each other, for entertainment and competition, and their exchanges are filled with details of country life: the music of the breeze in the pines, the playful sound of a waterfall, the flora and fauna, tasks such as milking, and lore such as that the meat of an unweaned kid tastes better. All the pastoral *Idylls* are imbued with escapism in the form of "the nostalgia, or hope, for simple virtues, uncomplicated living, plain home-grown food, basic country values."[7] Of course, country life never has been as ideal as this fantasy, produced for an urban elite by the court poet of Ptolemy II's Alexandria. Theocritus instigated the pastoral dream that led, via Virgil, to Poussin's Arcadia.

The evidence for the kind of tragedies that were being written in Athens and elsewhere at the time is exiguous, but bears out these generalizations about escapism. As far as we can tell, they tended to emphasize technical and musical virtuosity over the depiction and problematization of ideal civic values, as their fifth-century predecessors had. The fifth-century masterpieces of Aeschylus, Sophocles, and Euripides were commonly revived, but only as great works of literature; we watch a Shakespeare production in much the same way nowadays, missing the copious references to contemporary events.

The new emphasis on the individual also informed sculpture and painting. While kings and commanders were still portrayed in propagandist ways that distinguished them as players of critical roles, a considerable gap opened up between this kind of public idealism and the increasingly large numbers of privately commissioned works of art, which aimed at the perfect execution of less weighty subjects, depicted as realistically as the writer or artist could manage. Coin portraits bridged the gap, with their subtle combinations of ideal and real.

Earlier in the fourth century, sculptors and painters had already begun to strive for a closer imitation of nature than the classical ideal allowed. Lysippus of Sicyon had introduced a new proto-Mannerist canon for the human figure, with longer legs and smaller heads, and positioned so that more than just the front of the body was visible. On this basis, sculptors began to experiment with more sensuous poses of the human form. The full range of emotions could now be expressed on face and body together—a satyr turning to look at his tail, a dancer dancing free. Realism—or at least the appearance of realism, as Lysippus is said to have quipped[8]—was the name of the game. Just as Lysippus was Alexander's court sculptor, so Apelles of Colophon (died ca. 295) was the only painter he allowed to do his portrait, and Apelles too was at the forefront of developing a new realism in painting—so much so that, as the story goes, Alexander's horse Bucephalas whinnied at its own image in one of his paintings.[9]

A new aesthetic was emerging. Poetry and the visual arts focused on technique and subtle displays of learning, and reflected each other. What was assonance in poetry and repeated motif in music became the periodic placing of color and form in painting; poetry in particular was full of such devices, designed to enhance its musicality, playfulness, and suggestiveness. Techniques such as filigree, chiaroscuro, and gilding were the visual counterparts of the wit and refinement of Hellenistic poetry. Poets returned the favor by valuing vividness, the ability to bring a matter directly before the mind's eye. The subjects of all media were similar: pets, plants, children, ordinary people, domestic scenes, comic characters, tragic characters—all portrayed with vigor, a love of detail, and psychological insight. In some cases, artists chose to make their emotional point by grotesquery and caricature (here we find hunchbacks, dwarfs, and cripples, for instance); in others, by pathos or a gentle eroticism. Realism or caricature were the goals. It was all a far cry from war.

MACEDON IN TURMOIL

Cassander's takeover of Athens was a major blow to Polyperchon, but worse was to follow. In the summer of 317, Polyperchon was in Epirus, with Alexander IV, negotiating with the Aetolians to the south and arranging for Olympias's return to Macedon. She had finally agreed to take up his offer of being the official guardian of her grandson. One wonders what the first meeting was like between Olympias and the boy king—and his Bactrian mother. Taking advantage of Polyperchon's absence, and his lack of success as a military leader, Adea Eurydice had her husband (a pawn, as throughout his life) write to all the major players, announcing that he was ordering Polyperchon to resign the regency and his command of the armed forces in favor of Cassander. At last she was operating with the degree of freedom she had tried to win at Triparadeisus. She was defeated then by Antipater, but clearly did not hold a grudge against his son. And now she was insisting that, in these troubled times, legitimacy lay with her and her husband, rather than with Alexander IV and Olympias.

The existence of two kings had always been anomalous, and potentially explosive. Now the two courts formed separate camps, and there could be no doubt in anyone's mind that the final showdown had begun. Only one of the kings would survive this crisis. Cassander made a flying visit to Macedon to formalize his assumption of the regency, but then returned to his campaigns in the Peloponnese, where he was trying to recover the cities that Polyperchon had gained the year before. He expected to wrap things up soon, and then return to Macedon, but in the event he got held up at the siege of Tegea.

It did not take Polyperchon long to gather his forces to attack Adea Eurydice in Macedon, with Olympias at the symbolic head of an army that consisted largely of troops lent by the Molossian king. With Cassander tied up in the south, Adea came out to meet them at the head of her troops. Her bid for power came to an abrupt end when she was deserted by her men, who had no desire to fight the mother and son of Alexander. They had to choose between two Argead kings, and the presence of Olympias tipped the scales away from the half-wit. Besides, Philip had not and was presumably not likely to father any heirs.

Adea Eurydice and Philip III fell into Olympias's ungentle hands, and found Polyperchon disinclined to interfere in her vengeance. She imprisoned them in tiny, windowless cells in Pydna, and set about a purge in Macedon. While removing dozens of potential enemies among the Macedonian nobility, she focused particularly on Antipater's family, claiming that she was avenging the poisoning of her son. She had Nicanor killed and scattered the ashes of another of Antipater's sons, Iolaus, who had been Alexander's cupbearer and therefore the prime suspect in the alleged poisoning. If Heracles and Barsine were in Macedon, this is presumably when they fled to Pergamum, where they took up residence under Antigonus's protection.

Olympias's purge sped to its inevitable conclusion, and she took the momentous step of killing Alexander's half brother, the legitimate king, and his royal wife. Reputedly, she sent nineteen-year-old Adea hemlock, a noose, and a sword, for her to choose. Adea chose the noose, but spited Olympias by using her own girdle.[10] The fact that

Philip was a king, and had been for over six years, did not deter Olympias; it was more relevant that he was the rival to her grandson, in whose name she was now the effective ruler of Macedon.

But this was her last stroke; Cassander had abandoned his war in the Peloponnese against Polyperchon's son Alexander, and was on his way north. He knew he could expect support from the same factions in Macedon that had allowed Adea to declare for him, but his enemies raised three armies against him, and must have been confident of victory. The situation was critical; it would make or break either Polyperchon and Olympias, or Cassander.

Cassander displayed tactical genius. First, he bypassed the Aetolians, who were holding the pass at Thermopylae against him, by transporting his army by boat around them. He then split his army into three: one division checked the Molossian king in Epirus, another did the same to Polyperchon on the southern border of Macedon, and while these two enemies were occupied, he marched with the rest of his forces on Macedon itself, where Aristonous, perhaps with little more than his baronial forces, gave in more or less without a fight and retreated to Amphipolis. Polyperchon's army was bribed away from him and he fled, ultimately to join his son in the Peloponnese, where a few cities remained loyal. One of Cassander's first moves as the new ruler of Macedon was to foment rebellion in Epirus against the Molossian king and install a puppet on the throne in his place. His victory was swift and overwhelming. He was perhaps a little over thirty-five years old, and he would rule Macedon for almost twenty years, until his death in 297.

CASSANDER TAKES CONTROL

Olympias took the royal court to Pydna, where she holed up with a considerable and loyal army. After Polyperchon's flight, she could pin her hopes only on her generals, but they had problems of their own. So, over the late autumn and winter of 317/316, Cassander besieged her forces in Pydna to the point of desertion and starvation, and Olympias was captured while trying to escape by ship. Pydna fell, and Cassander gained by force the right to be the protector and guardian of the young king. Aristonous held on to Amphipolis until ordered by Olympias to give up the unequal struggle, but both Olympias and he were promptly killed by Cassander, despite assurances of safety.

In Olympias's case, Cassander felt the need to cover himself with a cloak of legality. He was no Argead, nor had he been a companion of

Alexander the Great, and he was uncertain of his standing among the Macedonian troops and barons, even though he could claim that he was killing the killer of the joint king of Macedon. So he got an army assembly to condemn her on the basis of a show trial, and, in order to make sure that no Macedonian loyal to the Argead line got cold feet, he had her put to death by relatives of those she had killed during her purge.[11] She was not quite sixty years old, and had been at or close to the center of Macedonian affairs since, as a teenager, she had become the bride of Philip II. Though the six-year-old king was too young to know it, the execution of his grandmother savagely reduced the chances of his full succession. She had been his principal and most influential champion ever since his birth.

Cassander's military skills had endeared him to the army, who always responded to a strong general, and over the next few years he continued to make war on his enemies in the Peloponnese and central Greece and to secure Macedon's borders. He was also generous in awarding his supporters positions of responsibility, where they could hold power and enrich themselves. But above all he chose the usual way to legitimize his rule—by associating himself closely with the Argead line. In the first place, he held elaborate state funerals for Philip III and Adea Eurydice, and even for Cynnane, six years dead. Philip and his wife are the probable occupants of the incomparable Tomb 2 at Vergina; on the hunt fresco that dominates the tomb, Philip was portrayed not as an imbecile, but as a Macedonian hero.[12] In the second place, he took as his wife a half sister of Alexander the Great called Thessalonice, who had been a member of Olympias's entourage.

Cassander was now de facto regent, even though, with Polyperchon still alive, there were delicate questions of legitimacy to be ignored by everyone. But no doubt he already envisaged his sons by Thessalonice occupying the throne of Macedon. He treated Rhoxane and Alexander IV badly, keeping them for years under house arrest on the citadel of the merchant town of Amphipolis, without pandering to their royal status. He gave out that their isolation in Amphipolis was for their own safety.

There is a fine line between regency and full kingship, as Philip II had found to his advantage. And Cassander very soon began to act like a king, above all by founding three cities within a single year, 316, the first full year of his reign. The two cities that were founded within Macedon—Cassandreia and Thessalonica—were Macedon's first major urban centers. Apart from Pella, the country was still almost entirely rural; Cassander's foundations represented a major step forward in Macedonian history.

Cassandreia was founded on the site of Potidaea, and incorporated other nearby villages, including the remnants of the once important town of Olynthus. Thessalonica, named to flatter his Argead wife, was founded by the amalgamation and incorporation of twenty-six small towns and villages at the head of the Thermaic Gulf; as the glorious future history of the city shows—it became joint capital with Constantinople of the Byzantine empire—the site was well chosen.[13] These two ports hugely helped Cassander to develop a navy. He also refounded the Boeotian city of Thebes; he needed a bulwark of loyalty in central Greece against the unremitting hostility of the Aetolians.

As well as serving practical purposes, all three of these foundations or refoundations were symbolic. Philip II and Alexander the Great had been the first to found cities in their own names and those of their family members. Cassander was implying that he was at least their equal—and even their superior: Philip had reduced Potidaea and destroyed Olynthus, and Alexander had razed Thebes to the ground. Cassander now dared to undo these acts of his Argead predecessors. Whether or not Alexander the Great had been right to judge that Antipater had regal pretensions, Antipater's son certainly did.

Hunting Eumenes in Iran

In the summer of 318, Antigonus, poised to invade Europe across the Hellespont, had chosen to leave Polyperchon to Cassander, while he set out instead to tackle Eumenes in Cilicia. Without a fleet after Byzantium, Polyperchon and Eumenes were isolated from each other and could be dealt with separately. The strategy turned out to be sound. Only a little over a year later, in the winter of 317/316, Cassander had Olympias under siege in Pydna, and Polyperchon had abandoned Macedon. Meanwhile, three thousand kilometers (1,800 miles) farther east, in the foothills of the Zagros Mountains of western Iran, Antigonus and Eumenes were poised for the third and final battle in one of the great forgotten campaigns of world history.[1]

In Cilicia, Eumenes had spent the kings' money well, to bring his forces up to strength. The word went out and mercenaries poured into the eastern Mediterranean ports, where his recruiters collected them. But Eumenes was still plagued by challenges to his leadership and felt he had to take steps to prove to Antigenes and the other Macedonian officers that he did not feel that he was their superior, despite the fact that Polyperchon had named him General of Asia. It was worth his while to appease them—he badly needed their Macedonian troops.

He came up with an extraordinary ruse. He claimed that in a dream he had seen Alexander the Great, dressed in his regal robes, giving orders to a council of senior commanders. Eumenes suggested, then, that he and the Macedonian officers should simulate this scene, and should meet, as such a council, before one of Alexander's thrones, on which would be placed the dead king's regalia. There was nothing very original about the dream; Perdiccas had used the regalia to similar effect at the first Babylon conference, and on the same occasion Ptolemy had proposed just such a council of peers. But the implicit message of such a dream at this juncture was that Alexander—that is, right—was still on their side.

In any case, from then on, that is what they did. They set up a tent, adorned with a throne and the regalia (all borrowed from the Cyinda treasury), and after sacrificing to Alexander as a god, they conducted their meetings as equals before the empty throne. At the same time, Eumenes endeared himself to the Macedonian veterans themselves by flattering them and making it clear that he had no designs on the throne, but wanted only to build on their extraordinary achievements and defend Alexander's kingdom. It worked well enough for him to be immune when both Ptolemy, in his sole intervention in the war, and then Antigonus went to work on the Macedonians. Ptolemy offered cash if they refused to cooperate with Eumenes, while Antigonus ordered them to arrest Eumenes and put him to death or be treated as his enemies. Eumenes heard of Antigonus's ploy before things got out of hand, and quieted the men down by reminding them that he, not Antigonus, represented legitimate authority. But it was a close call.

In the late summer of 318, at Antigonus's approach from Asia Minor, Eumenes broke camp and moved south to Phoenicia with his army, now numbering fifteen thousand. Ptolemy's fleet and garrisons withdrew at his approach. Knowing how vital control of the Aegean was to Polyperchon—without it, he would be less of a threat to Cassander and no threat at all to Asia Minor—Eumenes used some of the money he had been given at Cyinda to commandeer as many ships as he could and send them on their way. But they got no further than Rhosus, a port on the border between Syria and Cilicia. After the bloody victory at Byzantium, of which Eumenes was unaware, Antigonus had ordered the remnants of his fleet south. At the first encounter, the Phoenician officers hired by Eumenes changed sides. Antigonus could safely set out in pursuit of Eumenes.

TURMOIL IN THE EASTERN SATRAPIES

Eumenes was still outnumbered by Antigonus, but circumstances had conspired to make it likely that he could acquire more troops, if he was prepared to travel for them. There was a major power struggle going on in the east, pitting Peithon, satrap of Media, against an alliance of most of the other eastern satraps. The ever-ambitious Peithon was trying to create an independent empire out of the eastern satrapies. He had already occupied Parthia, and now he began to threaten Peucestas in Persis. Once they had been colleagues, as members of Alexander's Bodyguard. Under the circumstances, it was not difficult for Peucestas to garner support; the local satraps united behind him and drove Peithon out of Parthia. At the time of Eumenes' approach, Peithon was in Babylon, soliciting Seleucus's help. He cannot have offered any justification other than self-interest for such a blatantly aggressive venture.

So when Eumenes left Phoenicia (promptly reoccupied by Ptolemy) and headed east at Antigonus's approach in the autumn of 318, he wanted to supplement his army either with Peithon's and Seleucus's troops or with those of Peucestas and his allies. The rights and wrongs of the eastern squabble did not concern him; he just wanted troops. Perhaps, at the present moment, Peucestas's forces looked more attractive. The satrapal alliance had an army of more than eighteen thousand foot and over four thousand horse. Although all the Successors' armies included a few war elephants—Polyperchon even had them in Greece—the satraps were blessed with no fewer than 114 of the beasts, a gift from an Indian king to one of Peucestas's allies.

Eumenes spent the winter of 318/317 aggressively on the borders of Babylonia and entered into negotiations with Seleucus and Peithon, but to little avail. As the official Royal General of Asia, he appealed to their loyalty to the kings, but they remained unmoved. Seleucus attacked Eumenes' command as illegitimate; the sentence passed against him at Triparadeisus still held, as far as he was concerned. But his thinking was probably influenced by the knowledge that Antigonus was due to arrive and that the army of Peucestas and his fellow satraps currently had control of the eastern satrapies. If Seleucus agreed to help Eumenes, he would immediately find himself surrounded by powerful enemies. So far from aiding Eumenes, then, Seleucus and Peithon tried once more to detach the Macedonians from their Greek commander. Once again, Eumenes survived the attempt.

Eumenes left Babylonia early in 317, having written ahead to Peucestas and the other satraps, asking them, in the name of the kings, to join him in Susa. Seleucus made a half-hearted attempt to impede his progress, but was more eager to get him out of his satrapy than to make trouble that kept him there.[2] By the early summer, both Eumenes and the satraps of the coalition had reached Susa. They agreed to unite their forces. The final phase of the Second War of the Successors would pit Eumenes and the eastern satraps against Antigonus, Peithon, and Seleucus. The entire eastern half of the empire was convulsed.

Eumenes now had a formidable force under his command, but his new allies were all men who were used to being in command themselves. The challenge to his leadership intensified. Peucestas was particularly insistent, since he had contributed the most troops and had as good a claim to seniority as Eumenes. And Antigenes seized the opportunity to renew his challenge, trusting in local support since they were in his satrapy. The only way Eumenes could get the senior officers to work with him was by resorting once again to the "Alexander Tent." By holding their daily meetings in the cultic presence of Alexander's ghost, and by remembering that Eumenes was the only one with official authorization from the kings to draw on the royal treasuries, they managed to put aside their differences long enough to come up with a workable plan. But the army remained fragile, with each satrap encamping his forces separately and supplying them from his own satrapy.

The unstable coalition decided to withdraw farther east, take up a good defensive position, and await Antigonus. It was nearly high summer, and the advantage would lie with whichever army did not have to travel in the extreme heat just before giving battle. Susa was abandoned except for the citadel with its treasury, which was strongly garrisoned and well provisioned. Eumenes and Peucestas deployed their forces along the far banks of the rivers to the north and east of the city, a few days' journey distant. They could patrol and protect the land all the way from the mountains to the sea, which was a lot closer in those days—an enormous amount of silting has shrunk the Persian Gulf. They waited for Antigonus.

PREPARATIONS FOR THE SHOWDOWN

Antigonus paused, without immediately following Eumenes east. The news that Eumenes had linked up with the eastern satraps made it imperative for him to increase the size of his army. He waited several months, over the winter and spring of 318/317, in Mesopotamia, where he raised both men and provisions, and negotiated with Seleucus and Peithon in Babylon. It seems likely that Antigonus did not ask the Mesopotamian governor's permission to occupy and strip his territory, for he fled east and joined Eumenes in Susa with a useful company of six hundred horse.

The interests of Seleucus and Peithon clearly coincided with those of Antigonus, and in May of 317 they came to an agreement, and Antigonus set out east after Eumenes. His army now consisted of 28,000 heavy infantry (including 8,000 Macedonians), at least 10,000 light infantry and about the same number of cavalry, and sixty-five elephants. He took Peithon and Seleucus with him too, but in subordinate positions. He was the undisputed commander in chief.

The journey to Susa was straightforward. Rather than delay, Antigonus left Seleucus to investigate the citadel while he continued after the enemy. But Eumenes sent a force to take him as he was crossing the swiftly flowing Coprates (the river, the modern Dez, has now been dammed), whose bridges the satrapal coalition had destroyed on their way east. By the time Eumenes got there, some ten thousand men had already crossed, many of them lightly armed and intent only on foraging. Eumenes overwhelmed them, taking four thousand for himself and killing hundreds more.

Antigonus had lost large numbers of men. He could not force a crossing, and he could not just stay in Susiana with his men idle and suffering from the heat that had already taken some lives. He disengaged and marched north to the relative cool of Ecbatana, about a month's journey. It was the capital of Peithon's satrapy, and enough money was stored there for Antigonus to keep his men happy. On the way they suffered further losses from hostile tribesmen, since he had chosen the short, difficult route to Media through the mountains rather than the longer route up the Tigris valley and along the Babylon–Ecbatana road. The point was to get his men to the relative cool of the mountains as soon as possible. It was late August by the time he reached Ecbatana, where he could lick his wounds, make up his losses, and improve his men's shattered morale.

The retreat to Ecbatana was highly risky, a sign of just how desperate Antigonus was after this first defeat. Ecbatana was too far north for him to be able to stop Eumenes from returning west. By retreating that far, Antigonus isolated Seleucus in Susa and allowed Eumenes and his allies to return and threaten Babylonia and Syria if they chose to. In Eumenes' camp, the senior officers were divided. Eumenes and Antigenes wanted to storm west, but the eastern satraps refused to abandon their satrapies.

If the satraps stayed in the east while Eumenes and Antigenes fought their way west, the chances were that neither division of the army would be strong enough to attain its objectives. Eumenes therefore gave in and stayed, though he too moved away from the worst heat. The army went to Persepolis, which had been one of the capital cities of the Achaemenid empire and was now the capital of Peucestas's province, nearly a month's journey away to the southeast. Peucestas had a further ten thousand light infantry waiting there, including a contingent of the renowned Persian bowmen. Peucestas allowed the men to forage as they wished in the countryside, and once they reached Persepolis he treated the entire army to a splendid feast. All the many thousands were seated in four vast concentric circles, from the rank-and-file soldiers on the outside to the senior officers and dignitaries on the inside. The center of the circle consisted of altars to the gods, including Philip and Alexander, where Peucestas performed a magnificent sacrifice. Secure on his own turf, he launched another attempt to undermine Eumenes' command.

The degree of disloyalty and contentiousness that Eumenes had to face from his fellow generals was quite extraordinary, but he responded with typical cunning. He produced a forged letter to the effect that Cassander was dead and Olympias in charge in Macedon, and that Polyperchon had already invaded Asia Minor. Clearly, news had not yet reached them of the true state of affairs in Europe, where, on the contrary, Cassander had Olympias under siege in Pydna. The letter restored the army's confidence, since they now believed that Eumenes' allies had the upper hand. Under these circumstances, it made no sense to undermine Eumenes' authority as Royal General of Asia, and he was briefly able to assert his authority as commander in chief.

All intrigues were sidelined, however, when news came that Antigonus had left Media and was advancing on Persis. Leaving a token force to defend Persepolis, Eumenes set out to meet him. Almost ninety thousand men and two hundred elephants were to clash on the edge of the Iranian desert. For the first time in western history, elephants would be involved on both sides of a battle.

THE FINAL BATTLES

For several days after the armies drew close to each other in the district of Paraetacene, late in October 317, nothing happened apart from a little skirmishing. The terrain (near modern Yezd-i-Khast) was rugged and unsuitable for a decisive battle. Antigonus continued his vain attempts to have Eumenes betrayed to him. Joining battle was also hampered by the fact that both armies soon became critically short of supplies, and many men were assigned to foraging duties. The nearest fertile district was Gabene (near modern Isfahan), some three days' journey away to the southeast.

Antigonus was about to set off there, but Eumenes heard of his plans from deserters. In return he sent false deserters to Antigonus's camp. This was the most common and effective way to feed the enemy with misinformation, in this case that an attack on Antigonus's camp was planned for that very night, so that Antigonus would be vulnerable if he was breaking camp as planned. Antigonus fell for it and stayed put, and it was Eumenes who left in the night and got a head start toward Gabene. When Antigonus discovered the ruse, he personally led a cavalry detachment to hold some high ground along the route, while Peithon brought up the infantry. Eumenes spotted the cavalry and, assuming that Antigonus's entire army had arrived, drew up his men for battle. The terrain meant that he could hardly be outflanked, but he had the disadvantage of facing uphill, so he waited. Before long, the rest of Antigonus's army arrived, and took up their positions.

Antigonus's heavy infantry in the center outnumbered Eumenes, but he took care that Macedonians would not directly face Macedonians, in case they refused to fight one another. He deployed his light cavalry in large numbers on the left wing, commanded by Peithon, and his heavy cavalry on the right, under the command of his son Demetrius, still only nineteen years old. His elephants were mostly posted on the right and in the center, whereas Eumenes had adopted a more orthodox and evenly balanced formation. Antigonus advanced down the hill toward the enemy lines, and battle was joined.

On Antigonus's left, Peithon's light cavalry were routed, after an exceedingly close-fought contest. In the center, the elephants proved ineffective and were withdrawn, and the phalanxes became engaged in a bloody battle. Here Antigenes' crack veterans did what they did best, and broke Antigonus's phalanx. But as they pressed forward, they opened up a gap between themselves and the left wing. Antigonus had kept the cavalry on his right wing screened by elephants, but now he ordered them to charge, and before long Eumenes' left was in disorder.

Both sides regrouped and faced each other again, but despite tactical movements and countermovements they could do little in the gathering gloom, and after nightfall the exhausted and hungry armies disengaged by the light of a full moon. Eumenes' men insisted on returning to their camp, leaving Antigonus in possession of the field and therefore of the battlefield spoils, the usual tokens of victory. But he had lost four times as many men as Eumenes and gained nothing. In fact, after seeing to his dead, he withdrew, leaving Gabene to

Eumenes for the winter, and went northeast to take up winter quarters in Media. The two armies were perched on two spines of the Zagros foothills, with an arid salt plain between them.

Eumenes' winter quarters were scattered. His army was as fragmented as usual, and separate divisions were encamped far and wide. And in those pre-Roman days, camps were scarcely fortified. This attracted Antigonus's attention, but even so, given that he was now outnumbered, the attack he planned was predicated on surprise. He decided not to wait for spring but to attack during the winter, and to come at Eumenes from an unexpected direction. He would take his army across the salt plain that lay between the two armies. This would cut his journey down to about nine days, as opposed to over three weeks if they went around the desert—and Eumenes in any case had pickets in place all along the routes approaching his position from other directions.

They set off around December 20. The plan was to travel by night and rest by day. The troops carried prepared rations and plenty of water for the arid desert. Antigonus issued strict orders that no fires were to be lit, despite the subzero temperatures at night. Any fires on the plain would cut through the darkness and be clearly visible from the surrounding hills. Everything went well at first. They were more than halfway across when the cold tempted some of the men to light fires. No doubt the men themselves were thankful for the warmth, but the point may have been to keep the elephants alive, since they would have been suffering badly. In any case, the fires were spotted by some local villagers, who warned Eumenes.

But it already seemed too late. Antigonus was only four days away, and the furthest-flung of Eumenes' divisions was six days away. Peucestas recommended a tactical withdrawal, to buy time. But Eumenes had fires of his own lit on the hills, enough to make it seem as though a major division of his army was protecting the direct route across the plain and occupying the high ground. Antigonus's men were compelled to turn, and they reached the edge of the desert north of Eumenes' position. Antigonus had lost the element of surprise, and Eumenes had gained the time to regroup his army.

The elephants were the last to reach the huge fortified camp Eumenes built. But by then Antigonus's troops were refreshed and on the move south, and he sent a strong unit of cavalry and light infantry to intercept the elephants. Eumenes deployed a stronger counterforce, and suffered nothing worse than a few losses and some wounded beasts. But morale in Eumenes' camp was lower than at Paraetacene. In the intervening period, rumors had reached them that Eumenes' commission had been revoked, when Adea Eurydice had her husband disown Polyperchon. But Antigenes compensated with a nice coup just before the battle. He sent some of his Macedonian veterans to shout out to Antigonus's Macedonians: "You assholes are sinning against your fathers, the men who conquered the world with Philip and Alexander!"[3]

They faced each other across several miles of salt plain; the battle would be fought on level ground, with the only difficulty the terrain offered being the terrible dust for which the salt plains or *kavirs* of the Iranian plateau are infamous. Antigonus adopted pretty much the same formation as at Paraetacene. Eumenes, in response, bulked up his left wing with the majority of the elephants and cavalry, and took joint command there with Peucestas. He was directly facing Antigonus, who commanded his right wing, as was usual. After the initial skirmishing, Antigonus and his cavalry attacked Eumenes' left. Peucestas caved in suspiciously quickly, but Eumenes took up the struggle and kept Antigonus at bay for a while. Meanwhile, in the center, Antigenes' veterans were as successful as at Paraetacene. It was a massacre: thousands of Antigonus's men died, compared with a few hundred of Eumenes'. Eumenes seemed assured, if not of outright victory, then at least of the upper hand, and he rode around to the right wing, to take command there for the final push.

But as it turned out, the decisive move had already taken place off the battlefield. Antigonus had risked sending a sizable cavalry squadron from his left wing around the battlefield, under cover of the choking dust cloud created by thousands of men and horses on the move, to take Eumenes' undefended baggage train. By the time Eumenes became aware of what had happened, it was too late to do anything about it. Night was falling, and Peucestas refused to join him for the cavalry push on the right.

Eumenes was forced to disengage. He had fallen foul of the very stratagem he had used against Neoptolemus in 320, but there was a more significant precedent. The same thing had happened to Alexander the Great at Gaugamela, and had evoked a famous *mot* from the Conqueror: he had ordered his officers to ignore the threat to their baggage, on the grounds that "the victors will recover their own belongings *and* take those of the enemy."[4] Eumenes gave the same response, in much the same words, but without the same result.

Antigonus's phalanx had been shattered, and Eumenes could fairly look forward to victory the next day. But the Macedonian veterans refused to carry on, knowing that their wives and children had been captured, and the satraps insisted on withdrawing, to fight another day. Unknown to Eumenes, they had already decided, before the battle, to do away with him after the victory they had expected. Eumenes' appeals therefore fell on deaf ears, and messengers were secretly sent to Antigonus's camp to enquire after the safety of the Macedonians' families. Antigonus promised their return—once Eumenes had been handed over.

Within a few days of his being surrendered, Eumenes and several of his senior officers were put to death. Antigenes came off worst, despite his advanced age (he was about sixty-five): he was thrown alive into a pit and burnt there, in revenge for the slaughter his veterans had wrought on Antigonus's men. Eumenes' grand army, elephants and all, deserted en masse to Antigonus. Ever loyal to Olympias, Alexander IV, and the legitimate Argead cause, Eumenes had proved himself an excellent general and the most successful of the loyalists. His death ushered in a new era, in which, rather than working for the surviving king, Antigonus and his peers would strive to establish their own rights to kingship. The deaths of Olympias and Eumenes left the world in the hands of men who owed no loyalty except to themselves.

HOUSEKEEPING

By the end of 317, then, Antigonus had carried out his commission. But it had been clear, ever since his purge of the Asia Minor satraps, that he had far outstripped his Triparadeisus commission. His mastery of Asia seemed solid, his ally Cassander was in charge in Macedon, and Ptolemy was quiet in Egypt. It almost looked as though a balance of power might emerge, miraculously soon after Alexander's death. After the battle, Antigonus retired to winter quarters near Ecbatana, with the bulk of his now huge army dispersed far and wide over Media or repatriated to their satrapies. In the spring he would head west, but first he had a little housekeeping to take care of.

Peithon was an ambitious man, and could have been a contender— one of the great few who strove for control of large chunks or even the whole of Alexander's empire. He had played a considerable role at both Paraetacene and Gabene, was popular with the troops, and was satrap of wealthy Media, one of the heartlands of the former Persian empire. He had become involved in Antigonus's war against Eumenes in the first place only as a means to renew his bid for independence for the eastern satrapies, with him as their king, and he spent the winter after Eumenes' defeat trying to persuade as many of Antigonus's troops as possible to stay in the east and work for him.[5] But Antigonus was not ready to lose the eastern satrapies, a valuable source of revenue. He summoned Peithon to Ecbatana and, assured of his safety, Peithon guilelessly went. He was promptly arraigned before a council of Antigonus's Friends, accused of treachery (of trying to detach some of Antigonus's troops for his own purposes), and executed. Some of his lieutenants went on the warpath in Media, but were soon crushed. With the same presumption of authority that he had already displayed in Asia Minor, Antigonus appointed a new satrap for Media.

Another residual problem was Antigenes' veterans. They had been nothing but trouble since Triparadeisus, and now, by betraying Eumenes to him, they had proved their corruptibility. They had been bound by oaths of loyalty to Eumenes, but they had broken these oaths, albeit when faced with terrible personal loss. But then, Eumenes himself had broken his oath to Antigonus at Nora. Antigonus decided to dissolve the regiment. He packed some of them off to the remote east, to serve in Arachosia. The rest he kept with him, but as he returned west in the spring, he dispersed them here and there, as settlers to police potential trouble spots within his territories. In Arachosia, they were given jobs more suitable to mercenaries—garrisoning frontier towns, scouting in enemy territory. Antigonus's ruthless instructions to the satrap were to make sure that they did not survive their missions.[6]

CHANDRAGUPTA MAURYA

Arachosia was indeed troubled. Chandragupta Maurya, a conqueror who has every right to be considered as great as Alexander, was in expansionist mood.

The Indian satrapies won by Alexander bordered on a vast kingdom, ruled by the Nanda dynasty. Even in 326 and 325, while Alexander had been in India, he had been approached by a young man called Chandragupta (Sandrokottos to Greeks) for help in overthrowing the unpopular dynasty. Whatever Alexander may have thought about this, the mutiny of his men in India meant that he was unable to comply. After his departure, Chandragupta unified the warring northern tribes and did it himself. With the overthrow of the Nandas, he inherited a ready-made kingdom as his base.

Macedonian control over the Indian satrapies was tenuous. Two satraps had already been killed by 325, one in an uprising and the other by assassination. Alexander's death allowed Chandragupta to foment further rebellion. By the time of the Triparadeisus conference in 320, the Macedonians more or less acknowledged the independence of the Indian satrapies by making no new provisions for them. By 317, still aged under thirty, Chandragupta had taken over the Indian satrapies, thus effectively controlling all northern India from the Khyber Pass to the Ganges delta, and was turning his attention northward, toward the satrapies that ringed his new empire from the Himalayas to the Arabian Sea.

So when Antigonus made himself master of Asia, he inherited a number of provinces that were under constant pressure from the young Indian emperor. He did little to defend the region, but it remained fairly stable for a while, as long as Chandragupta was more concerned with securing what he had already gained. Unlike Alexander, Chandragupta put in place a complex, detailed, and precise administrative pyramid, to cover military, fiscal, and civil functions throughout his empire. He made his capital at Pataliputra (modern Patna) on the Ganges.[7]

Antigonus was little interested in the far east of his kingdom, and the satrapies there were left pretty much to their own devices until Seleucus reconquered them. This brought Seleucus into direct conflict with Chandragupta, and in 304 a great battle was fought. Seleucus was defeated and forced to cede to Chandragupta eastern Arachosia, Gandaris, Paropamisadae, and parts of Areia and Gedrosia. These provinces were never recovered, nor was any attempt made to do so. Chandragupta then expanded south until he controlled almost all of India, and Pakistan and Afghanistan up to the Hindu Kush. His empire was larger than British India. Seleucus kept a permanent ambassador at Chandragupta's court, a man called Megasthenes. We have no more than a few fragments of his account of India,[8] unfortunately, but it seems to have contained a warning against trying to defeat the Maurya empire. Chandragupta himself resigned the throne and dedicated his final years to religious devotion. He died in 298, and his empire continued for more than a hundred years, until the rise of a new dynasty in 185 BCE.

LORD OF ASIA

In the spring of 316 Antigonus started out from Ecbatana on his journey home. At Persepolis, he set up a kind of court—only a kind of court, because one night in 330 Alexander had gone along with a drunken escapade to destroy the main royal palace.[9] Antigonus summoned the eastern satraps from Eumenes' coalition and dictated their futures from his throne, in a manner deliberately reminiscent of the imperial power Antipater had assumed at Triparadeisus. Many satraps retained their earlier posts; not surprisingly, Eumenes' chief ally, Peucestas, found himself out of a job. The fact that he was allowed to remain alive at all is powerful evidence that his poor performance at Gabene was deliberate, that he had been suborned. At any rate, Antigonus took him back west with him on his staff, and he remained as a close adviser first to Antigonus and then to his son Demetrius. It was a climbdown for the former Bodyguard of Alexander, but it was safe: though he more or less drops out of the historical record, we still hear of him alive in the 290s.[10]

When Antigonus reached Susa, he appointed a permanent satrap there as well. Seleucus, who had already returned to Babylon, was no longer needed; the garrison commander of the citadel of Susa had surrendered as soon as news arrived of Eumenes' defeat. And so the treasury of Susa fell into Antigonus's hands. With Eumenes' death, none of the treasurers of Asia would refuse to open their doors to their new master. Antigonus helped himself to the resources stored at Ecbatana, Susa, and Persepolis, to the tune of twenty-five thousand talents (about fifteen billion dollars), and the territories he controlled, at their largest extent, brought in an annual income of a further eleven thousand talents.

Antigonus's wealth fueled his ambition and his ambition fed his wealth. Apart from anything else, he was able to maintain a huge standing army of forty thousand foot and five thousand horse, at a cost in the region of 2,500 talents a year. He brought west with him on his return from the eastern satrapies all the bullion he had taken from the east, and stored it in his key treasuries in Cilicia and Asia Minor. He was not intending to return that far east, and needed the money to retain control of his core realm, Asia west of the Euphrates. For the next dozen or so years, this heartland of his was remarkably free of warfare (though he was often at war beyond its borders), and he used this time of peace to develop and administer it, while still keeping an eye open, as did all the Successors, for occasions for expansion.[11]

But even though Antigonus ruled the entirety of the former Persian empire, apart from Egypt, he was not yet ready to call himself king, not while Alexander IV was still alive. That would have invited trouble—certainly from his rivals, who would pounce on the chance to use it against him, and probably from his troops, many of whom were still fiercely loyal to the Argead line. He allowed himself to be recognized by his native subjects as the successor to the Achaemenid kings and Alexander (who had also used the title "Lord of Asia"),[12] but in public he maintained the fiction that he was just some kind of super-satrap, the Royal General of Asia, holding the former Persian empire for the kings.

Antigonus was now living up to his alternative nickname—not just "the One-Eyed," but "Cyclops," after the famous one-eyed giants of myth. Both he and his son Demetrius were exceptionally tall and strongly built, but now Antigonus had become a metaphorical colossus too. Would the others tolerate it? Could a balance of power emerge, so soon after Alexander's death? It did not take Antigonus long to show that he was not interested in balance—he wanted the totality of Alexander's empire.

Antigonus, Lord of Asia

Fʀᴏᴍ ꜱᴜꜱᴀ, ᴀɴᴛɪɢᴏɴᴜꜱ journeyed west to Babylonia, with all his bullion and booty carefully guarded in the caravan, the moving equivalent of the strongholds that made up the empire's treasuries. The size and strength of the army, and its voraciousness, were plain tokens of Antigonus's naked ambition. Woe betide anyone who stood in his way, or who might even have the potential to stand in his way. Seleucus was the next to find this out.

When Antigonus reached Babylon, Seleucus honored him as a king, but it was not enough to appease the great man. The relationship deteriorated until Antigonus demanded from Seleucus, as though he were king and Seleucus a mere satrap, an account of his administration of the satrapy, and an audit of his finances. With considerable courage, Seleucus resisted Antigonus's bullying. He said he had been awarded Babylonia legitimately at Triparadeisus (subtly reminding Antigonus that the Triparadeisus conference was also where *he* had received his commission), in recognition of his services to Alexander, and that Antigonus did not have the right to interfere. In effect, he claimed a kind of seniority to Antigonus, who had scarcely been involved in Alexander's campaigns, since he had been posted in Asia Minor throughout. At the same time, Seleucus sensibly made plans to escape, and before long he fled for safety to Egypt with his family and a small escort.

In Egypt, Ptolemy welcomed Seleucus as a friend, but was no doubt also aware of the propaganda value of sheltering someone who could be portrayed as a victim of tyranny. When Seleucus reached Egypt, he told Ptolemy that Antigonus now wanted "the entire kingdom of the Macedonians"—sole rule of Alexander's empire.[1] It was the truth, and it meant that no one could feel safe from Antigonus. Ptolemy wrote to Cassander and Lysimachus, enlisting their support in the attempt to restore Seleucus, and at the same time Antigonus wrote to all his opponents, reminding them that they had all been allies for the war against the Perdiccans, and insisting that they honor that agreement. He was asking, in effect, that they connive at the deposing of Seleucus, but this act had already come to symbolize the insatiable scope of his ambitions. As he must have expected, his pleas fell on deaf ears.

From Babylonia, Antigonus marched to winter quarters in Cilicia. All the parties spent the winter preparing for the renewal of war; it was a good time to be a mercenary. In the spring of 315 Antigonus set out for Syria; on the way he was met by a delegation of representatives of Lysimachus, Ptolemy, and Cassander. They presented Antigonus with an ultimatum, which was a strange mixture of undisguised ambition and justified indignation. The justifiable part was that they demanded the return of Babylonia to Seleucus. The rest was no more than a demand that he share the spoils of his victory over Eumenes with them, on the grounds that it had been a joint war, triggered by agreement at Triparadeisus. Specifically, they wanted some of the fortune in bullion that Antigonus had brought back from the east. Lysimachus also wanted Hellespontine Phrygia (a big gain for him, since it would give him territory on both sides of the Propontis); Antigonus had seized it in 318, but none of them had any right to dispose of it as if it were private property. Ptolemy wanted official recognition of his annexation of Palestine and Phoenicia; and, for reasons that are obscure, Cassander wanted Cappadocia and Lycia.

Antigonus would have been left with severely reduced territories west of the Euphrates, but with mastery of the eastern satrapies. Communication would have been difficult between the two halves of his empire, and his hold on Asia Minor tenuous. The subtext of the allies' demands was the suggestion that he take himself off east. But Antigonus had gone too far to do anything other than reject the ultimatum and accept the inevitability of war with his former friends and allies. He saw himself as Alexander's heir, which made the others rebel satraps. And so began the so-called Third War of the Successors (315–311), pitting Antigonus and his son Demetrius against Lysimachus, Ptolemy, Seleucus, and Cassander.

SECURITY MEASURES

Antigonus was surrounded by enemies, but he had the resources to mobilize sufficient means of violence to keep them at bay. His first priority was to dissuade Cassander from leaving Greece. He went about this both defensively and aggressively. For defense, he sent his nephew Polemaeus to Asia Minor, where Cappadocia had declared for Cassander. Polemaeus extinguished such thoughts of independence, and then continued northwest to the Black Sea coast. Having intimidated Zipoetes, the ruler of Bithynia, into neutrality and ensured that the Greek cities in the region would not cause trouble, he established himself on the Hellespont to guard against a possible invasion from Europe.

Meanwhile, Antigonus's fleet succeeded in securing some of the Aegean islands. The first outcome of this was the formation, over the next few years, of many of the Cycladic islands into a league, allied to Antigonus. The sacred—and increasingly mercantile—island of Delos became the center of the league, and was therefore lost to Athens, which had controlled it for much of the fourth century; it remained free for almost 150 years, until the Romans restored it to Athens. The formation of the league was good for the islands, since it gave them self-government and greater bargaining power, and good for Antigonus too, since it simplified his dealings with them. In due course of time, Antigonus would form other groups of cities within his empire into leagues as well.

In addition to these defensive moves, Antigonus also took direct action against Cassander. He sent Aristodemus of Miletus, one of the Greeks in the inner circle of his court, to the Peloponnese with plenty of money and instructions to establish a working relationship with Polyperchon and his son Alexander. Eight thousand mercenaries were raised and Polyperchon was named "General of the Peloponnese" for the Antigonid cause, with the job of opening up a second front in Greece, to keep Cassander occupied there. Alexander sailed south for a meeting with Antigonus to confirm the arrangements—specifically, no doubt, the division of the spoils.

Along with these measures against Cassander, Antigonus took steps to challenge Ptolemy's naval supremacy. As a first step toward gaining a fleet, he persuaded the Rhodians to build ships for him, from raw materials that he would supply. We can only guess what arguments were used to turn the Rhodians, who were theoretically neutral, although for commercial reasons they were closest to Ptolemy. Rather than argument, the decisive factor was probably fear of what would happen to them if they refused. Rhodes was not only an island state, and their possessions on the mainland opposite the island were vulnerable. Antigonus also sent agents to Cyprus, where the currently dominant king was an ally of Ptolemy. If Antigonus's intention was to gain control of the island, he failed, because Ptolemy responded in strength, and was able over the next few years to make the island effectively his. But if his intention was simply to tie up some of Ptolemy's forces, the plan worked perfectly, and Antigonus was able to move south against Ptolemy's possessions in Phoenicia.

Given that Ptolemy's annexation of Palestine and Phoenicia in 320 had been achieved relatively easily and that Eumenes' visit in 318 was brief, the region had last seen major trouble in 332, when the prolonged resistance of Tyre and the lesser resistance of Gaza had provoked Alexander the Great to atrocities that were repellent even by his standards: a mass crucifixion on the seashore at Tyre and having the garrison commander of Gaza dragged behind a chariot. The garrisons that had been installed by Ptolemy now withdrew in the face of Antigonus's overwhelming army and its reputation, taking Ptolemy's Phoenician fleet with them.

City after city capitulated without resistance, but, probably gambling on Antigonus's current naval inferiority, the garrison of Tyre chose to resist. Tyre was the most important city in the region, a major mercantile center (especially for the Arabian spice trade) with a good port. It had taken Alexander seven months to take the stubborn island city, and then only after he had demolished the mainland town and used the rubble to build a causeway across the few hundred meters separating the island from the mainland. It was to take Antigonus fifteen months, but until his control of the sea was as secure as his hold on the land, there was little he could do against blockade runners. Even so, the siege was curiously unadventurous. Alexander, for instance, had made use of a specialist naval siege unit for his assault on Tyre, but Antigonus preferred to establish a simple blockade rather than take the city by storm.

Antigonus badly needed this stretch of coastline. As long as he lacked a fleet that could challenge Ptolemy's, his territories would be vulnerable to seaborne raids, or even invasion, and the merchants who left his shores would be harassed or worse. All the facilities and the expertise he needed could be found in Phoenicia's flourishing shipyards and ports, and the raw materials, especially the famed (and rapidly diminishing) cedars of Lebanon, were not far inland. Antigonus's propaganda, designed to terrify his enemies, let it be known that he was preparing a fleet of five hundred warships and, unrealistically, that they would be ready that very summer. For this purpose, he established three shipyards in Phoenicia and another in Cilicia; we have already seen that the Rhodians were building a few more for him. The whole eastern Mediterranean seaboard was dedicated to this one task. While maintaining the siege of Tyre, Antigonus also cleared the Ptolemaic garrisons out of cities as far south as Gaza, thus gaining another wealthy mercantile port.

ANTIGONUS'S RESOURCES

With the annexation of Phoenicia and Palestine and the alliance of Polyperchon and Alexander, in 315 Antigonus was at the height of his power. In addition to the eastern satrapies, he controlled all Syria, all Asia Minor, and southern Greece. He had capital reserves amounting to billions of dollars (mostly left over from the treasuries of the Achaemenid empire), and a very healthy annual income from taxes. A slim volume wrongly included in the corpus of works by Aristotle gives us some idea of the range of taxes Antigonus employed, since it lists six forms of tax exacted by his satraps: on agricultural produce, on livestock, on natural resources, on profits from trade, on profits from the local sale of agricultural produce, and finally a poll tax.[2] As the Achaemenids had done before him, Antigonus left it up to his satraps or governors to raise the taxes from their subjects and pass the revenue on to him for use and redistribution.

A preserved inscription affords us a window onto Antigonus's economic intentions. The cities of Teus and Lebedus in Asia Minor had asked permission to import grain from abroad. In his reply Antigonus explicitly says that he does not usually allow this, since he would rather they took grain from within his own realm, but that in this case he magnanimously gives his permission.[3] He wanted to be an exporter, not an importer of grain. But he also recognized that foreign grain was cheap; he himself had forced the price down by his embargo on it.

Mountains within his realm held minerals and metals, and grew every kind of timber he might need; there was no shortage of fertile river valleys and plateaus; he commanded almost all the overland and sea–river trade routes from the east to the Mediterranean; and he could call on enough manpower to meet any emergency. All the Successors did their best to make their lands self-sufficient, not just because this was the instinctive goal of ancient economic policy but because they did not want to help their rivals by paying them for imports. Antigonus even developed Syria's native papyrus production, so as not to be so dependent on Egypt even for that.[4] In Antigonus's case, self-sufficiency was not an altogether unrealistic goal, and many communities within his empire made considerable profits from trading surpluses or exporting commodities that were unavailable elsewhere.

Antigonus now had a healthy slice of the grain market, and controlled almost all the main sources of timber. Just as his inroads into the grain market put commercial pressure on Ptolemy, since Egypt was by far the largest grain exporter in the eastern Mediterranean, so Ptolemy was also his target of his attempt to monopolize timber. This was precisely what the annexation of the Phoenician ports was for: to enable Antigonus to build a fleet and to deny Ptolemy access to timber. Egypt itself had no timber to speak of, and Ptolemy was forced to rely on imports from his ally in distant Macedon and on the less productive but closer forests of Cyprus, with their pine and cedar. Before long, Antigonus would make Cyprus a primary target.

This is not the last time we will see Antigonus using economics as a form of warfare against Ptolemy, his rival in the eastern Mediterranean. And he had good reasons to be money-minded. His realm could be approached by enemies from three directions. A vast army was needed to defend it—and if the opportunity arose, to expand it. Such an army was very expensive; Antigonus was simply making sure that he had the means.

THE PROCLAMATION OF TYRE

In the early days of the siege, Antigonus was reminded of his naval weakness when Seleucus deliberately sailed past at the head of a Ptolemaic fleet. No doubt some of the ships peeled off to deliver supplies to the semi-beleaguered town before rejoining the main fleet. Its mission was to establish the island of Cos as a secure Ptolemaic base, and from there to raid Antigonid possessions in Asia Minor. When Polemaeus moved into the region in response to these raids, Seleucus withdrew. But first he stopped at the famous sanctuary of Apollo at Didyma near Miletus, where the shrine had recently been magnificently refounded by Alexander the Great, since it had proclaimed him a son of Zeus. The oracle reputedly hailed Seleucus as "king";[5] it was only a little premature.

Polyperchon's son Alexander reached Antigonus at Tyre, and not long after his arrival, Antigonus launched a propaganda offensive against Cassander. He summoned an assembly of all the Macedonians he had under arms, or who had become military colonists in the area, and issued the "Decree of the Macedonians," more commonly known as the "Proclamation of Tyre."[6] The first task of the assembled Macedonians was to try Cassander in absentia for all his anti-Argead crimes: killing Olympias (though, ironically, she had been condemned herself in just such a show trial by Cassander's Macedonians), detaining Rhoxane and Alexander IV (whose release "to the Macedonians" Antigonus demanded), forcing Thessalonice to marry him, rebuilding Thebes, and so on. This was a more public version of the bullying tactic Antigonus had tried out with Seleucus the previous year. But Cassander was never going to submit; his war with Antigonus lasted another fourteen years.

The deal with Polyperchon and Alexander became clear too. The appointment of Polyperchon as "General of the Peloponnese" was meant to replace, not supplement, his regency. Antigonus now declared that he had himself "taken over responsibility for the monarchy," so that, in addition to being "Royal General of Asia," he was now also the self-proclaimed legitimate regent. Antigonus recognized that Polyperchon's claim to the regency was empty, and that by virtue of his control of the king, Cassander had usurped it. It was Cassander, then, who was named as the pretender. There could hardly be any doubt that Antigonus's intention was to rule the entire Macedonian empire.

The final article of the proclamation declared that the Greek cities were to be free, autonomous, and ungarrisoned. Antigonus had already begun to foster such autonomy in the cities within or just outside his reach, but now he was making it official policy. It was good propaganda and good sense. He needed the goodwill of the cities, so that they would supply him with Greek manpower and expertise, and it was cheaper to manage the cities without garrisons.

In the short term, however, the chances of Greek freedom were remote, even within Antigonus's own domain, since he must have garrisoned many of the cities of Asia Minor and the Cycladic islands in case of invasion. But of course, as well as being a manifesto, the declaration was aimed, as Polyperchon's had been a few years earlier, at his enemies. He was still trying to secure the loyalty of the Greek cities of Cyprus, by encouraging those that were ruled by princelings loyal to Ptolemy to throw them out, and he needed to undermine Cassander's hold on the cities of Greece. The proclamation economically served more than one purpose.

Cynicism is easy, but Antigonus does seem to have done his best to keep this promise of autonomy within his own realm—as well as using it as a sweetener for potential allies. It was not always possible, however. I have already referred, a little earlier, to a couple of letters from Antigonus, written around 303 BCE to the cities of Lebedus and Teus. Antigonus wanted to unite the two communities at or near the site of Teus, while Lebedus was to be altogether abandoned. It is clear from the tone of the letters that Antigonus was pushing this plan through against the will of the inhabitants, and that his intention was to ensure that his coffers would continue to be filled by taxes from the new joint city. In practice, the cities' "freedom" was often an illusion.

But Antigonus's declaration worried Ptolemy enough for him to respond immediately with a proclamation of his own, affirming *his* commitment to the freedom of the Greek cities. Coming from Ptolemy, this is doubly strange: in the first place, he was already master of Greek cities, in Cyprus and Cyrenaica, in which he had installed garrisons, and so the speciousness of the propaganda was self-evident; second, Cassander had cities on the Greek mainland under his sway, just as Antigonus did in Asia Minor and Greece, so Ptolemy risked damaging the interests of his ally as much as those of his enemy (supposing anyone took his manifesto seriously). It is hard, then, to know what to make of Ptolemy's declaration. But if, as is likely, he had his Macedonian troops approve the proclamation, as Antigonus had done, then at least part of the point was not to let Antigonus get away with claiming to be the official spokesperson for Macedon. Whoever controlled Macedon and the king in theory controlled Egypt, as one of the satrapies of the king's empire.

As they often do in times of war, the abstract generalizations of these manifestos disguised horrors. Antigonus was encouraging, and Ptolemy was in danger of encouraging, the democratic elements within the Greek cities controlled by Cassander to rise up against their administrations. Any who did so would embroil their cities at the very least in the banishment of prominent citizens, and very likely in assassination and even civil war. Old feuds were refreshed, and in a number of Greek cities atrocities were carried out in the name of one political system or the other. In the summer of 315, for instance, very shortly after the Declaration of Tyre, five hundred democratic rebels were rounded up and massacred at Argos by Cassander's garrison commander.[7]

CASSANDER IN GREECE

In response to Antigonus's proclaimed usurpation of power in Macedon and to his rapport with Polyperchon and Alexander, Cassander needed to act quickly to stabilize his core territories in Greece. An attempt to win Polyperchon over to his cause failed, and in the summer of 315, while Antigonus was busy at Tyre, Cassander reinvaded the Peloponnese with the help of a Ptolemaic fleet of fifty ships. A swift and successful campaign netted him a number of new possessions, including Corinth's southern port.

After attending the famous athletic games at Nemea, Cassander returned to Macedon, but he had not finished with the Peloponnese. Almost immediately, he sent his most trusted general Prepelaus back south, and Prepelaus succeeded in detaching Polyperchon's son Alexander from the Antigonid cause. He was appointed "General of the Peloponnese" for Cassander. We are told that Alexander's reason for changing sides was that this position was all he had ever wanted,[8] but this is implausible, since he could expect to inherit the Antigonid title before long from his elderly father. He must have reckoned Cassander's position stronger in the Peloponnese. The decisive factor was probably that Alexander's chief stronghold was Corinth, and Cassander now controlled the more important of its two ports.

By the end of 315, all the northern Peloponnese was under Cassander's control. Polyperchon was reduced to holding Messenia in the southwest with his mercenary forces, and Sparta in the southeast was currently too trivial for anyone to bother with. The Ptolemaic fleet had no more work to do in the area and it sailed for home, defeating on the way a small Antigonid fleet and army as it passed through Caria.

Cassander had defused the immediate threat to his realm, but had not done enough to enable him to carry the war into Antigonid territories in Asia Minor. The next year, 314, started disastrously for him when Aristodemus first persuaded the Aetolians to make an alliance with Antigonus, and then, on his way back to the Peloponnese, undid much of the good Cassander had done there the previous year. The Aetolian alliance was important not just in itself, but because the Aetolians were allies of at least some of the Boeotian states, who had lost land and power when Cassander refounded Thebes and had accordingly allied themselves with Macedon's most implacable enemies. Central Greece effectively became a no-go area for Cassander, and he was cut off from the Peloponnese. He had no choice but to trust his

General of the Peloponnese, the renegade Alexander, to take care of matters there, while he himself was restricted to campaigning against the Aetolians and the Illyrians.

Eliminating the threat of the Illyrians on the western borders of Macedon was a solid gain, but otherwise things were not going well for Cassander. Aristodemus had done a brilliant job for the Antigonid cause in the Peloponnese. In the autumn, Antigonus succeeded in detaching the islands of Lemnos and Imbros from Athens, which helped him to command the grain route from the Black Sea region to Greece; the islands were also good sources of grain themselves. And then the Peloponnese, already a powder keg, had its fuse lit by the assassination of Alexander under mysterious circumstances. His generalship and alliance with Cassander had lasted less than a year. Cassander immediately lost the vital strongholds of Corinth and Sicyon, which were taken over by Alexander's wife, the formidable Cratesipolis, in a bid for semi-independence. She did manage to hold her little realm together for a few years—but then the Acrocorinth, the craggy hill overlooking the plain of Corinth and commanding the isthmus, has proved its strategic importance time and again over the centuries.

THE CARIAN THEATER

Asander had been appointed to the governorship of Caria immediately after the death of Alexander the Great and confirmed in the post at Triparadeisus. For years, he had apparently been a loyal friend of Antigonus, but something had happened to make that change. Wealthy and cultured, Caria had a history of spawning independent dynasts, and perhaps Asander had ambitions in that direction—ambitions that would justly make him afraid of retaliation by Antigonus. Perhaps his only crime was, like Seleucus, to fail to submit to Antigonus's assumption of seniority. At any rate, late in the summer of 315 he declared for the anti-Antigonid alliance.

This was, of course, intolerable to Antigonus. Apart from his obvious desire to keep Asia Minor as a unified whole, Caria would make a perfect bridgehead for an invasion of Asia Minor from Egypt or Cyprus, where Ptolemy was concentrating his forces. Antigonus ordered Polemaeus into the region. Polemaeus arrived late in 315, in time to winter on the borders, but for much of the following year Asander managed to keep him at bay, with his own not inconsiderable army supplemented by a mercenary force donated by Ptolemy. Toward the end of 314, perhaps in response to a personal visit we happen to know that Asander made to Athens, when he provided the city with money to raise troops, Cassander sent Prepelaus to Caria with a force that might have broken the deadlock.[9] But it was wiped out by the indispensable Polemaeus, who was emerging as one of the best generals of the time.

The stalemate in Caria continued, but Polemaeus had done his job. He had contained the situation in Asia Minor long enough for Antigonus to wrap up affairs in Phoenicia. The fleet was built, and with its help Antigonus finally brought the siege of Tyre to an end, so that the whole Phoenician seaboard was under his control. The precariousness of Cassander's position in Greece also made the timing right. And so Antigonus decided to leave the Middle East in the hands of his relatively untried son Demetrius, now aged twenty-two, while he marched to Caria to deal with the traitor himself—and then to see what could be done about Cassander.

The Restoration of Seleucus

ANTIGONUS'S PLAN, on returning to Asia Minor, was not just to retake Caria. If he defeated Lysimachus, whose main job was to hold the straits against invasion from Asia, he could get to Macedon; if he defeated Cassander, Ptolemy would be isolated and he could finish him off at his leisure. He therefore left Demetrius a relatively small force—a mere twenty thousand, including two thousand Macedonian infantry, five thousand horse, and forty-three elephants—with which to hold Ptolemy at bay. He took the bulk of the army north, while his fleet sailed around Asia Minor to join him. After a tough crossing of the Taurus, Antigonus arrived only in time to winter in Celaenae, but his ships encountered a fleet of Cassander's, originally sent to support Prepelaus in Caria, and captured every single vessel. Cassander's Carian expedition had been a complete disaster.

Antigonus massively outnumbered Asander on both land and sea, and early in 313 the terrified rebel came to terms. He would be allowed to remain as governor of Caria, but strictly as Antigonus's subordinate, with no troops under his personal command and no garrisons in the cities. He gave his brother to Antigonus as a hostage, but a few days later, realizing that he could not live as Antigonus's pawn, he changed his mind, freed his brother, and wrote urgently to Ptolemy and Seleucus for help. Not surprisingly, Antigonus was furious. He broke up his winter quarters and attacked Caria by land and sea. It was an outstanding campaign, a true blitzkrieg with coordinated land and sea operations. In a matter of weeks all Caria—or the coastal regions, at least, which were all that counted—fell to Antigonus and his generals. Asander fled or was killed; we hear nothing of him again.

With Asia Minor once more secure, Antigonus could focus on Greece, which lay open to the might of his new fleet. Cassander felt the threat and was prepared to negotiate, but the talks came to nothing, and Antigonus put into effect his invasion plan. First, in an attempt to tie up Lysimachus's forces, he fostered an uprising among the Greek cities within Lysimachus's Thrace, which had never been content under Macedonian rule. The cities threw out their garrisons and entered into an alliance with the local tribes, Lysimachus's constant enemies.

Lysimachus rose to the challenge. He advanced rapidly, and at the threat of siege all but one of the rebel cities capitulated. A joint Thracian and Scythian army failed to react quickly enough to help, and Lysimachus went to face them. He persuaded enough of the Thracians to desert, and then crushed the rest. The final rebel city, Callatis, held out and was intermittently under siege until 309, but the uprising was effectively over.

Antigonus sent help, but Lysimachus left a holding force at Callatis and went out to meet this new threat. The Odrysian king, Seuthes III, saw an opportunity to renew his bid for independence and reneged on the peace treaty he had negotiated a couple of years previously with Lysimachus. He occupied the mountain pass through which Lysimachus would have to march to meet Antigonus's forces. But Lysimachus, fully living up to his reputation for military genius, repulsed first Seuthes and then the Antigonid army. Seuthes was forced to come to terms, and the renewed pact was sealed by an exchange of brides.

Lysimachus's brilliance had foiled Antigonus so far, but would he be capable of halting a full-fledged invasion? Antigonus laid his plans carefully. He sent his nephew Telesphorus to the Peloponnese with a small fleet and a large army, with which he mopped up all the remaining Cassandrian garrisons in the northern Peloponnese except for Sicyon and Corinth, held for Cassander by Cratesipolis. But Telesphorus failed to prevent Cassander from securing the island of Euboea as his first line of defense against the imminent invasion. Antigonus dispatched Polemaeus with a substantial force. With the help of his Boeotian allies, Polemaeus as usual did brilliantly: he gained control of much of Euboea and, on the mainland, even briefly threatened Athens.

Once Polemaeus had established himself, Antigonus recalled much of the fleet from Greek waters and, as the winter of 313/312 approached, moved north toward the Propontis and Europe. Cassander had no choice but to withdraw to Macedon to face the threat of invasion via Thrace, leaving an insufficient force in Euboea, under the command of his brother Pleistarchus, to combat Polemaeus. Meanwhile, again at Antigonus's instigation, the Aetolians and Epirotes continued to make trouble for Cassander, and he had to dedicate even more of his forces to a campaign in western Greece. He had barely enough troops in Macedon to offer resistance to Antigonus's threatened invasion.

But Antigonus's northern feint came to nothing. He approached the independent city of Byzantium for an alliance. That would give him a foothold in Europe and a chance to establish himself there over the winter. But, at Lysimachus's prompting, the Byzantines preferred to stay neutral, and Lysimachus had both the time and the manpower (his army had been swelled by the mercenary troops he had defeated) to prepare his defenses. Antigonus decided against forcing a crossing, in uncertain winter weather, into well-defended territory, and distributed his troops to winter quarters in the region of the Propontis. The invasion was planned for the following year, across the Hellespont, as soon as the weather improved.

THE BATTLE OF GAZA

The months of the winter of 313/312 brought respite for Cassander, but his situation was still desperate. For the first time since the Lamian War in 322, little of southern Greece, with the notable exception of Athens, was under Macedonian control, and Antigonus's assurances of freedom had revived a militant spirit of independence among the Greek cities. It would take a miracle to stop Antigonus. The most obvious move would be for him to come at Macedon via Thrace while Polemaeus marched north from central Greece, and that was surely what Antigonus had in mind for 312. But nothing is certain in war.

First, the Antigonid impetus was blunted by internal squabbling. Polemaeus had succeeded in Euboea, where Telesphorus had failed. Not unnaturally, Antigonus gave Polemaeus overall responsibility for Greece. But Telesphorus, in the Peloponnese, took himself off in a huff at this, and created a separate enclave for himself in Elis. His behavior there, such as robbing sacred sites to pay his mercenaries, was winning the Antigonid cause no friends, and demanded attention. Polemaeus soon brought his brother (or cousin) back into their uncle's (or father's) fold, but in the meantime he was not available to support Antigonus's invasion. Fortunately for Antigonus, neither Polyperchon nor Cratesipolis seems to have been in a position to exploit the situation further; they rarely had the manpower for more than defensive work.

Ptolemy proved to be Cassander's second savior. He had been distracted in 313 and for the first part of 312. He had had to quell a rebellion by the cities of Cyrenaica, and he finally secured the last cities in Cyprus that held out against him. The only anti-Antigonid action he and Seleucus took was to raid Cilicia on their way back from Cyprus; Demetrius rushed to the rescue from Syria, but arrived too late. But by the autumn of 312 Ptolemy's preparations were ready, and he launched a massive invasion of Palestine by land and sea. His purpose was to recover Palestine and Phoenicia for himself, and to ease the restoration of Seleucus to Babylon.

It was late in the autumn, and if Demetrius had known about the buildup of enemy forces at Pelusium, he had assumed that nothing would happen until the following spring. After his Cilician expedition, he had dismissed his men to winter quarters, and he now had to reassemble them to meet the invasion. As Ptolemy and Seleucus advanced north from Egypt, they were intercepted by Demetrius at Gaza. The town bore twenty-year-old scars from the time when Alexander had razed it to the ground and massacred its inhabitants, but it was still the final destination of major caravan routes from the east, and spices left its harbor for destinations all over the Mediterranean. Antigonus had left Demetrius with a cluster of senior advisers, who urged caution, but Demetrius was young and hot-headed, with extraordinary good looks and charm that led him to believe that he could get away with anything. He imagined, perhaps, the fame that would accrue to him if he defeated two of Alexander the Great's generals. The armies deployed for battle on the plain south of the town.

In the center, where the infantry phalanxes were deployed as usual, Demetrius was outnumbered. This did not overly concern him, however, since he planned for his cavalry to sweep all before them. He massively bulked up the cavalry contingent on his left wing; the right wing was correspondingly weaker, but if things went well, it would not be used at all. Given its weakness, he had it "refuse"—deploy at an angle back from the main line of battle—so that it would be harder to outflank. He posted his elephants along the whole front of the line at its weak points. Ptolemy and Seleucus had also bulked up their left wing, so when their scouts brought back information about Demetrius's disposition, they had to make some hasty adjustments. They had no elephants themselves, but they knew how to deal with Demetrius's beasts: they sowed spiked caltrops, like a minefield, in front of their line, and posted their light-armed troops out in front with plenty of javelins.

The action began, as Demetrius had intended, on his left, Ptolemy's right. Thanks to Ptolemy's last-minute adjustments, the two wings were closely matched in numbers and commitment, and the overwhelming charge that Demetrius had hoped for became bogged down in a fierce and close-fought struggle. In the center, his elephants were foiled by the caltrops and became vulnerable to the skill of Ptolemy's skirmishers. Most of the mahouts were shot down, and the elephants were captured. When Demetrius's cavalry realized that their infantry phalanx was now vulnerable to Ptolemy's superior numbers, many of them turned to flight. Demetrius, left almost isolated, had no choice but to break off as well. A retreating army was vulnerable to massacre, but they kept due order and made it safely back to Gaza. At that point, discipline broke down as the men poured into the city to rescue their baggage, and when Ptolemy's troops came up they were able to take possession of the city. Demetrius fled by night farther north, abandoning Palestine to Ptolemy.

It was the decisive battle of the war. Demetrius lost only a few hundred, mainly cavalrymen, on the field of battle, but almost all his foot soldiers surrendered and were incorporated by Ptolemy into his own forces. The loss of the entire Syrian army in the east was bound to draw Antigonus from Asia Minor. He had taken up winter quarters in Phrygia, but it was clear that, as soon as he could, he would march south, back across the Taurus Mountains—to see, it was said, how Ptolemy would fare against an adult adversary, rather than a beardless youth.[1] The invasion of Greece was postponed indefinitely. The miracle for which Cassander had been praying had taken place.

THE RETURN OF SELEUCUS

Ptolemy was briefly triumphant. He had recovered Palestine and was hungry for the rest. Early in 311, before Antigonus could arrive, he sent one of his generals north to see to the final eradication of Demetrius from Syria. But Demetrius had stripped all the available towns of their garrisons, and put together enough of a force to dare to meet Ptolemy's army in battle, and this time it was he who won the decisive victory, and augmented his army with captives and his treasury with booty. Perhaps Antigonus's trust in his son was not misplaced after all. And so, when Antigonus arrived in the spring, Ptolemy retreated to Egypt, abandoning all his gains.

Before leaving Asia Minor, Antigonus had negotiated a truce with Lysimachus and Cassander. Both of them were ready to talk terms, Cassander because the war was going so badly for him and Lysimachus because, as so often, he needed to focus on the hostile tribes of the Thracian interior. Ptolemy's withdrawal therefore introduced a lull in the fighting. Antigonus chose to use it for an attack on the Nabataeans.

These seminomadic Arabs would make dangerous enemies on his flank when he chose to invade Egypt, but profit was on Antigonus's mind more than strategic considerations. War was always the Successors' chief source of income, and as well as short-term plunder, Antigonus probably intended to try to take over the Nabataean trade in frankincense and bitumen. Nabataean business had made Gaza wealthy, and now that he controlled Gaza, Antigonus wanted to cut out the middlemen. Ptolemy's lands were otherwise the main source of bitumen (which was used as a cement and for waterproofing wood), and Antigonus naturally had no desire to enrich his enemy by paying for it. For the first time in history a Middle Eastern petroleum product was the cause of warfare. But three successive raids by Antigonid forces either came to nothing or ended in disaster. At one point, they succeeded in plundering Petra (at this stage still little more than a sacred and safe haven, not yet a glorious rock-carved city), only to be ambushed on the way back.[2]

Seleucus, meanwhile, had also taken advantage of the lull in the fighting. One of the casualties at Gaza had been the Antigonid satrap of Babylonia; Seleucus's realm was available and relatively undefended. In the spring of 311 he was given a thousand men by Ptolemy and set out from Palestine to Babylonia. Given the small size of his force, and the hostility of the lands through which he journeyed, this was an incredibly bold move. He had to encourage the faint-hearted, who must have thought he had taken leave of his senses, by reminding them that Apollo had already hailed him as king, which implied that he would be successful in this venture. And in fact the loyalty he had won in Babylon as satrap from 320 to 315 served him well, and he was able to recover his province and double the size of his army with relative ease. The Antigonid garrison of the city took refuge in one of the city's two citadels, but soon surrendered to Seleucus's siege. The date of his return—1 Nisan 311, in Babylonian terms; some time in April of that year, in ours—became the foundation date for his reign, and remained the standard chronological marker in the east until the Roman period.

THE PEACE OF THE DYNASTS

The main objective, the restoration of Seleucus to Babylonia, had been attained, and the war lost energy. Ptolemy was ready to join his allies in making peace with Antigonus; he had already been chased back to Egypt, and the armistice Antigonus had in place with Lysimachus and Cassander left him critically exposed. Antigonus too wanted peace: he had to do something about Seleucus's recovery of Babylonia, but that would be difficult as long as he was still at war elsewhere. All the main parties, then, desired peace. In the autumn of 311 their representatives met (we do not know where) and terms were agreed. After four years of warfare, nobody had gained much, and the "Peace of the Dynasts" more or less recognized the status quo from before the war. Cassander was recognized as General of Europe and Protector of the King until Alexander IV attained his majority; the fiction that all this was happening for the good of Alexander's heir was still being maintained. Lysimachus kept Thrace but renounced his claim to Hellespontine Phrygia; Ptolemy kept Greater Egypt (by now Egypt, Cyprus, Cyrenaica, some subject towns in Arabia, and a few possessions in the Aegean) but renounced his claim to Palestine and Phoenicia.

This was all a serious climbdown from the provocative demands they had presented to Antigonus in the spring of 315, in the ultimatum that triggered the war. Moreover, the Lord of Asia was confirmed in his title: all Asia was explicitly reserved for Antigonus. You could say that Antigonus won; at any rate, he certainly did not lose, except in so far as his further ambitions had been thwarted. He regained the territory that Ptolemy had taken after Gaza, and he had won some new allies and territories in Asia Minor, the Aegean islands, and Greece. He was not rebuked for his kingly ways. He effectively controlled all Asia from the Hellespont to Gaza, and east into Mesopotamia; he was also nominally in control of the eastern satrapies, though Seleucus's return to Babylon made it more difficult for him to maintain the connection.

The lack of mention of Polyperchon in the treaty is understandable, since he was by now a spent force, and was pursuing an independent policy in the Peloponnese without (for the moment) seeking alliances with any of the others. The lack of mention of Seleucus is also readily comprehensible; this was a meeting for peace, and Seleucus was still at war. In ceding all Asia to Antigonus, the war-weary players were betraying Seleucus by condemning him to the status of rebel. They

FIGURE 1. Alexander the Great. A Roman copy (1st century BCE/CE) of a Greek bronze dating from ca. 330 BCE. Despite his Roman cuirass, the distinctive hairstyle—over the ears, and with a quiff at the front—is what immediately marks the horseman as Alexander.

FIGURE 2. Olympias. A gold medallion purportedly depicting Alexander's mother. One of a series, it was struck to commemorate games held by the Roman emperor Caracalla (third century CE) in honor of Alexander and Olympias, as his putative ancestors.

FIGURE 3. Ptolemy I of Egypt. A tetradrachm dating from after 305, when Ptolemy, as king, began to have himself portrayed on his coins instead of Alexander or some other deity. The bust presents him as virile and experienced, and the eagle on the reverse suggests a connection with Zeus.

FIGURE 4. Seleucus I of Asia. This exceptional bronze bust formed part of the collection of the owner of the so-called Villa of the Papyri at Herculaneum. It is based on an original from the third century BCE, possibly even within Seleucus's lifetime.

FIGURE 5. Demetrius Poliorcetes. A Roman copy of a Greek original; there are perhaps enough elements of individuality about the portrait to regard it as reasonably accurate. But the budding bull's horns emerging from the young king's head demonstrate his alignment with the god Dionysus.

FIGURE 6. A Lysimachan "Alexander." The message of this tetradrachm, minted between 297 and 281, is that Alexander's rule has passed on. The obverse shows Alexander as the son of Zeus Ammon, but the reverse shows Athena holding out Victory, who is crowning the first letters of Lysimachus's name.

FIGURE 7. The Taurus Mountains. The massive Taurus range divided Asia Minor from Cilicia and Syria, and was therefore a critical border. This photograph shows one of the rare passes across the mountains, at an altitude of well over a thousand meters (over 3,500 feet).

FIGURE 8. The Acrocorinth. This strategic hill, a little south of the ancient city of Corinth, dominated the surrounding countryside and the land entrance to the Peloponnese across the Isthmus. The fortifications visible in this photograph date from the thirteenth or fourteenth century CE.

FIGURE 9. The Temple of Apollo at Didyma. The ancient oracular sanctuary near Miletus had fallen into disrepair, but Seleucus paid for it to be rebuilt on a massive scale. The temple measured 118 × 60 meters (385 × 200 feet), and each of its many columns stood almost 20 meters (65 feet) tall and was about 2 meters (over six feet) in diameter at the base.

FIGURE 10. The Arsinoeion. A reconstruction of the building (perhaps a hotel) erected in the sanctuary of the Great Gods on Samothrace between 299 and 281 and funded by Arsinoe, the wife of Lysimachus, and later of Ptolemy Ceraunus and Ptolemy II.

FIGURE 11. Indian War Elephant. This harness plate of partly gilded silver, with a diameter of about 25 cm (a little less than 10 in.), dates from the third or second century BCE and may come from Bactria. The style of the helmets marks the mounted warriors as Greek.

FIGURE 12. Salamis Commemorative Coin. The naval battle of Salamis in Cyprus in 306 BCE was the high point of the career of Demetrius the Besieger. On the obverse of this tetradrachm, minted in Salamis itself, we see Victory, sounding the signal to advance; the reverse shows Poseidon, with the legend "King Demetrius."

FIGURE 13. The Lion Hunt Mosaic, Pella. This exquisite floor, from the last quarter of the fourth century BCE, is one of the finest examples of early Greek pebble mosaic. Hunting was a popular pastime for Macedonian aristocrats and kings and a favorite subject for paintings, sculptures, and mosaics.

FIGURE 14. Ivories from Vergina. This miniature ivory relief, from the couch found in Tomb 3, the "Prince's Tomb" at Vergina (ancient Aegae), clearly displays the Hellenistic love of realistic detail, as the woman looks up trustingly at the jolly, bearded man during a procession led by the god Pan on the left.

FIGURE 15. Wall Painting from Vergina (detail). The discovery of the magnificently decorated tombs at Vergina in 1977 revolutionized our knowledge of late classical and early Hellenistic painting. The north wall of Tomb 1 showed a popular theme, the rape of Persephone by Hades, the god of the underworld, who drives her away in his chariot.

FIGURE 16. The Fortune of Antioch. This is a small Roman copy of a famous monumental original, commissioned by Seleucus I when he founded his new capital city in Syria. The Orontes River (which flowed through the city) swims at the goddess's feet; she is crowned with the fortifications of the city, and she holds sheaves of wheat in her hand.

were saying, in effect: "Let Antigonus and Seleucus sort it out between them." It took another few years for them to do so.

Of course, no one believed that this was the peace to end all wars. Warfare was so central to the Successors' ideology that all their treaties should be regarded as temporary truces rather than as treaties as we understand them. Never has Ambrose Bierce's definition of peace as "a period of cheating between periods of fighting" been more appropriate.[3] Antigonus undoubtedly retained his desire for universal dominion, and they would all be looking out for the others' weaknesses, but the peace brought a brief respite. This phase of the war—the so-called Third War of the Successors—had been particularly intense.

The treaty also reaffirmed the right of the Greek cities to autonomy—which is to say that it affirmed the right of any of the Successors to wield the slogan against any of his rivals, since all of them had Greek cities in their territories. Not long after the treaty came into force, Antigonus sent a letter to the cities under his control, which was also meant to be read further afield, within his enemies' territories.[4] In this letter, he expressed his abiding concern for their welfare and suggested that those cities that were not already organized into a league (as the Cycladic islanders were) should contemplate doing so. Despite the fact that he was a tax-hungry ruler, always trying to finance new ventures (warfare and the foundation of cities were the two most expensive), Antigonus had a good record with the Greek cities. Now he was trying to capitalize on this goodwill to gather more cities into his alliance. At the same time, his rather crude purpose was to provide himself with an excuse if he ever felt the need to make war on any of the others, especially Cassander, who had a record of garrisoning the cities under his control. The respite provided by the Peace of the Dynasts would indeed be brief.

THE BABYLONIAN WAR

None of the leaders was personally present at the peace conference. Antigonus and Demetrius, at any rate, still had pressing military matters on their minds. Babylon was vital for anyone wishing to control an empire that spanned all of Asia. It was rich in men and supplies, as well as being a meeting point for major overland and sea-to-river routes. The resources of the eastern satrapies would be less easy to exploit without control of Babylonia. Seleucus's presence there struck at the heart of Antigonus's empire, and he was bound to do something about it. Unfortunately, the details of the Babylonian War that ensued are extremely hazy, because no extant historian bothered to report it (except for a very brief mention of its first phase by Plutarch),[5] and we have to rely on information gleaned from a very few cuneiform texts whose first purposes were not always historical, and which survive only in fragments.

Seleucus was of course extremely vulnerable in Babylon. His ally Ptolemy had withdrawn to Egypt, and Antigonid forces could have swept in from Syria if they had not been occupied in their futile attempts against the Nabataeans. Above all, Seleucus needed more men. He recruited a few Macedonian veterans, the remnants of those dispersed by Antigonus in 315, but he found his main opportunity when, despite being hugely outnumbered, in the autumn of 311 he beat off an attack by two of Antigonus's eastern satraps. His victory, in a surprise night attack, was so complete that he was able to add ten thousand foot and seven thousand horse to his forces. By the end of 311 he had taken over the neighboring province of Susiana, and was making no attempt to disguise the fact that Media and then the satrapies farther east were his next targets.

Late in 311, fresh from his failure in Nabataea, Demetrius invaded Babylonia. Elsewhere, his father's representative was signing the Peace of the Dynasts. The governor Seleucus had left in charge of Babylon while he was campaigning farther east evacuated the civilian population in order to concentrate on defending the two citadels, but half of the city, which was divided by the Euphrates, fell to Demetrius's army. Demetrius left Babylon in competent hands and returned to Syria, but if he thought he had won the war, he was mistaken. Seleucus's governor waged a guerrilla campaign in the countryside to impede the passage of supplies to the city, and Seleucus was already on his way back. After his arrival, it took him only a few days to recover the second half of the city.

In the summer of 310 Antigonus counterattacked from the west with a full-scale invasion, but although he came to occupy large areas of Babylonia for some months, Seleucus held him at bay. There was "panic in the land," according to an astronomical diary for September 310,[6] perhaps referring to the initial reaction to Antigonus's invasion; a few months later, there was still "weeping and mourning in the land."[7] The cuneiform texts also bear witness to galloping inflation, as even the bare necessities of life became scarce and expensive.

The war seems to have seesawed. Antigonus had the early successes; his troops broke into Babylon and drove Seleucus out after fierce street fighting, and at another point he captured a nearby town and allowed his troops to plunder freely. At the end of August 309, Seleucus met Antigonus in an indecisive pitched battle, but surprised his troops in their camp at dawn the next day and inflicted a defeat on them. It must have been a decisive defeat, because Antigonus withdrew to Syria and refocused his energies on more peaceful pursuits, such as building his new capital city, Antigonea. Apart from anything else, he was now over seventy years old, and his great weight, we may guess, was putting a strain on his heart.[8]

Even in the absence of evidence, it seems safe to say that Antigonus and Seleucus must have entered into a treaty, because for a while afterward they each went about their separate businesses without infringing on each other's territories. Antigonus abandoned the eastern satrapies, and over the next few years Seleucus gained control of them one by one, by conquest or by reaching a modus vivendi with the incumbent ruler. The troublesome Indian satrapies and some satellite territories were ceded to Chandragupta, as we have seen, probably in 304. Given the enormous size of the territories involved, and how few troops Seleucus had started with, this is a truly astonishing beginning for a kingdom that was to last, in some form or another, for 250 years. What is not surprising is that he was pleased to be invested with the honorific name that he bore for the rest of his life—Nicator, the bringer of victory, the only one to have successfully challenged Antigonus's rulership of Asia.

Warfare in Greece

THE PEACE WAS never stable; it only gave the contenders the opportunity to rally. Even while the treaty was being negotiated, Antigonus and Demetrius were already involved in the lengthy business of trying to evict Seleucus from Babylonia and prevent him from taking over the eastern satrapies. That in itself did not transgress the peace, because Seleucus was not included in it. But no more than weeks elapsed before Ptolemy helped his friend Seleucus by sending him fresh troops and by invading Antigonid Cilicia on the pretext that Antigonus had installed garrisons in Greek cities there and so had broken the terms of the peace agreement. As it happened, Demetrius was able to repulse Ptolemy's general, but the fragility of the situation was already clear.

Cassander had the best reasons for relief. He had been on the ropes, but the peace gave him a respite, and then his recovery was enormously helped by the defection in 310 of Polemaeus from the Antigonid cause. Polemaeus was simply disgruntled. Perhaps he had expected the peace conference to name him as satrap of central Greece or something; perhaps he felt that Antigonus's preference of Demetrius underrated the invaluable service he had provided in Greece and Asia Minor. At any rate, he declared his central Greek enclave independent, made Euboea his headquarters, and expanded his sway into Hellespontine Phrygia as well, thanks to his friendship with the governor there. Worst of all, he safeguarded his position by entering into an alliance with Cassander, thus depriving Antigonus of access to much of central Greece and opening it up for his enemy. Antigonus immediately sent an army to

Hellespontine Phrygia to recover the province and its control of the easiest crossing to Europe, but for the time being ignored Greece.

The upshot of these partial enterprises was a slide to war. The Fourth War of the Successors has a dramatic ending in 301, but no clear beginning. It was to be the decisive war, or, rather, the decisive phase of the war that had in effect been going on since 320.

THE END OF THE ARGEADS

There was still a major obstacle to the Successors' increasingly obvious ambitions. The Peace of the Dynasts had proclaimed, as had all previous general agreements, that the current administrations were temporary, and had named the expiration date: in five or six years' time, Alexander IV would come of age and inherit the lot. Already there were murmurs in some quarters of Macedon that it was time for the boy to be brought out of seclusion and taught to rule. But of course in reality none of the Successors wanted to cede power to Alexander, now or in the future. They read the treaty clause "when Alexander comes of age" as "if Alexander should come of age." They had risked everything to get where they were; they had not the slightest intention of handing it all over to the new king in a few years' time. For years Cassander had kept him and his mother in comfortable custody in Amphipolis; in 310 or 309 he had the teenager poisoned, along with his mother Rhoxane.

There was a telling lack of protest or reaction from the others. Surely this, if anything, should have triggered war. From time to time, when it had made practical sense, they had all professed themselves loyal to the Argead line. Where was the Antigonus of 315, who had condemned Cassander for killing Olympias? Had he and the others given Cassander the nod at the 311 conference? Probably nothing needed to be said openly; they would all benefit from the freedom of no longer being constrained by the existence of a royal family to whom they owed nominal allegiance. "Since there was no longer an heir for the empire," Diodorus observed, "all those who held nations or cities began to hope for royal power, and began to regard their subordinate territories as a spear-won kingdoms."[1] From now on, the Successors made less use of the magic of the Argead name to legitimate their positions; they were in effect kings in their own right, with kingdoms consisting of what they could gain and hold by force of arms. And, before long, they would all begin to style themselves kings.

The precise date of Cassander's removal of the boy king is uncertain. His basic tactic was obfuscation; he already had him and Rhoxane in seclusion, and the killings were carried out in secret by a trusted agent. He may even have denied that they had died, or spread the rumor that they had escaped, because coins and documents from various parts of the empire still used the name of Alexander IV for a few years yet.[2] Even though Cassander had been the one who ordered the murders, the victims were later buried in a suitably royal fashion (in Tomb 3, the "Prince's Tomb," at Aegae), and presumably by Cassander himself—a public act designed not just as a display of piety, but also as a brazen way of disassociating himself from their deaths. Moreover, by Macedonian tradition, the burial of a king was undertaken by the next king: Cassander was further staking his claim to Macedon.

The removal of Alexander IV did not quite end Cassander's problems with the Argead dynasty. Waiting in the wings was Heracles, the bastard son of Alexander whose claim to the throne had been half-heartedly defended by Nearchus at the original Babylon conference. Since then he had been more or less ignored; no one needed a third possible king, and especially one with dubious credentials. But the death of the last legitimate king brought Heracles, who had now almost come of age, out of the shadows. He was resident in Pergamum, and in 309, presumably with Antigonus's compliance, Polyperchon summoned him to the Peloponnese. It was a good time to play this trump card, since Cassander had just been further weakened by a major invasion by tribes from the northwest.

Seventy-five-year-old Polyperchon revived his dreams of glory, after a miraculous year or two of relative peace on the Greek mainland and a hiatus of four or five years in his own activities, and marched north toward Macedon with an army of twenty thousand to proclaim Heracles king. He had prepared the way over the previous months by soliciting as much support as he could from the Greek states (the most important gain was realliance with the Aetolians) and within Macedon itself. He established himself in the canton of southwest Macedon of which he was the hereditary ruler, and prepared to do battle with Cassander.

Cassander defused the threat. He avoided combat (in case his men were tempted to desertion by the prospect of an Argead king) and used diplomacy instead, offering the old soldier peace, the restoration of his estates in Macedon, and the great gift of several thousand Macedonian troops, if he would consent to be his military governor of the

Peloponnese—the generalship Polyperchon had once held for Antigonus. Polyperchon accepted this grant of semi-independent rulership. The betrayal of Antigonus was easy, because for some years Polyperchon had been pursuing an independent course in the Peloponnese. One hopes that he at least hesitated over the other consequence of his rapport with Cassander, the removal of Heracles. Polyperchon had him and his mother Barsine strangled during a banquet. It was a terrible act, and became a paradigm of the evil consequences of moral weakness.[3]

It was the end of the Argead line, which over three hundred years of rulership had produced some remarkable Macedonian kings, culminating in Philip and Alexander. Though Argead blood still flowed in the veins of Cleopatra's children by her Epirote first husband, there were no remaining children of male Argeads. The Successors were now truly free to divide among themselves the spoils of Alexander's empire.

PTOLEMY'S OPPORTUNITY

Cassander's position in Greece was greatly strengthened by his alliances with Polemaeus and Polyperchon. He had given Polyperchon enough troops to make serious trouble for the Antigonids in the Peloponnese, and he could hope that in central Greece Polemaeus could contain the Aetolians. His road to recovery, however, was fated to be less smooth. Polemaeus, acting with unusual fickleness even in these days of tested loyalties, seems to have become rapidly dissatisfied with his alliance with Cassander. Perhaps the elevation of Polyperchon disturbed him, or perhaps he had come to see Cassander's cause as hopeless in the long run. At any rate, he made the momentous decision to abandon Cassander when he responded positively to an approach by Ptolemy.

Demetrius's repulse of Ptolemy's army from northern Syria in 311 did not dampen the Egyptian ruler's ambitions. In the years 310 and 309, he continued to attack Antigonus, his only rival at sea. He brutally reestablished his hold over Cyprus, against Antigonus's intrigues there, and continued to make war on Antigonid territory in Lycia and Caria from his bases on Cyprus and Cos. Demetrius did what he could to defend southwest Asia Minor while his father was tied up in Babylon. He saved Halicarnassus, for instance, when it was being besieged by Ptolemy's troops in 309. But Ptolemy's gains were considerable, and, given Rhodian neutrality, he effectively dominated the approaches to the Aegean.

The usual picture of Ptolemy makes him only moderately ambitious, at any rate compared to an Antigonus.[4] He was certainly cautious: he refused the regency in 320, and meticulously created buffer zones around his core territory, as if he entertained no ambitions beyond securing Egypt. But, by hijacking Alexander's corpse, he had declared himself Alexander's heir—and Alexander's heir should inherit Alexander's aggressiveness.

Rather than having moderate aims, it is more reasonable to think that he was just being patient. And there is no way to explain his actions at this time except as indicating a sustained program to gain control of Greece. First, he softened up the Greek cities under Cassander's and Lysimachus's control in 310 by asking them not to be tempted by the Antigonid promise of freedom, and to join his alliance instead—a move that was designed to undermine not just his old enemy Antigonus but also his former allies, Cassander and Lysimachus. Then he gained control of the southern approaches to the Aegean, and then he detached Polemaeus from Cassander. Moreover, he even approached Cleopatra, resident in Sardis, to ask for her hand in marriage. She agreed; they saw themselves soon being enthroned as the king and queen of Macedon.

Polemaeus sailed to Cos to discuss the terms of the pact with Ptolemy. The island had entered into an alliance and trading agreement with Ptolemy, and was currently Ptolemy's advance post in the Aegean. Ptolemy's son, the future Ptolemy II, was born there in 309, where his mother could get the best medical attention then available. Praxagoras of Cos was still alive, and laying the foundation for the remarkable anatomical work of the next century: the discovery of the nervous system and of the diagnostic value of the pulse, and the differentiation of the functions of the inner organs. While Polemaeus was there, however, Ptolemy forced him to kill himself. The pretext given out to the public was that Polemaeus was intriguing with Ptolemy's army officers to divert their loyalty from Ptolemy to himself, but it is just as likely that Ptolemy wanted to eliminate a future rival in Greece. Yet another great general was undone by dreams of empire.

Greece was in considerable turmoil, then, when Ptolemy set sail, toward the end of 309, with an invasion-sized force. On the way, he detached the island of Andros from Antigonus's Cycladic League. Greece was ripe for invasion: Cassander was in recovery, Lysimachus's focus was still restricted to his own province, Antigonus was battling Seleucus in Babylon, and Demetrius was in Syria. Even Polyperchon was helpless; on his way back from Macedon the previous year, after the assassination of Heracles, he had been pinned in central Greece by the Boeotians, and he had not yet arrived in the Peloponnese. He may even have returned to his mini-kingdom in Macedon.

Ptolemy landed unopposed at Corinth. Since as a matter of policy Antigonus had not installed garrisons in the Peloponnesian cities under his control, Polyperchon's absence meant that there was no effective force in the Peloponnese. Cratesipolis was terrified into surrendering Corinth and Sicyon. Making Corinth his base, Ptolemy planned "to free the other Greek cities as well."[5] It is likely that he intended to revive the old Hellenic League, or League of Corinth, that had been founded by Philip II.[6] All the Successors competed with one another for Greek manpower; the revival of the league, with Ptolemy at its head, would compel member cities to provide him with troops when he needed them, and deny them to his rivals. Ptolemy would have complete control of the sea.

It was indeed a great opportunity for Ptolemy—an opportunity for grand imperial power—but it came to nothing. The response to Ptolemy's appeal by the Greek cities was less than tepid. The Peloponnesian cities were already free, and felt no need to exchange one overlord for another; the mainland cities that might have been interested were simply too few to make a difference, and too vulnerable to Cassander, now that Polemaeus was dead, to be able to respond positively. And then new crises loomed for Ptolemy elsewhere. First, Antigonus returned to Syria at the end of his unsuccessful war with Seleucus. Second, Ptolemy's governor of Cyrenaica launched a bid to take over the whole North African coast from Cyrenaica to Carthage as his own independent empire. As it turned out, the rebellious governor was assassinated by his allies before his plans had come to fruition. But it was clear that the extent of Ptolemy's commitment in Greece would make him vulnerable elsewhere, and he was concerned about his enemies' ability to exploit this.

So he came to terms with Cassander and returned to Egypt, leaving garrisons in Sicyon and Corinth. He may even just have rehired the mercenaries Cratesipolis had been using to protect her enclave. Of course, garrisons and his talk of Greek freedom were somewhat incompatible, but with conditions as they were in the Peloponnese, the cities may even have asked for them. Ptolemy had had a fleeting glimpse of supreme power, but in the end he gained little. He even lost Cleopatra. On Antigonus's orders, she was prevented from leaving Sardis to join her future husband, and was soon killed.

Poor Cleopatra, always on the edge of greatness. Her brother's death in 323, when she was already a royal widow in her early thirties, condemned her to become a pawn in the Successors' bids for legitimation. She was the perfect catch, a queen in her own right and the sister of the Conqueror; she held the key to all the Successors' ambitions. Leonnatus had accepted her, but died before the marriage; then Perdiccas too had prematurely died. At one time or another other Successors had sounded her out with a view to marriage. Finally, aged about forty-five and past the age for child-bearing, she awarded herself to Ptolemy, only to be thwarted by Antigonus's determination not to allow such a prize to fall into anyone else's hands.[7] But he tried to disassociate himself from the murder by a show trial of the killers and by awarding Alexander's sister a noble funeral. He remembered the trouble that the killing of Cynnane had given Perdiccas.

DEMETRIUS ON THE OFFENSIVE: ATHENS

In the west, with Polemaeus out of the way and fresh alliances in place with Ptolemy and Polyperchon, Cassander could look forward to building up his strength again in Greece. However, he was unlikely to receive much help from his allies, who were obliged to help him in emergencies only.[8] Besides, for the foreseeable future Lysimachus was engaged as usual with freedom-loving tribes within his province; he was also in the process of building a new capital city, Lysimacheia, on the neck of the Thracian Chersonese. And Seleucus, who had also been a member of the anti-Antigonid coalition in the last phase of the war, was for the present too focused on the east to jump into this affair. He was in the early phases of the protracted campaign to subdue and stabilize the eastern provinces.

Antigonus decided in 307 that the time was right for a preemptive strike against Cassander, with the immediate purpose of reestablishing a solid base in Greece and the longer-term purpose of making Greece his once and for all, now that it had been abandoned by Ptolemy. We could take this as the true start of the Fourth War of the Successors, in the sense that intermittent warfare was replaced by a fight to the finish. At any rate, as if we can isolate affairs in Greece from what was happening elsewhere, it was the start of what is called the Four-Year War on the Greek mainland.

Perhaps the most blatant transgression of the supposed freedom of the Greeks was the presence of Cassander's tyrant Demetrius of Phalerum in Athens—not because there were not tyrants or oppressive regimes elsewhere, but because Athens was Athens. Continuing to proclaim the freedom of the Greeks, Antigonus sent his son Demetrius, with a fleet of 250 ships and a purse of 5,000 talents (around three billion dollars), to restore democracy in Athens. It was clear that the Antigonids meant business.

While the main fleet sheltered at Cape Sunium, at the beginning of June 307 Demetrius took twenty ships and sailed north up the Saronic Gulf. Little notice was taken of such an unthreatening flotilla; the ships were assumed to be Ptolemy's, heading for Corinth. At the last minute, Demetrius turned and sailed straight into Piraeus. Cassander's garrison commander chose inaction, and within a few days Demetrius of Phalerum's position in Athens had become untenable. He was granted safe conduct out of the city to Thebes, where he lived for the next ten years. By then it was clear that he was never going to get back to Athens, and he made his way to Alexandria in Egypt. He might have been pleased to know that his grandson would hold a position of authority in Athens in the 260s.[9]

In the short term, however, Cassander could send no help, because he was tied up with a campaign in Epirus, and the loss of Athens was compounded by the loss of Piraeus, where the garrison fell rather rapidly in August 307 to Demetrius's assault. At the next assembly of Athenian citizens, through his agents Demetrius declared the city free, and guaranteed not to impose a garrison. He razed to the ground the Piraeus fortress, the hated symbol of foreign occupation. He also promised them timber, grain, and cash, all vital commodities of which Athens was always short and often starved. He returned the islands of Lemnos and Imbros, which his father had taken from them seven years earlier. Most importantly, he restored the democratic constitution that had been suspended ten years earlier.

The Athenians were jubilant—and obsequious. They silenced politicians who were opposed to the Antigonid cause, awarded Antigonus and Demetrius divine honors as savior gods, instituted an annual festival in their joint names, and appointed a priest for their cult; even Phila, Demetrius's first wife, gained cult honors as Aphrodite, the goddess of loving marriage. They addressed both Antigonus and Demetrius as "kings,"[10] and two new civic tribes, named after them, were added to the ten that had stood since the beginning of Athenian democracy two hundred years earlier. They even wove Antigonus's and Demetrius's features into the sacred robe with which the cult statue of Athena, the city's goddess, was ceremonially draped. When a freak storm burst on the procession bearing the robe toward Athena's temple, the robe was ripped.

There were of course those who chose to see this incident as ominous, but there was a sense in which Antigonus and Demetrius were truly Athens's saviors (though Demetrius of Phalerum's regime had scarcely been harsh), and deserved at least some of the honors they received. By restoring the democracy, they restored Athenian pride. It also helped that Athenian shipyards were soon busy rebuilding the fleet that Cassander had repressed. No longer would all that Athenian naval expertise go to waste. But the restoration of democracy was more symbolic than real, and rearmament was not meant to help Athens itself. During his periods of residence in the city, Demetrius treated it as the capital of his kingdom, and expected his orders and even his whims to be carried out. Athens, under Demetrius, was to be the western capital of the Antigonid empire.

THE MUSEUM OF ALEXANDRIA

By the early 290s, Demetrius of Phalerum found himself, as I have just said, in Egypt. Until his death some dozen or so years later, he was Ptolemy's right-hand man for one of the most ambitious projects undertaken by any of the Successors—the establishment in Alexandria of the Museum (literally, a shrine to the Muses, the goddesses of art, literature, and culture) and its library.[11]

Alexandria became Ptolemy's administrative capital in 313, the tenth anniversary of his regime.[12] The occasion was probably marked by the removal of Alexander's body from Memphis to its new home, the shrine known merely as the *Sēma*, the Tomb. Most of the city had been built by then, and it was already a thriving center of commerce. The city was divided into three sections, according to population: Greek, Egyptian, and other (chiefly Jewish). The first of these was by far the most magnificent, especially since a great deal of it was occupied by the palace compound, strikingly visible on the shoreline as one sailed into the harbor. All the buildings Ptolemy valued most were in close proximity to one another: the palace itself, the *Sēma*, the barracks, the harbor and its warehouses, and the most important temples, including the Museum. No expense was spared on these and other great buildings. Alexandria was designed to display the majesty of the Ptolemies, as Versailles was built by Louis XIV for the Bourbon dynasty. Absolute monarchs have always spent enormously on such displays.

The Museum functioned both as a temple of learning (literally, since its director was also its high priest) and as a residential college for scholars, focusing particularly on science and literature. All expenses were covered by the king. Their major resource was to be the library. This was not a separate building; the book-rolls were stored on shelves in the Museum itself.

Ptolemy's intentions in establishing the library were typically ambitious: first, to collect a copy of every single book ever written in Greek, wherever possible in original editions, and second, to translate into Greek the most important books written in other languages. The second aim led, most famously, to the translation within the Museum of the Old Testament into Greek. The work was undertaken by a group of about seventy Jewish scholars, which is why the Greek Old Testament, still considered the definitive version, is called the Septuagint, or "Translation of the Seventy," *septuaginta* being the Latin for "seventy." The project was begun under Ptolemy I—the first five books of the Bible were perhaps already translated in Alexandria during his time—and was completed about 150 years later. The Septuagint then became the body of law for the Jewish community of Alexandria.[13]

It is impossible to estimate the number of papyrus rolls the library contained at any given time, and many books occupied more than one roll. If each roll held about thirty thousand words, this book, for instance, transcribed onto papyrus, would make three rolls. It is possible that it came to hold well over half a million rolls, little enough by today's standards (the Library of Congress holds more than thirty-three million books and sixty-three million manuscripts, let alone other forms of media), but an incredible achievement in the ancient world. Even during the reign of Ptolemy I, it probably held about fifty thousand. By the end of the third century the catalogue alone ran to 120 volumes; it contained not only the title of the work, but the name and a brief biography of the author, listing all his other works, the opening line of every work, and the number of verses if the work was poetry. It was an inventory of Greek literature and thought. The library was finally burnt to the ground in 641 CE, but by then it had long been sadly neglected; apart from anything else, the city (and especially the palace compound by the sea) had been devastated by a severe tsunami on July 21, 365 CE.[14]

As soon as the books began to arrive and to be studied, it was clear that there were many different versions even of well-known texts such as Homer's epic poems, the first and foundational works of western literature. A certain amount of editorial work on Homer had taken place in sixth-century Athens, but it was clearly inadequate; and even though there were standard texts of the major Athenian tragedians,

Aeschylus, Sophocles, and Euripides, these texts were riddled with actors' interpolations. The problem was compounded by the fact that librarians were prepared to pay well for texts, to the delight of forgers and the bane of future scholars. In any case, in Alexandria, the necessity of classifying every work for the catalogue had to be supplemented by the attempt to establish authentic texts of the work of every author, at least partly by drawing up rules for the use of the Greek language. Thus was literary scholarship born. This may be where we can distinguish the signature of Demetrius of Phalerum. He belonged to the Peripatetic school of philosophy, founded by Aristotle, and encyclopedic thoroughness was one of the hallmarks of the school.

The library of Alexandria was not entirely without precedent. It is just possible that scientific research had become institutionalized in Babylonian temples in the fourth century.[15] Certainly, private collectors had begun to accumulate libraries; Aristotle's in Athens was especially famous (the library in Alexandria went to considerable pains to acquire it), and there were others. What was unprecedented, however, was the sheer scale of the project. As the Hellenistic period progressed, other cities came to establish fabulous libraries—those of Antioch and Pergamum, especially—but none ever compared with the library of Alexandria. Ptolemy's intention fell little short of an attempt to monopolize Greek literary and scientific culture.

It was always part of the Egyptian mirage that they were an old race, whose scribes kept records of the distant past,[16] but more important to Ptolemy was the fact that Macedonian kings had long patronized Greek artists, philosophers, and scientists. From this perspective, the establishment of the Museum was simply a vast extension of this kingly function. Patronage was no longer to be governed by the particular whims of the king, but institutionalized and passed down from generation to generation of Ptolemies.

All over the Hellenistic world, royal patronage was the main engine of cultural development in science, mathematics, medicine, technology, art, and literature. Philosophers generally stayed away, in horror of the opulence of court life. The kings had the money, and their cultural gestures enhanced their prestige as tokens of the extent of their resources. The painted Macedonian tombs of Vergina and elsewhere, tombs for the rich from the late Classical and early Hellenistic period, vividly show the connection between wealth and the development of fine art.

Patronage was not just necessary but an honor, a sign that a poet or scientist had won or deserved international renown. Hence artists and writers were expected to pay for their privileged and comfortable life-styles with the occasional work or passage in fulsome praise of the king.[17] And nowhere were artists or scholars treated better than in Alexandria. In due course of time, there even came to be a daughter library in the city, for the use of scholars not settled by the Ptolemies themselves in "the birdcage of the Muses."[18]

The erudition that the Museum fostered had a powerful impact on the kind of literature that was written in Alexandria. A lot of poems were so incredibly learned that only the author could be expected to get all the allusions. In addition to learned references, obscure words and neologisms abounded. Whereas in the past poems had been written for public performance and accompanied by music, they were written now also for private readers, who had the time to linger over texts and pick up at least some of the allusions and nuances. Shorter verse forms predominated, and so anthologies began to be put together, allowing readers to compare within specific genres. To a certain extent, Alexandrian literature was a kind of refined game between author and reader. It is not surprising that clever tricks such as the use of acrostics and the writing of concrete poetry (poems where the overall shape of the lines on the page make a specific shape—a cup, say, for a poem on a cup) first make their appearance in Alexandrian writers.

Overclever verse can of course be horribly frigid, and this would certainly be a fair description of some Alexandrian literature, but erudition and beauty are not necessarily incompatible, and there is plenty to charm and delight in Alexandrian literature. The best of it preserves the spirit of the Museum in which it was written in its attempt to honor the past by echoing, imitating, and parodying the old masters, while at the same time developing new forms and directions. A writer's display of erudition mirrored in miniature the ostentation of the whole Museum. Wit, learning, experimentation, and technical mastery were the hallmarks of Alexandria.

The End of Antigonus

Tʜᴇ ᴀɴᴛɪɢᴏɴɪᴅꜱ ᴡᴇʀᴇ still immensely powerful. Even the fact that they had been forced to cede the east to Seleucus helped them in the sense that they were now fighting on only two fronts. In Greece, the Four-Year War pitted Demetrius against Cassander, and in the eastern Mediterranean the old antagonism between Antigonus and Ptolemy remained just as fierce as ever. Antigonus and his son were still on the offensive. Demetrius's recovery of Athens was meant to be a platform from which to regain control of Greece—and then to take Macedon. Meanwhile, Antigonus was determined to deprive Ptolemy of Cyprus—and then Egypt.

Nothing is certain in war, but even so, with their vast resources and their aggression, they might have succeeded against only these two rivals. But what if Lysimachus got involved as well? They might defeat two, but could they defeat three? And would Seleucus remain quiet? If he succeeded in conquering the eastern satrapies, would his ambitions be satisfied? These were the decisive questions of the Fourth War of the Successors (307–301).

DEMETRIUS ON THE OFFENSIVE: CYPRUS

Once Demetrius was established in Athens, the Athenians set about repairing their fortifications, and Demetrius secured the city by means of an alliance with the Aetolians and by expelling Cassander's garrison from nearby Megara. But just when he was poised to launch a major offensive in Greece, Antigonus recalled him. Demetrius was reluctant to leave. He took what steps he could to secure Athens and other Antigonid allies against the certainty of counterattack by Cassander, and tried to suborn the Ptolemaic garrison commander of Sicyon and Corinth. But the man stayed true, and Demetrius simply had to abandon Greece for the time being. Over the next few years, Athens was subjected to repeated assaults by Cassander and his generals, "in order to enslave the city," as an Athenian inscription tendentiously puts it[1]— that is, presumably, in order to reinstate Demetrius of Phalerum, who had done such a good job of keeping Athens secure for ten years.

The mission for which Antigonus recalled his son was to finally take Cyprus from Ptolemy. Antigonus was too old to take charge himself; Demetrius was now his military right arm, and the chance of gaining Cyprus made even the prospect of success in Greece seem less urgent. The two sides had intrigued and fought over the island for ten years or more, but for several years it had been effectively part of Greater Egypt and in the firm grip of Ptolemy's brother Menelaus. But Antigonus was preparing to sweep the Ptolemaic forces off the island once and for all. Cyprus was a good source of grain and salt, minerals (especially copper—hence the metal's name—and silver), and timber, all of which Antigonus was anxious to secure for himself and deny Ptolemy. It also had a long history of shipbuilding and seamanship. Its command of the eastern Mediterranean is such that successive British governments have been moved to lie and cheat to retain their influence and military presence there.[2]

Ptolemy's possession of Cyprus was a major obstacle to Antigonid control of the sea. Even so, it seems strange that Antigonus recalled Demetrius from Greece when he was doing so well and was poised to do better. If something had happened to create at that particular time an opportunity for invasion, we do not know what it was. More probably, that was the deal Antigonus had offered Demetrius in the first place—that he was to go to Greece and do what he could, but be ready to return once Antigonus had mustered the forces and armament needed to take the island.

At any rate, Demetrius left Athens early in 306 and linked up with the invasion force in Cilicia. On the way he asked the Rhodians for help, and they refused. The invasion was launched as soon as the weather permitted. Demetrius's land army swept across the island from the north, ultimately pinning Menelaus inside the city of Salamis, while his navy came up to command the harbor mouth. A full siege ensued, with the help of professional siege engineers imported from Asia Minor. Siege towers had been in use for over thirty years, but for Salamis Demetrius built one that was tall enough to overtop the city walls and large enough to contain, as well as hundreds of troops, heavy artillery on the lower decks and lighter catapults on the upper levels.

The defenders fought back heroically, while anxiously waiting to be relieved. Ptolemy arrived in force; he and his brother had twenty-five thousand men under their command, against Demetrius's fifteen thousand. Whoever won this battle was going to dominate the eastern Mediterranean. In the greatest naval battle for a hundred years, involving almost four hundred warships, Demetrius crushed Ptolemy's fleet off Salamis before it could make land. Ptolemy fled back to Egypt, while on the island his brother surrendered, followed by the commanders of all the remaining Ptolemaic garrisons. Demetrius allowed Menelaus to return to Egypt with his family and property intact, an exchange of courtesies initiated by Ptolemy after Gaza, when he had returned Demetrius's regalia and captured courtiers.

This was the star campaign of Demetrius's career, and he was not quite thirty years of age. He more than doubled his forces by capturing Ptolemy's mercenaries while they were still in their transport vessels at sea, and by taking over the garrison troops too. At a stroke, Ptolemy lost almost half his available forces, and without his previously unchallenged naval superiority it was impossible for him to defend his carefully constructed bulwark in southwest Asia Minor and the Aegean. The Antigonids recovered all their losses, and held Cyprus for the next ten years. Since Ptolemy had also withdrawn from Phoenicia in 311, he was reduced almost to the territories he had inherited in 323. Even worse, he was currently denied access to all the most convenient sources of ship-quality timber. We will find Ptolemy playing a reduced role for the next few years.

THE ASSUMPTION OF KINGSHIP

Immediately after the capture of Cyprus, Antigonus took the step which had been inevitable since the murder of Alexander IV: he allowed himself to be proclaimed king. This was done in a highly theatrical manner. Antigonus was in northern Syria, supervising the construction of Antigonea, when the news arrived of Demetrius's conquest of Cyprus. The envoy, Aristodemus of Miletus, approached in a stately manner, and his first words were: "Hail, *King* Antigonus!"[3] A diadem was quickly found by those of his courtiers who had been primed, and was tied reverently onto his head. An army assembly ratified his royal status by acclamation.

By return of post, so to speak, Antigonus sent a second diadem to Demetrius in Cyprus, proclaiming him joint king—an unmistakable sign that Antigonus was intending to establish a dynasty. Within a very few years, all the other major players had also taken the title of king (and not long after, in a break from Macedonian tradition, their wives began to style themselves "queens"). In part, this was a reaction to the Antigonids' move—they could not be allowed to get away with claiming the entire empire. A telling anecdote, however, shows that the Antigonids regarded only their claim to kingship as authentic; at best the others were, or should be, their subordinate officers. They were true kings in the sense that they wanted all of Alexander's legacy for themselves, while Seleucus was just "commander of the elephant squadron," Ptolemy "commander of the fleet," and Lysimachus a miserly "treasurer." Cassander was not even worth mentioning.[4]

But the several declarations of kingship were, above all, declarations of independence; the Successors were no longer satraps within someone else's empire but kings in their own right, obedient to themselves and to no other authority. The timing of this assumption of royal status is significant; had he lived, Alexander IV would have come of age in 305, aged eighteen. Cassander therefore had to admit openly by then that the king was dead—hence the "big bang,"[5] the phenomenon of all the Successors beginning to style themselves kings in a very short space of time.

As a result of the assumption of kingship, territorial divisions became clearer. Plainly, they could not all be kings of one empire. By declaring themselves as royal as Antigonus and Demetrius, the other Successors were claiming possession of the territory they currently occupied—and to whatever else they could win by the spear. There no longer was any single Macedonian empire that held the loyalty of officers or men. The disintegration of the overall empire meant that their loyalty became more parochial, something to be given only to themselves or their paymaster, their king.

The Successors may by now have felt their territories to be relatively settled, but they still wanted more. That was their job as kings. Royal status was gained by war and maintained by war, and all Hellenistic kings, in our period and beyond, presented themselves, even by the clothes they wore, as men of war. In a never-ending, bloody cycle, military success brought wealth (from plunder and indemnities) and increased territory, which enabled a king to create more revenue, to pay for more troops, and hence to gain more military successes. That was the royal ideology; that was why the kings always clashed with one another. It took years for this destructive cycle to be broken, and for a balance of power to be recognized that would allow heredity rather than victory to determine kingship. Heredity was irrelevant to the Successors because they were the pioneers; their achievements, not their blood, made them kings.

The major contenders had often acted like kings before; they had even come close to naming themselves as such (Antigonus was already "Lord of Asia," Ptolemy the de facto pharaoh of Egypt), or being acclaimed as such (Seleucus at Didyma, Antigonus and Demetrius at Athens), but these few years saw the official birth of the kind of monarchy that became the constitutional norm in Hellenistic times, when a dozen dynasties spawned over two hundred kings and queens. Almost two centuries of development were to follow, but even at this early stage many of the characteristics of Hellenistic monarchy are evident. Its roots lay not just in the Successors' common Macedonian background but in the more autocratic blend of eastern and Macedonian kingship that, as we have seen, Alexander had developed. It was the beginning of the model of absolute kingship that was inherited, via the Roman principate, by medieval and early modern European kings.

A king in the Macedonian style was the possessor of all the Homeric, manly virtues, and liked his subjects to know it. Lysimachus let it be known that he had killed a savage lion, Seleucus that he had wrestled a bull to the ground with his bare hands; hunting and fighting are the most common motifs in royal artwork; statues of kings, and written descriptions, portray them as young and virile (whatever the truth), and by far the most common way of sculpting kings was as heroic nudes. The culture of heavy drinking that all Macedonian nobles took for granted was part of the same spectrum of virility.

But the chief manifestation of his virility, and a king's chief virtue, was military prowess.[6] It was always thus in premodern societies: "A Prince," Machiavelli wrote in 1532, "should have no care or thought but for war . . . and should apply himself exclusively to this as his peculiar province."[7] Hence, in every case where we know the details, the Successors' assumption of kingship followed significant military success. The conquest of Cyprus was the trigger for the Antigonids; the repulse in 306 of the Antigonid invasion of Egypt for Ptolemy; for Seleucus, the subjugation of the eastern satrapies, complete by 304; successes against native Thracian dynasts for Lysimachus; and (speculatively) successes in the Four-Year War for Cassander.

The charisma of successful military leadership was so important that, whatever other noble qualities the king might possess, if he was poor or unlucky at warfare he risked being replaced, as Perdiccas's failure in Egypt led to his assassination. But a king needed other attributes. He had to display generosity, not just in rewarding his troops and especially his courtiers (who expected to get very rich indeed) but in making time to hear petitions, for instance. There is a nice story about Demetrius: an old woman repeatedly asked for a hearing, and when Demetrius replied that he was too busy, the woman said, "Then don't be king."[8] Seleucus is said to have remarked that the endless bureaucracy and paperwork involved in kingship would put people off if they knew of it.[9] The king had to find the balance between accessibility and maintaining by ceremonial means the dignity of his position. Other forms of generosity included charitable deeds and sponsoring cultural activities within their courts and kingdoms, acting as arbitrators in disputes within their kingdoms, founding cities to help alleviate poverty, and providing financial aid to cities.

A king made sure that his subjects were aware of his kingly qualities by means of magnificent processions and frequent campaigns, by donations and monuments, by getting poets to praise him and painters and sculptors to portray him, and by establishing priests of his or his dynasty's cult. The apparent altruism of some kingly qualities is illusory; everything fed back into maintaining the position of the king himself. Sponsoring cultural activities, for instance, or performing magnificent sacrifices to the gods, were forms of display that enabled a king to gain and maintain stature at home and abroad. Nevertheless, it was the appearance of altruism that made it possible for individuals and communities to petition kings, since the pretence had to be followed through. Political thinkers added an ethical dimension, that kings should rule for the good of their subjects and not themselves, but the Successors almost totally ignored it. They were setting up empires, not protectorates.

The name of the game was income generation, and ultimately there was only one beneficiary: the king himself. As a rule, the Hellenistic kings owned their kingdoms as their personal fiefs; hence, for instance, in 133 BCE the last king of Pergamum simply bequeathed his entire kingdom to the Roman people. All individual landowners, and every institution such as a landowning temple, were just more or less privileged tenants. The kings could give and take away at whim.

Early Hellenistic monarchy was absolute, an extension of the king's power as commander in chief out on campaign; Seleucus is said to have held that "What the king ordains is always right."[10] Treaties were made with the king in person, not with his state, so that on his death all treaties became null and void. There was not even a permanent council of advisers, but rather a loose group of "Friends," who were as likely to meet and conduct business over drinks as in a council session. The use of the term "Friends" or "Companions" for a king's closest advisers and bodyguard again reveals the personal nature of early Hellenistic kingship. The glory of victory was personal too: it was Ptolemy who won a victory, not "Egypt." It showed that he was favored by the gods, and, if the victory was significant enough, almost a god himself. Absolute monarchy suited the Successors perfectly. They took it to be a license to give their ambitions their head.

ANTIGONUS ON THE OFFENSIVE: EGYPT

Victory was an essential part of the ideology of the early Hellenistic kings. Victory proved that a king was indeed the right man for the job. But the gods signally failed to smile on the Antigonids' next venture. Just a few months after their capture of Cyprus, taking advantage of the cooler weather and intending to catch Ptolemy still reeling, Antigonus and Demetrius launched an all-out attack on Egypt, by land and sea, with a monstrous army. Ninety thousand men and eighty-three elephants marched south from Syria by land, while 150 warships with their crews of forty thousand shadowed the army's route. From Gaza onward, every man in the land army was required to carry his own provisions for ten days, which was sufficient for crossing the northern Sinai desert, while a huge camel train supplied by friendly Arabs bore fodder for the animals, water, and extra grain. Ptolemy had made his headquarters at Pelusium, where he waited.

Despite poor weather at sea, most of the fleet, and all of the Antigonid land army, managed to rendezvous at the Nile early in November, with Ptolemy's forces on the other bank. The navy had suffered, however: they had found few places to put to land, and had become short of water and food. Antigonus well knew, especially from the example of Perdiccas, how hard it was to force the Nile. The plan was that Demetrius was to sail beyond the Nile, to get behind Ptolemy and create the opportunity for the land army to cross the river. But Ptolemy's defenses along the coast on the far side of the river were just too good, and Demetrius was again unable to land.

On his way back to rejoin the land army, another storm sank a few more ships. As his fleet commander stressed, the weather was unlikely to improve this late in the year, and Antigonus could not maintain his troops for long in the desert. He decided to withdraw. He may have been ill as well as dispirited, and he was certainly feeling his advanced age. It should have been his last campaign; he no longer belonged on the battlefield.

DEMETRIUS ON THE OFFENSIVE: RHODES

The original plan was to make another attempt on Egypt in 305. But first there was the question of Rhodes. Its links with Egypt, both formal and informal, were firmly founded on the fact that the Rhodians acted as brokers for the export of Egyptian grain to Greece. But Antigonus too was now an exporter of grain, and it is quite likely that one of his main reasons for wanting to take the island was to force it to deal only in his grain, not Ptolemy's. In any case, it was spoiling Antigonid control of the eastern Mediterranean and it had refused to support the invasion of Cyprus. But the last straw was that, during the Egyptian invasion, Rhodian ships had repulsed an Antigonid attempt to interrupt the transport of grain from Egypt. In a blatant attempt at self-justification, Antigonus chose to interpret this as an act of war. He wanted Rhodian wealth for himself, and he wanted to interrupt one of Ptolemy's main sources of income; the islanders appealed in vain to the clause in the 311 peace that guaranteed autonomy for Greek states.

Taking the island was supposed to be easy; it would all be over in a matter of weeks, and then the Antigonids could turn their attention back to Egypt. In the event, however, Rhodes held out for over a year, and absorbed so much energy that the invasion of Egypt became an impossibility. By the time it was all over, Ptolemy had been able to regroup. It was one of the turning points of the war.

Demetrius appeared off the island in the summer of 305 with a huge fleet. The Rhodians hastily agreed to break off their alliance with Ptolemy and enter into one with Antigonus, but Demetrius now added unrealistic further demands. The Rhodians prepared for a siege. As well as strengthening their defenses, they wrote to Antigonus's enemies for help. All three responded, but Ptolemy above all: he wanted the siege to go on for as long as possible, to give him time to recover, and over the course of the siege his blockade-runners brought in troops as well as supplies and money, often just in the nick of time. It was impossible for the Antigonid fleet to entirely surround the large island, especially at night, so that blockade-running was relatively easy. Demetrius even hired pirates—often some of the best sailors in the Mediterranean—to increase his naval strength, but supplies still got through.

Demetrius began from the sea, making use of the technology perfected at Salamis to bring up ship-mounted siege engines, and before long also managed to occupy and fortify a spit of land. Repeated assaults were thwarted by Rhodian bravery and naval skill; on one occasion, their ships managed to sink two of Demetrius's floating siege engines—only to find, a few weeks later, that Demetrius had built an even larger monster. But this was destroyed in a storm, and the Rhodians seized the opportunity also to drive the Antigonid troops off their beachhead.

By the beginning of 304, Demetrius had gained little, and the Rhodians had good reasons to congratulate themselves for their heroic resistance. But it was not over yet. Demetrius decided to switch directions and attack from the land. For this purpose, he had an even larger siege tower constructed than he had used at Salamis. It was forty meters (130 feet) high, armored and bristling with artillery, some of which was capable of firing missiles weighing up to eighty kilograms (175 pounds) almost two hundred meters (650 feet). The moat was being filled, and numerous battering rams and catapults were built. The artillery would strafe the battlements while the rams pounded the towers and sappers undermined the walls. Attempts by neutral states to arbitrate an end to the fighting came to nothing. As Lawrence Durrell once wrote, Demetrius gave the would-be arbitrators his answer precisely by building this enormous siege tower.[11]

The Rhodians resorted to extreme measures, and while Demetrius's engineers were busy, they constructed an entire second wall inside the one that was under threat, tearing down the marble walls of public buildings to supplement their supply of stone. Meanwhile, their ships continued to achieve extraordinary successes at sea, despite their small numbers. Above all, Demetrius was never able finally to secure the harbor mouth.

Demetrius began his assault. Rhodian countermines foiled his sappers, and although they were eventually driven back onto their newly built interior wall, they counterattacked and damaged the monster siege tower. This bought them enough time to repair their defenses and prepare new ones. The assault was renewed, and it all seemed to be going Demetrius's way. He planned to bring things to an end with a night attack through the breaches his engines had made. His men penetrated well into the city, but were bloodily repulsed. Demetrius began to prepare another assault, which would surely be the final one—but his father called him off. It was costing them too many men; besides the situation in Greece was rapidly getting worse, and he was needed there. Rhodes had survived.

In gratitude to Ptolemy for keeping them supplied with men and food, the Rhodians instituted his cult as a savior god. Demetrius gained a new title too: Poliorcetes, the Besieger. Despite his failure, the title was not ironic. The siege technology he had applied was truly impressive and innovative. As always, warfare accelerated the rate of technological advances—though for the time being only warfare benefited from man's ingenuity. Archimedes' screw, accurate water clocks, the rotary olive press, amazing gadgets for entertainment—all the remarkable, peaceful developments of later decades lay in the future, with the notable exception of the mechanical snail that by the command of Demetrius of Phalerum had led a procession in Athens in 308, excreting slime.[12]

The Antigonids agreed to recognize Rhodian autonomy, and the Rhodians agreed to help the Antigonids in any of their campaigns, except against Ptolemy. This was some gain for the Antigonids, but hardly compensation for what they had lost—not just money, men, and prestige, but the opportunity to attack Egypt. There was, not un-naturally, delirious joy in Rhodes at the outcome. The most striking manifestation of this was the construction of the Colossus, one of the seven wonders of the ancient world, to stand near the harbor mouth (not *over* the harbor mouth, as some fanciful pictures have it). They raised money in part by selling siege equipment abandoned by Demetrius's forces.

The Colossus was a bronze statue of their presiding deity, Helios, the sun god; it stood thirty-two meters tall (about 105 feet), and was built on such a scale that only those with the longest reach could get their arms around even one of its thumbs. They matched the Besieger's gigantism with their own, and made the point by using a local man as chief designer. At any rate, they were right to celebrate, because Rhodian neutrality was the foundation for the island's subsequent prosperity. But the symbol of the foundation of that prosperity snapped at the knees and fell during an earthquake in 226 BCE. The toppled remains were a tourist attraction for hundreds of years, until they were removed in the seventh century CE after the Arab conquest of the island.

THE END OF THE FOUR-YEAR WAR

The situation in Greece was indeed dire, from the Antigonid perspective. Polemaeus's defection and subsequent death had let Cassander back into central Greece, and he had compelled the Aetolians to break off their alliance with Athens. Early in 304 Cassander put Athens under siege, and in addition to the usual hardships, the city was disturbed by political feuding between Antigonid supporters and opponents. Athens came dangerously close to falling. Cassander's brother Pleistarchus even managed at one point to breach the walls before being repulsed by the cavalry.

Demetrius arrived in force and landed in central Greece. Cassander abandoned the siege at his approach and retreated to Macedon. The Aetolians and Boeotians swiftly came to terms, and Demetrius marched south. Athens was saved—at least from Cassander's predations. But Demetrius was a king now, and expected to be treated as such. At least he continued to benefit the city in material terms.

Demetrius spent the winters of 304/3 and 303/2 in the city he considered his royal seat. Since the Athenians had already agreed, by making him the founder of one of their civic tribes, that he was more or less a god, he set up house in the Parthenon—the temple of Athena, his "older sister."[13] More specifically, he seems to have considered himself an avatar of Dionysus (which licensed a series of celebrations). Two of his concubines were identified with Aphrodite; they must have been good at their work. All our sources insist that Demetrius was a good-looking man,[14] and he was never short of women to share his bed. Menander wryly listed the famous beauties of the day and ended: "You've had 'em all."[15] Even his cohorts were awarded heroic honors as the liberators of Athens, while a cult was established at the very spot on Attic soil where Demetrius had first descended from his chariot on arrival, as if it were a divine epiphany. By now he had three cults in Athens; before long, after Sicyon fell to him, the Sicyonians added a fourth.

Militarily speaking, Demetrius was unstoppable. Having driven Ptolemy's garrison out of Sicyon in the spring of 303, he went on to do the same at Corinth, where Cassander's general Prepelaus had hugely reinforced Ptolemy's garrison. At the specific request of the Corinthians themselves—or so his propaganda stressed—Demetrius installed his own garrison on the Acrocorinth instead. Ptolemy had only briefly kept a toehold on mainland Greece, but the Antigonid garrison remained in place for sixty years, a thorn in many sides.

The Four-Year War ended later that year with the defeat of Cassander's brother Pleistarchus in the Peloponnese. Polyperchon watched helplessly from Messenia. Fortune had briefly made him a major player, but, lacking sufficient killer instinct and megalomania, it was not a role for which he was temperamentally suited. His story has a relatively happy ending, however; this "jackal among lions"[16] died, within a year, of nothing more serious than old age.

While in the Peloponnese in 303, Demetrius found time also to add to his collection of wives the sister of Pyrrhus of Epirus, a young woman called Deidameia—an important catch, because she was a cousin (once removed) of Olympias and had previously been betrothed to Alexander IV. Pyrrhus was the ambitious king of the Molossians, the most powerful Epirote tribe, and hence head of the Epirote League. The Epirotes were lining up once again against Cassander.

Demetrius was poised to invade Macedon itself. Cassander sued for peace, but the Antigonids rebuffed him by demanding unconditional surrender. After all his success in Greece, in spring 302 Demetrius refounded Philip II's Corinthian League, with him and his father (and then their successors) as life presidents. This was exactly what Ptolemy had tried and failed to do a few years earlier. A large number of Greek states were involved, so that Demetrius effectively controlled Greece; Sparta refused to join, but Sparta was so insignificant at the time that it made little difference. The immediate aim of the league was to defeat Cassander, and as long as they were on a war footing, the Antigonids retained a firm grip on the league.[17] Since the league lasted only a couple of years, we have no way of knowing quite how it was to function in peacetime. The league duly appointed Demetrius commander in chief, and he marched north against Cassander. It looked as though the final showdown for possession of Macedon itself was about to take place.

THE BATTLE OF IPSUS

The intransigence of the Antigonids in their peace talks with Cassander may have been a mistake; since all-out war was now inevitable, Cassander summoned help. Lysimachus was very ready to oblige, especially since Cassander seems to have offered him Asia Minor as his reward. The Antigonids made efforts to placate him, but every one of their successes increased the likelihood that he would be the next target of their aggression, once they held neighboring Macedon as well as Asia Minor. The decisive difference between this phase of the war and earlier was precisely Lysimachus's greater involvement, since for the first time for years he was relatively free of trouble within Thrace itself. And he was such a great general that it was he who led the anti-Antigonid forces.

Ptolemy, of course, was a natural ally (though in the event he was not especially helpful), and Seleucus had at last freed himself from his eastern wars and offered his assistance too. At the conclusion of their conflict, Chandragupta had given him five hundred elephants and their handlers, a stupendous gift, though not as valuable as the territories Seleucus had had to give up. He would bring most of the beasts west with him. Cassander, Lysimachus, Ptolemy, Seleucus—it was the same grand anti-Antigonid alliance as in 315–311.

Cassander sent an army under Prepelaus to Lysimachus and marched south from Macedon. He confronted Demetrius in Thessaly, but the campaign was ineffective from both sides. They built enormous military camps and eyeballed each other, but both armies were so terrifyingly huge that neither was in a hurry to start the offensive, but preferred to wait for news from Asia Minor. Cassander commanded over thirty thousand men, Demetrius over fifty-five thousand. Both had good supply lines and were securely encamped on high ground. Neither had a good reason to risk battle against such formidable forces. The battle that should have taken place for control of Macedon never happened.

In the early summer of 302, Lysimachus invaded Asia Minor. It was the first time for many years that Asia Minor had seen war. While he headed east into Hellespontine Phrygia, Prepelaus took an army south down the coast. Both had the same aim, to win over as many as possible of the Greek cities of Asia Minor before the Antigonids had a chance to respond. They quickly gained a few important cities, and some significant allies among the Antigonid governors of Asia Minor who were terrified into surrendering. But those cities that were not immediately threatened, or felt they could endure a siege, preferred to wait and see what would happen rather than risk Antigonid wrath if they gave in prematurely.

Antigonus, feeling the burden of his eighty years, was forced to break his retirement and move north into Asia Minor. He knew he was no longer fit for battle, and had been involved in more peaceful pursuits. In fact, he had been about to stage a superb international athletic competition, to prove to the world that Antigonea was a Greek city to be reckoned with, but he had to cancel it. It was as shocking— and as expensive, in terms of compensation—as if the host nation of a modern Olympic festival canceled at the last moment. But Antigonus was never one to duck a fight.

Once Antigonus reached Asia Minor, Lysimachus's and Prepelaus's tactics had to change: they were no match for him in the field—not until Seleucus arrived. As Antigonus advanced, threatening their supply lines, they fell back north, avoiding pitched battle by keeping safe behind a series of entrenched camps. This also served the purpose of drawing the Antigonid forces farther away from Seleucus's arrival point in Asia Minor, which they knew to be Cappadocia. They held Antigonus at bay at Dorylaeum, and then winter intervened and both sides separated. While Antigonus retired to Celaenae, Lysimachus and Prepelaus fell back on the plain south of Heraclea Pontica. Lysimachus confirmed his alliance with Heraclea—and its detachment from the Antigonid cause—by marrying its current ruler, Amastris. Control of Heraclea gave him an extra source of timber, but also an extra lifeline back home to Thrace, the importance of which became clear that very winter.

In order to be certain of victory, Antigonus needed reinforcements. He ordered Demetrius to make a truce with Cassander, so that he could join him in Asia Minor. Once Demetrius had set sail, Cassander recovered Thessaly, retained a force to protect Macedon, and sent a second tranche of troops by land under his brother Pleistarchus to support Lysimachus and Prepelaus. Meanwhile, Demetrius landed at Ephesus, recovered the city immediately, and then moved up the coast, undoing all Prepelaus's gains. He made his winter quarters at Chalcedon and guarded the strait.

So when Pleistarchus and his army reached the north coast of the Propontis, they found that Demetrius had already secured the southern coastline. Pleistarchus therefore marched up the west coast of the Black Sea to Odessus and prepared to embark his forces there and sail for Heraclea. There were not enough ships at Odessus for a single crossing. The first contingent made it safely to Heraclea; the second was captured by Demetrius; the third was smashed by a storm, with Pleistarchus among the few who made land safely. Fully six thousand of the twenty thousand troops he was bringing died or fell into Demetrius's hands. But during the winter, news arrived that Seleucus had reached Cappadocia. Even an Antigonid raid on Babylon from Syria had failed to deflect him from his purpose. He had avoided the route through Syria and traveled to Cappadocia via Armenia.

In the meantime, while Antigonus's Syrian army was busy in Babylonia, Ptolemy played his part by invading Phoenicia. But on receiving misinformation that his allies were losing the war in Asia Minor, he prudently or lamely withdrew for the winter to Egypt, leaving garrisons in the cities he had taken. It was not much of an effort, and Tyre and Sidon, the most important ports, remained in Antigonid hands. Seleucus, by contrast, had made an epic journey in a few months, and so was waiting to join up with Lysimachus when he marched south in 301 from his winter quarters.

Battle was joined at Ipsus in Phrygia; each side was commanded by two kings and fielded about eighty thousand men. It was the greatest battle of the Successors numerically, and the most significant. Lysimachus and his allies would either crush the Antigonids or be crushed by them. If they lost, only Ptolemy would stand in the way of the Antigonids' long-held desire for world domination.

But it was an outright victory for the anti-Antigonid alliance. Octogenarian Antigonus died appropriately in a shower of javelins, while Demetrius escaped by the skin of his teeth. Hostile propaganda afterward said that he had performed badly—that he had raced with his cavalry too far in pursuit of a fleeing enemy contingent to be in a position to support his father when the crisis came. But it is equally likely that Seleucus's elephant drivers skillfully blocked the attempts of Demetrius's victorious cavalry to return to the battlefield and relieve his father. Demetrius's cavalry, on the right wing, had been expected to win; details of the battle are uncertain, but it may even have been a deliberate tactic by Lysimachus and Seleucus to let him drive their left wing back far enough for them to deploy their elephants to block his return. Then, while he was held at bay, Antigonus and his men either surrendered or were cut down. Demetrius prudently fled, but his heart must have been filled with dread, anger, and sorrow in equal measures: he and his father were famously close.[18] So died one of the most determined, successful, and gifted of the Successors. At the age of sixty, circumstances had given him the opportunity for imperial rule; he had seized it eagerly and had exercised vast power for twenty years. To minds not already besotted with power, Antigonus's fall from such a great height might have taught moderation.

The Kingdoms of Ptolemy
and Seleucus

ONE OF THE most important effects of the battle of Ipsus was that it left Seleucus and Ptolemy in firm control of their kingdoms. This is a good point, then, at which to pause from war narrative and take a closer look at those kingdoms, insofar as we have evidence. Many conclusions must remain tentative, but we are even worse off for other Successor kingdoms. Seleucid Asia and Ptolemaic Egypt remain our best chances for investigating the important topic of what the Successors made of their realms once they had carved up Alexander's empire.

After Ipsus, the Ptolemaic kingdom remained unchanged, in terms of core territory, until the Roman takeover in 30 BCE. The Seleucid kingdom suffered more from shifting borders, and there were mountain tribes in several parts of the empire that were never altogether tamed. We have already seen that in 304 Seleucus ceded the satrapies bordering India to Chandragupta, and he and his descendants had to put up with several independent or semi-independent kingdoms in Asia Minor, such as Bithynia. For much of the third century, Persis was semi-independent, and around the middle of the third century, the Seleucids lost Bactria, which went independent under Greek leadership. Worse was to follow: the Parthian satrap declared his province free of Seleucid rule in 246, but within ten years had lost it to invaders from the north, who held it for thirty-five years. Seleucus's great-great-grandson, Antiochus III, recovered it, but only temporarily, and by the middle of the second century BCE the invaders had annexed Media, and Babylonia and Mesopotamia became the front line of their ongoing war with the Seleucids. The remains of the Seleucid empire were finally broken up by the Romans in 62 BCE, and the Euphrates became the border between the Roman and the Parthian empires.

We have a a lot more evidence for Egypt, thanks to the preservation of papyri in the dry heat, than we do for Asia. Almost all this evidence, however, dates from later than the first forty years of the Hellenistic period with which I am concerned in this book. It may be legitimate, in some cases, to project what we know from a later period back on to an earlier period, but this can be no more than intelligent guesswork. As the history of early modern Europe shows, the processes whereby states become increasingly centralized, territorialized, and bureaucratized are complex and develop over time, but we do not have enough evidence for early Ptolemaic and Seleucid history to see the processes in detail. At any rate, I shall assume that, in our period, the administration of the kingdoms was in the process of development rather than settled. Ptolemy and Seleucus spent a great deal of their time on a war footing, and it is likely that their first administrative measures were designed mainly to ensure that their kingdoms were internally stable enough to guarantee them sufficient income to continue to make war.

In each case, as one would expect, the administration blended Macedonian with local institutions.[1] In Asia, "local" largely meant Achaemenid, since Antigonus's regime had left hardly a mark (or, if it did, it is impossible to distinguish it), but the Persians themselves had necessarily worked with local subsystems in the further-flung parts of their empire. Egypt held a mix of Egyptian and Achaemenid systems, since it had intermittently been under Persian administration for two hundred years. In each case, the Macedonians came as conquerors, with their own way of doing things, but in order not to ruffle too many feathers, and to keep their lives simple, they took over local structures, which had proved their effectiveness for decades, if not centuries. It follows that we should expect to find both similarities and differences between the administrations of the two kingdoms, with the similarities being due to the Macedonian background and the similar situations in which the kings found themselves, and the differences to inherited local practices or other local conditions, such as the relative sizes of the two kingdoms.

Egypt was a relatively self-contained unit, both geographically and ethnically; it consisted of the Nile delta and a thin fertile strip a thousand kilometers (620 miles) up the river, never wider than thirty kilometers (twenty miles) at any point, and bounded by desert to the east and west. Seleucid Asia, however, was a sprawling empire, consisting of huge territories and varied peoples, each with its own traditions and subcultures. In modern terms, they held much of Turkey, Lebanon, Syria, Iraq, Kuwait, Iran, Afghanistan, and bits of Uzbekistan, Turkmenistan, and Tajikistan. Seleucus and his son achieved the remarkable feat of coming as conquerors and holding all this together for fifty years before it began to break up in the east. The size of the empire meant that wherever the king happened to be at the time was the center. In Ptolemy's case, after 313, the center was Alexandria, but Seleucus had palaces or residences all over the kingdom. He was most likely to be found in Antioch, but Susa, Seleucia-on-the-Tigris, Celaenae, and Sardis were also royal residences.

THE MACEDONIAN BACKGROUND

Macedon basically consisted of a large and fertile plain to the west of the Thermaic Gulf, ringed by mountains (Upper Macedon). The country was rich in all the essentials: timber, grain, and minerals. It was still very largely rural, with a history of barons and princelings ruling cantons of upland farmers and peasants. These cantons were subject to frequent raids from their neighbors; as a result, military prowess was a dominant virtue in Macedonian culture, and kings and barons were expected to be powerful and successful war leaders as well as performing their administrative and religious duties. Each local princeling relied on the advice of a group of close friends, but was the sole decision maker. Every man bearing arms had the right to assemble, but such an assembly had little independent power; it was formed at the ruler's behest, and its job was to approve his decisions.

When Philip II united the country under central leadership, he retained the same essential structure: king, friends, assembly of citizens. The assembly consisted of whatever citizens were to hand; out on campaign, then, it consisted of however many Macedonian soldiers were to hand. Citizenship and military obligation were very closely allied: in order to be a citizen, you had to be awarded a grant of land by the king, and being the king's tenant in this way simultaneously committed you to paying your taxes and serving in the army when needed. Sons inherited their father's obligations along with the land. The king nominally owned all the land (at least in the sense that it was his to dispose of), but parceled it out as he chose. The assembly was not the source of the king's legitimacy, but could be a critical factor at times of uncertain succession, or if a king proved weak. We have already seen this, at Babylon after Alexander's death. The increase in the use of army assemblies by the Successors is a sign of their insecurity; it was a kind of insurance.

But the overriding dynamic of any Macedonian king's administration lay not so much in his relations with the peasantry and soldiers but in his relations with the barons, many of whom formed his inner circle of advisers and lieutenants. In the first place, these Friends were military leaders in their own right, in command of divisions raised from their own cantons. Even the king's relations with the army, then, were largely mediated by his barons. Since the barons also ruled regions of Macedon, they formed the basic structure of the state, and they also took on any other jobs within the administration that the king required. There must have been a bureaucracy, to promulgate decisions, arrange for the shipment of goods, conscript troops, and so on, and there were local administrative structures for each town and canton, but there was no overall administration as such other than the king and his Friends.

In theory each king's power was absolute, but in practice he had to defer to his advisers; after all, he could not know everything that was going on everywhere in the kingdom. He also had to defer to the general populace, in the sense that it helped to retain popularity if from time to time he did so. However, few of those who presented themselves at court got to see the king in person rather than, at best, one of his Friends. The barons therefore acted as intermediaries not only between the king and the army but between the king and his citizens. Without the barons' goodwill he could hardly function.

In critical situations, a Macedonian king might also decide to call an assembly so that his subjects would be fully informed as to what was about to happen, and have fewer grounds for complaint afterward. So, for instance, when Alexander the Great revealed his plans to march farther east than anyone had expected, he first ran the decision past his men;[2] and we have seen how several of the Successors had their troops conduct show trials of their opponents to legitimate their wars and assassinations.

Macedon was a tempered monarchy, then, but not a constitutional monarchy. The king was the executive head of state and the chief religious official. It was his right to decide matters of policy, both foreign and domestic (such as levels of taxation); it was his right to form and break alliances and to declare war and peace, and he was commander in chief of the armed forces. He was also the chief judge, with the power to decide whether or not to hold a trial in any given situation, or even whether to order a summary execution. The Homeric model of kingship was close; in Homer's poems, the elders advise, the people listen and shout out their views, but the final decisions rest entirely with the king.[3]

The king's position could be likened to that of a head of a household: he was decidedly the head, but there were plenty of occasions when he had to negotiate potential opposition to see that he got his way. A lot depended, then, on the personality and will of the king. If he was passionate enough and committed enough to a project, there was no person and no body that could stop him. He could do whatever he could get away with.

SECURITY, ECONOMIC EXPLOITATION, AND APPEASEMENT

The Successors' default administrative model was the Macedonian system, but their immediate predecessors, Philip II and more especially Alexander the Great, had shifted the model more in the direction of autocracy. Their unprecedented successes gave them unprecedented authority, so that they were less afraid of overriding the wishes of their Friends. The same goes for the Successors, as long as they were successful. Ptolemy and Seleucus were certainly successful, and autocratic.

Apart from their shared Macedonian background, other similarities between the Ptolemaic and Seleucid administrations stem from the simple fact that they both came as conquerors, and like conquerors of all epochs had three immediate concerns: security, economic exploitation (control of resources), and appeasement (or legitimation of their rule). These three concerns are interconnected: their kingdoms would not be secure unless they appeased the native elites, nor would they be secure unless they could maintain armies; but armies needed the money economic exploitation could provide, which in turn required a compliant native population. Unlike many later colonialists, these conquerors saw the stupidity of terrorizing or even exterminating the native populations.

As conquerors, and as Macedonian kings, Seleucus and Ptolemy owned their kingdoms as their private estates; as "spear-won" land, it was theirs to dispose of as they wanted. "Tax" was the equivalent of rent to a landlord; huge swaths of land were crown territory, farmed by royal appointment, with all the profits, not just a taxed percentage, swelling the king's coffers. All resources were concentrated in the hands of the king and then redistributed. Neither Ptolemy nor Seleucus was ever quite a despot, however, and their power was diffused through the hierarchical structures beneath them. Nor were they simply bandits; they took thought for the future, and wanted their sons and grandsons to succeed to functioning and profitable kingdoms after them.

One of the redistributions the kings made was to give away some of their land to temples, cities, and even deserving individuals, who, depending on the size of the donation, could thus become barons within the kingdom, with estates that might encompass several villages and many tied serfs. This was a way for the kings to attract the loyalty of powerful men, and at the same time it brought more land into production and into the taxation system. The villages and farmers on the estate paid tax to the estate owner, who passed on what he owed to the royal treasury. These estates were not always heritable and alienable; they remained nominally crown territory, and in certain circumstances—presumably extreme ones, such as disloyalty—the king could repossess the land. The king could thus assure himself of the continued loyalty of the Greek and Macedonian elite within his kingdom.

Both Seleucus and Ptolemy also settled their troops on the land; in the Macedonian fashion, these soldiers, and then their descendants, owed military service to the crown, and always formed the core of the kingdoms' armies. This was an economical policy; it was expensive to maintain a standing army, but a pool of soldiers was needed for emergencies, and the royal coffers would profit from the taxes paid by such people as farmers. The policy also made the men grateful to their king, and hence they or their sons would be more likely to respond willingly to any future call-up. A typical allotment consisted of two or three pieces of land, to be used for different agricultural purposes. The size of the allotment depended on its fertility and on the rank of the settler; officers and cavalrymen, higher up the social scale, as usual got more.

Ptolemy settled mercenaries throughout Egypt, wherever such a settlement might help to develop agriculture, police a district, or secure a trade route. Above all, he drained the Fayyum marshes southwest of Memphis specifically for the purpose of settling his mercenaries— thousands of them, during his reign alone. The draining of the marshes shows in miniature the combination of local and Macedonian expertise: the Egyptians had long been expert at irrigation, and the Macedonians brought new developments in drainage engineering. It was a massive project, as great in its way as the building of Alexandria; the water level of Lake Moeris was lowered by radial canalization, and these new canals served to irrigate the reclaimed land. The amount of land in use was trebled. Many of the new settlers, however, preferred to live as absentee landlords in the Greek cities of Naucratis (founded as a Greek emporium in the second half of the seventh century BCE), Ptolemais (founded by Ptolemy ca. 310 on the site of an earlier Greek settlement), and of course Alexandria. Memphis too had long had a substantial Greek population. After the battle of Ipsus, the settling of mercenaries on allotments was extended throughout Greater Egypt, to Cyrenaica, Cyprus, and Phoenicia. Ptolemy now felt that these were more securely his possessions.

The size of Seleucus's territory meant that he had many more trouble spots and trade routes to police and protect. He established far more mercenary settlements, ranging from fortresses to cities; perhaps as many as twenty cities were founded in the first two generations of Seleucid rule. The cities would attract further immigrants and help to cohere the districts in which they were founded, as plants fix soil on a hillside. In Egypt, only Ptolemais really served the same function, since it was founded in the Thebaid district of southern Egypt, which had a perennial tendency to regard itself as a separate state, and so contained a large garrison as well as serving as the administrative center for the region.

Seleucus too founded his cities in agriculturally rich areas, which could then be exploited and taxed to the maximum, and intermarrying with the local population was encouraged (though not imitated by any king after Seleucus himself). Seleucus offered incentives such as payment of removal costs, grants of grain, and relief from taxation for the first few years, to help the immigrants get started; and as soon as he felt it was feasible, he allowed the land to be alienable—not just passed down from father to son, with implicit renewal of the tenancy at each break, but disposable outside the family. Ptolemy was forced to follow suit, or risk losing out in the market for mercenaries.

Mercenaries felt themselves well rewarded by being set up as farmers, and gave their loyalty accordingly. Many of them had left home in the first place because there was insufficient land for them to prosper there. They had won their share of the booty taken in war, and now they and their sons had financial security for life. In Seleucus's case, the fact that the Greek settlements were spread thinly over a vast empire meant that he had to take steps to ensure that this loyalty endured. He had the sons of his settlers trained at his military headquarters in Apamea. The son remained in training until his father was withdrawn from the reserve, at which point he returned to his allotment and took his father's place in the reserve, ready to be called up. The culture of the school shaped his loyalty to the king. Ptolemy felt no need for such provisions.

Not unnaturally, the settlement of foreigners on this scale could disturb local sensibilities, so both Ptolemy and Seleucus took care to confiscate land only from those who were too weak and scattered to organize armed resistance, or where it was scarcely used. Hence, for instance, the draining of the underused Fayyum. Wherever possible, they gave away crown land.

Resentment was also offset by the fact that the new cities increased the demand for agricultural products and local farmers' profit margins. Many of the immigrants were content to let former owners continue as tenant farmers, and they increased productivity by introducing new crops and new techniques wherever possible, such as double-cropping and the use of iron plowshares. The extensive irrigation systems of Egypt and Babylonia were also serviced and extended; they were essential in these regions, which could not rely on rainfall. But the newcomers also learned; the seeding plow, which placed seeds in regular furrows, had long been in use in Babylonia, but not in mountainous Greece, whose small amount of good arable land was sown by hand. Overall, the coming of the Greeks and Macedonians did not make as much of a difference as might be thought. Even in a remote area like Bactria, recent archaeology has shown that the incoming Greeks expanded land use only by 10 percent.[4]

Ptolemy's kingdom comprised about 23,000 square kilometers (8,880 square miles) and a population of about four million; Seleucus's, at its largest extent, occupied over 3,750,000 square kilometers (about 1,500,000 square miles) and had a population of about fifteen million. The immigrant population was never more than 10 percent in either kingdom. They were heavily outnumbered. And so they took more radical measures to avoid displeasing at least the more powerful among the native populations—the merchants and landowners, and especially the priests, who were in effect the only political group in both Egypt and Babylonia. If resistance was going to emerge, it would most likely be fomented by the priests, as the leaders of their people—and as the managers of wealthy temple estates with a lot to lose. A king who did not have the support of the priesthood would not last long; he would not even be considered a true pharaoh.

First, as successful defenders of their realms, the kings brought peace and prosperity, which went a long way toward mitigating any hatred their arrival might have caused. Second, existing temple-run lands (which could be massive estates, including a number of villages along with their workshops and farmland) and large privately owned estates generally remained in place—which is to say that the king graciously granted that much of his spear-won land to the temples and landowners. Their side of the bargain was loyalty, or at least passivity. Ptolemy and Seleucus also both undertook programs of refurbishing old temples or building new ones, and made certain to take part in the appropriate local ceremonies and celebrations. Their Persian predecessors had rarely acted with such diplomacy toward the Egyptian priesthood.

Third, both of them employed natives in responsible positions in the administration. How could they not? They needed collaborators, people who spoke the languages and were familiar with the way things worked at a local level. They needed to guarantee a smooth transition to the new dispensation, so that taxes would begin to flow in as quickly as possible. But they fell short of Alexander's notion of an empire governed by both Macedonians and natives; under Ptolemy and Seleucus, natives rarely rose very high in the administration. Few provinces of Asia and none of the forty-two counties (or "nomes") of Egypt, for instance, ever had a native governor. The top jobs, and positions at court, were reserved for Greeks and Macedonians.

Nevertheless, as the years and decades passed, the native elite became more and more hellenized, in the familiar colonial process whereby the closer one gets to the ruling class, the more cultural differences are eradicated. To this extent, the upper levels of society were permeable by natives. Otherwise, in both states, hellenization was superficial; people were proud of their traditions and were encouraged in that pride by their priests. The gymnasia that sprang up all over Egypt and Asia, and resources such as the Museum in Alexandria, were intended primarily for Greek use, not to hellenize the natives. Just as the gymnasia in classical Greece had been for the aristocratic elite, so the gymnasia of every town and even large village in the new world were for the new elite, Greeks and other nonnatives, with rare exceptions for successful social-climbing natives. As in British India, there were formidable barriers to full assimilation.[5]

Fourth, they interfered as little as possible in native traditions. Both Egypt and Seleucid Asia were Janus states, in which local religious practices, artistic conventions, and so on continued unabated alongside newly introduced Greek forms. Successor imperialism was happily unaccompanied by the phenomenon familiar from later empires of missionary conversion of the natives to a "better" religion; Greek religion was scarcely dogmatic, and like polytheists from all times its practitioners were tolerant and found it easy to identify their gods with native gods.

In both Egypt and Seleucid Asia, two sets of laws—native and Greek—ran in parallel for the two populations; the language of the case documents determined in which court the case was heard. The kings were likely to intervene in local law only if their revenues were threatened. Both kingdoms used two official languages (Greek and Aramaic; Greek and demotic Egyptian) and even had double calendrical systems. Year One of the new era that was ushered in by Seleucus's recovery of Babylon began on the Babylonian new year—but also on the Macedonian new year, which fell about six months earlier. In Egypt, the gap was considerably greater; Ptolemy began to count his regnal years in Greek from his first gaining the province in 323, but native Egyptians counted from 305, when he formally became an Egyptian pharaoh. He was King of the Macedonians, but Pharaoh of the Egyptians, the first pharaoh of the thirtieth, final, and longest-lasting dynasty of the ancient kingdom of Egypt. Ptolemaic Egypt and Seleucid Asia were not fully Greek states but slightly awkward amalgams.

The fact that local systems were allowed to run in parallel to the conquerors' preferences indicates a considerable degree of local autonomy—more in Asia, because of its sheer size. There were plenty of crossover points, but the Greek-speakers kept themselves apart as much as possible. Their tolerance of the continuation of local administrative institutions mirrored their cultural isolation from the native populations. The separation between conquerors and subjects was most marked in the founding of new Greek enclaves, and best epitomized by the fact that the full title of the city of Alexandria, distinguishing it from all the other Alexandrias around the world, was not "Alexandria in Egypt" but "Alexandria by Egypt." The title reeks of the supremacism inherent in the imperialist mentality. It is an often repeated but still telling fact that Cleopatra VII (the famous Cleopatra), the last Macedonian ruler of Egypt, was also the first to learn the Egyptian language.

Despite these measures, however, the fact that there was little trouble, at least for a good while, was due as much as anything to the long history, in both Egypt and Asia, of foreign occupation. Many of the native populations, especially in Asia, were so remote from the king that their lives hardly changed; they simply exchanged one distant master for another, while continuing to give their immediate allegiance to the same landowner for whom they had been working before.

Ptolemy's and Seleucus's regimes were authoritarian in nature, backed up by a strong military presence. Their appeasement measures could do no more than prevent passive acquiescence from escalating into active resentment. In Asia, where the Persians had been the top dogs, Seleucus tactfully let their heartland, Persis, retain a greater degree of autonomy than other provinces of his empire; Macedonians were described there in one document as "the demons with disheveled hair of the Race of Wrath."[6] In Egypt, Ptolemy took the precaution, after the Battle of Gaza in 312, of not employing a native Egyptian contingent in his army; his great-grandson, Ptolemy IV, took the momentous step over a century later of rearming native troops, and the cost was the first native rebellion in Ptolemaic times. The core of the Seleucid army, however, was made up right from the start of native troops, armed and trained in the Macedonian manner.

TAXATION

The program of appeasement was, of course, self-interested; what the kings were interested in was the generation of income. Both Seleucus and Ptolemy employed a large number of forms of taxation, from percentages of agricultural produce (different percentages for different products) to a monetary tax on certain other products, and even forms of poll tax. Border tolls and harbor dues were imposed. Seleucus took tribute from the Greek cities within his realm and also imposed a tax on slaves. In short, the kings exploited every area they could in order to maximize their income.[7]

In general, central government interfered less in the lives of Greeks and other nonnatives (who all came to be classified as "Greeks" in both Asia and Egypt, provided they had received a Greek education), and they were taxed at a lower rate. This policy naturally risked increasing resentment, but it encouraged hellenization, and so helped to ensure an efficient and educated bureaucracy. Privileged organizations such as temples received the same kind of preferential treatment, at least for a while—the hands-off approach taken by both Ptolemy and Seleucus was gradually diluted by later kings, who were able to bring the temples more fully into the royal bureaucratic system, and even took to despoiling them for cash.[8] One is reminded of the way fifteenth- and sixteenth-century European kings expanded their power at the expense of the nobles and the Church. It would have been inexpedient for the Ptolemies and Seleucids to have done so straightaway, just as, in England, the dissolution of the monasteries had to wait until the reign of Henry VIII.

Alexander the Great had looted, or liberated, something in the region of five thousand tons of bullion from the Achaemenid empire—comparable to the weight of all the gold stored in Fort Knox—and a great deal of this had been and continued to be turned into coin. The money was used for the whole range of royal expenses, from paying troops and building ships to founding cities and, especially in Alexandria, maintaining a fantastically splendid court. Alexandria was like a gigantic maw, fed by the produce of the Egyptian countryside and the toil of native laborers; already by the middle of the third century it had a population of two hundred thousand. The income generated by taxation was enormous, but so were the kings' expenses, and in addition to taxes they raised money by selling surpluses abroad and by profiting from the trade in luxuries that passed through their kingdoms—spices from Arabia, gems from the east, gold and ivory from Sudan and from across the Sahara.

Both countries had been to a degree monetized before the coming of the Macedonians, but this process increased at a rapid rate. Along with founding cities, it was one of the main ways in which the kings asserted their kingship and marked the regime change. The natives had to learn to sell at least some of their goods for cash and to accept their wages in cash, because not all their taxes could be paid in kind—some were to be paid in coin. Likewise, when the European imperial nations carved up Africa in the nineteenth century, they introduced coinage to many places which had never used it before, and for the same reason: to facilitate the payment of tax in a form that could readily be used by the central authority.

In due course, both the Ptolemies and the Seleucids developed state-run banks, whose primary purpose was to receive cash payments of tax and thus to act as the equivalent of the royal granaries where tax in kind was stored. Seleucus even encouraged the payment of taxes on cereal crops in cash rather than kind. City building was an important plank in this program, since the surrounding rural population could sell their goods in town for cash, with which they could then pay taxes. Both Ptolemy and Seleucus minted gold and copper or bronze coinage, but silver was the preferred metal—rare enough for the coins to have value, but common enough for even people low down the economic scale to participate in the monetary economy.

The relatively small size of Egypt meant that Ptolemy could control revenue collection more than was possible for Seleucus. Cereal farmers, for instance, were given their seed grain every year from the royal granaries, and by accepting it they accepted the obligation to repay a fixed percentage the following year. Every year, once the flood had subsided, a land survey was undertaken to determine how much good soil the flood had left that year, so that the Ptolemies knew roughly how much income to expect and could plan ahead. A vast and complex bureaucracy was put in place, if it did not already exist, from the court down to villages, to process such information and ensure the regular collection of taxes.[9] Within each nome or county, three separate officers, each at the head of his own pyramid of assistants, were responsible, respectively, for agricultural production, finances, and record keeping. All of them reported to the king's finance minister in Alexandria, the *dioikētēs*. Censuses were carried out to determine who was to pay the poll tax and at what rate. Capitation tax was initiated by Ptolemy and imitated by Seleucus to the best of his ability, since accurate censuses were impossible in his kingdom.

The efficiency of the system under the first two Ptolemies meant that Egypt was regularly the wealthiest of the Successor kingdoms. In Ptolemy I's time, it had an estimated annual revenue of about fifteen thousand talents of silver (about nine billion dollars) and eight million artabas of wheat (perhaps 320 million liters, or 72,500,000 U.S. gallons).[10] Seleucus took in more (about thirty thousand talents a year), but the natural defenses of Egypt meant that Ptolemy could spend less on the armed services, which, along with city building, were regularly the biggest drain on Seleucus's finances. As a result, Seleucus's capital city, Antioch, glittered less brilliantly than Alexandria; he had more urgent demands on his resources.

Another economic measure Ptolemy put in place before the end of the fourth century was to break away from the monetary standard that had been adopted, following Alexander's lead, all over the empire. Egyptian coins were minted to a considerably lighter standard, and no other coinage was allowed within the realm. All foreign coin brought into Egypt by commerce was surrendered and reminted to the Ptolemaic standard. This somewhat isolated Egypt from the rest of the world, but it "established a royal monopoly of exchange which was extremely profitable to the treasury."[11] Imports were thereby discouraged, while exports could be sold abroad on the higher standard and then recoined at the lower standard, making an extra profit. Egypt was short of silver anyway; one way and another, this was one of Ptolemy's masterstrokes.

But there was a limit, even in bureaucratized Egypt, to the degree of central control that could be exercised, and more flexible systems were put in place that accommodated existing native institutions. Alexandria intervened more directly in the lives of the new settlements in the Fayyum depression and around Ptolemais than it did elsewhere, where taxation was locally organized, as it always had been. A lot of the complaints that one reads in the papyri from native farmers were complaints against petty Greek prejudice and local corruption, not against the king in Alexandria.[12] As long as the taxes came in, Ptolemy was content to let things carry on in the time-honored fashion, or develop in a haphazard way.

The collection of taxes was also decentralized, in keeping with the usual Greek system—or rather, the Greek system was grafted, somewhat awkwardly, on to local systems. The contract for the year's taxes in a specific product was put up for sale. Tax farmers, wealthy men who were able to post a large surety bond, and often operating as a consortium, underwrote a guarantee of the revenues for a year from a specific tax. If what they collected fell short of the sum bid, the farmers were bound to pay the difference, but if there was the expected surplus, they retained it. But in Egypt (and probably also in Asia), they were not responsible for the actual collection of the taxes in at least some non-Greek areas, which was left in the hands of local agents. In Egypt, the crown similarly licensed the sale of certain key products such as flax, beer, salt, and some oil crops. As with tax farming, this served to protect the Ptolemies from unforeseen variations in revenue.

The size of Seleucus's kingdom meant that he could not exercise even the limited degree of control that Ptolemy sought. He inherited workable systems and let them continue. In Asia Minor and Syria, Antigonus had replaced the Persian satrapies with smaller, more manageable units that would not give their administrators great wealth, power, or pretensions. Seleucus was therefore able to exert more administrative control there than farther east, where he retained the old satrapal system of the Achaemenid empire. Satrapies and even cities were allowed to retain many of their own institutions. A city in Syria would not necessarily feel itself part of the same "empire" as a city on the borders of Afghanistan or one in Asia Minor.

Just as in Ptolemaic Egypt, a hierarchical pyramid spread out under Seleucus. The first layer was occupied by trusted family members, who were awarded special commands, such as oversight of all the eastern satrapies (Antiochus) or of western Asia Minor as a whole (Achaeus). The second layer was occupied by his Friends, men we could call his ministers of state, chiefly with broad financial responsibilities; for such an enormous empire, there were very few such dedicated ministers. The third layer was occupied by the military and financial administrators of satrapies and other regions and by the city authorities. Each of these layers of officers had considerable power within their domains, while being answerable to the next level above; each officer had a considerable network of junior officials under him. As in Egypt, the jobs of all officials within the hierarchy were chiefly to ensure security and the smooth collection and storage of taxes.

PLUS ÇA CHANGE . . .

The Janus nature of Seleucid Asia and Ptolemaic Egypt—the choice not to impose uniformity—meant that kings had to be adaptable in their official discourses. It depended on who they were talking to: should they be king, conqueror, or god? In Egypt, if they presented themselves as kings, should it be in the Macedonian style or as a pharaoh? In some parts of the empire, they presented themselves as promoters of hellenization and spoke of defending the empire against barbarians; other parts, however, were populated precisely by "barbarian" peoples, and so in these areas the kings came across as preservers of local traditions and guarantors of freedom.

The degree to which long-established local systems were taken over, and kept separate from the instruments reserved for the new elite, meant that, in this sense, the coming of the conquerors made little difference. The greatest impact was in the acceleration of processes that were already taking place: goods could travel farther and more easily (though, apart from luxuries and hard-to-acquire necessities, most trade remained fairly local relative to the size of Alexander's former empire as a whole), peripheries were brought into a closer relationship with the center, monetization rapidly increased.

Societies remained essentially unchanged in their ancient agricultural forms, only with an additional layer of Macedonian and Greek practices. Hellenization and collaboration with the new rulers were encouraged, but not required, because the new rulers could easily get by with mere acquiescence from the majority of their subject populations. Both Ptolemy and Seleucus were necessarily conservative, since the last thing they needed was to arouse opposition. They supported and even reinvigorated local institutions, and made their subjects' lives easier and more profitable overall. They were authoritarian rulers and could easily have been despots, but both of them chose the less risky course of appeasement, so that at the same time they could accelerate change in the area that concerned them most—improving the state's profitability and taxations systems. Their measures worked, in the sense that there was no real trouble in either of their kingdoms during their reigns, or indeed for many years afterward. They managed the most difficult of tricks—a smooth transition to foreign occupation and rule.

Demetrius Resurgent

THE EARLY HELLENISTIC period is studded with extraordinary personalities, but none of their stories is more amazing than that of Demetrius the Besieger over the next few years. It simply should not have happened. After Ipsus, the Antigonid cause seemed hopeless: Antigonus was dead and Demetrius in flight, his forces few and scattered. But then, if anyone was going to stage a remarkable recovery, it would be Demetrius, the most energetic and flamboyant of the kings. Within seven years, he had seized the throne of Macedon and, even if unrealistically, revived his hopes of imperial power.

It may be that some of our amazement would be mitigated if we could fill more of the gaps in the record. The narrative of the historian Diodorus of Sicily has sustained us so far, but his account ends on the eve of the battle of Ipsus, and the rest of his history, as of all others of the period, is lost. We are condemned to try to piece the picture together out of incomplete and often disparate fragments—of literature, and of archaeological and epigraphic data. Informed guesswork is sometimes the way forward. At least in Demetrius's case some of the problems are offset by the fact that he earned a Life in Plutarch's collection. But Plutarch was a biographer, not a historian, and he chose as his subjects men who could serve as paradigms to emulate or avoid. For Plutarch, Demetrius was a model of wasted talent.

AFTER IPSUS

Ipsus was a critical battle, but only in a counterfactual sense: *if* Antigonus had won, there would have been little to stop him achieving his ambition of ruling all Alexander's empire, or at least of bequeathing that distinct possibility to his son. But the fact is that Antigonus lost, and so Ipsus was critical only in that it stopped him. In other respects, little changed. True, ever since Alexander's death, warfare had been given its impetus because someone aspired to rule over the entire empire: Perdiccas at first, and then Antigonus. After Ipsus there was at least the possibility of less warfare and more consolidation, so that a balance of power could emerge, but that did not happen immediately. It is illusory to think that Antigonus's death "marks the final passing of the idea of an empire reviving that of Alexander."[1] The remaining Successors, and Demetrius above all, still entertained imperialist ambitions, as we shall see. They did not see Antigonus's death as ending grand imperialist dreams; they saw it as creating space for *their* dreams. But first they had some consolidating to do. All Ipsus did was slow things down for a while.

After the battle, "the victorious kings sliced up Antigonus's domain like an enormous carcass, each taking his portion."[2] The prisoners of war, and the three thousand talents Antigonus had brought from Cilicia, were divided among the victorious kings, but it was by partitioning the Antigonid realms that they made really significant gains.

Lysimachus, who had commanded the coalition forces, was the biggest winner, since he was awarded all of Asia Minor up to the Halys River. Asia Minor was not a whole, however. There were independent cities such as Heraclea, and the princelings of Cappadocia had taken advantage of the constant warfare to gain a kind of independence. The countries on the south coast of the Black Sea, protected by the sea on one side and formidable mountains on the other, had never been fully under Macedonian control, if at all. Bithynia had always been independent, and it is testimony to the survival skills of its ruler, Zipoetes, that he held his territory for forty-seven years, from 327 until his death in 280. A noble Persian called Mithradates had recently established himself in Pontus. Both Bithynia and Pontus turned out to be successful kingdoms, which lasted until, respectively, 74 and 63 BCE. Paphlagonia too had attained a similar kind of independence, but Lysimachus soon brought it within his sway. All these dynasts valued their independence, but had to accept the fact that they were surrounded by bigger fish than themselves.

Essentially, Lysimachus now held, in addition to Thrace, pretty much the same territory that Antigonus had held in 318, before his expansion eastward. It had been the foundation of Antigonus's power; it could do the same for Lysimachus too. He was only sixty, or a little over; he had some time. His most valuable new possessions were the Asiatic Greek cities, famed for their wealth (from both commerce and natural resources) and rich in manpower. After Ipsus, many cities were cowed into surrendering of their own accord, but Antigonid garrisons remained in Ephesus, Miletus, and elsewhere. No doubt many cities had built or repaired their walls over the past few years of peace in their land, in preparation for just such an emergency. Lysimachus's first job was the subjugation of these cities, to consolidate his hold over Asia Minor and gain the ability to exploit its wealth. It took a few years of almost unremitting effort.

Cassander (who traveled from Macedon to Asia Minor to attend the post-battle conference) gained nothing, but Greece was left vulnerable by Demetrius's departure and the collapse of the Hellenic League he had revived a couple of years earlier. Cassander clearly expected to recover Greece, and just as clearly expected no interference from the others while he did so. In other words, he expected recognition of his kingship of Macedon, even after eliminating the last Argeads to obtain it. He got this, but no more; after all, he had not been present on the battlefield. By the same token, Ptolemy officially gained nothing either, but there was no resentment against him on the part of the others for the meager part he had played in the final campaigns. He had done his bit by fighting off the Antigonid invasion of Egypt a few years earlier.

Cassander's brother Pleistarchus, however, who had taken part in the battle, was given Cilicia as his personal fiefdom. This may have been at Cassander's insistence, since he looked out for his family's interests: he also had a dotty brother called Alexarchus, who was allowed to found a utopian community called Ouranopolis, "The Heavenly City," on the Athos peninsula, within Macedon. He dressed as the sun, and his citizens were the "children of heaven." Official documents were written in a complex, archaic form of Greek—"too difficult even for the Delphic oracle."[3] In an era of literary utopias and escapist literature, one eccentric tried to make it real.

Seleucus added Mesopotamia and Syria to his enormous kingdom. The stretch of Mediterranean coastline he gained was critically important, but his pleasure was not unalloyed. First, northern Syria was an undeveloped region. The small population was relatively prosperous, but almost entirely rural, with only one city (Antigonus's half-built Antigonea) and a few scattered trading towns—and Seleucus had rivals to the north and south. Second, the cities on the coastline south of the Eleutherus were currently in Ptolemy's hands (with the extra anomaly that Demetrius held Tyre and Sidon), and, having finally reestablished himself in the region, Ptolemy was disinclined to make way for their new owner. Trouble therefore brewed once again for Phoenicia, but postwar fatigue on both sides gave Ptolemy the chance to settle in. Seleucus made out that he refrained from attacking Ptolemy out of friendship, but everyone knew that the real reason was that he was in no position to challenge Ptolemy at sea.

The known world, as it emerged from the settlement, appeared relatively stable. All the kings had core territories and sons who seemed destined to become kings after them. Phoenicia, Greece, and the western seaboard of Asia Minor were the most likely trouble spots in the short term, as the kings sought to gain firm control of the areas they had been allotted. But such consolidation was not their only focus; they still looked out for opportunities for expansion. What emerged after Ipsus was not so much a balance of power as a balance of fear. They also reverted to the default Successor position of helping one's neighbor only in the direst emergencies—and then only if significant gains could be made out of it.

DEMETRIUS'S SITUATION

Demetrius fled from the battlefield with several thousand men, chiefly members of the cavalry contingent he had been commanding. He holed up in Ephesus, where he had a garrison, and took stock of his position. His last remaining strength was his command of the sea. He had a substantial fleet. He held Cyprus, Tyre, and Sidon; most of the original Cycladic League and other strategic Aegean islands, including Euboea; a few places on the Hellespont and the Aegean coast; and the most important ports on the Greek mainland. He had sufficient funds to be able to retain his men and maintain his fleet. He could certainly still make a nuisance of himself at sea, even if he was a spent force on land. It was not in his nature to give up. He determined to stay in the game, the only game he had ever known in his harsh life. He felt he had enough strength at sea to survive by moving between his safe havens and by making raids as the opportunity presented itself. He decided, then, on a course of grand piracy.

Demetrius set sail from Ephesus for the city he had come to regard as the center of his kingdom, Athens. But, possibly prompted by Lysimachus (who was to woo Athens with benefactions over the next few years), the Athenians turned against him. Embarrassed by their earlier obsequiousness, they passed a resolution that they would from now on strive for neutrality. One of Demetrius's wives, Deidameia, was still resident in the city, along with his eighteen-year-old son by Phila, Antigonus Gonatas, who was being educated in the university town; the Athenians bundled them off to Megara.

An Athenian delegation found Demetrius on Delos. He accepted their insulting decisions with good grace, or icy calm, and asked for the return of some warships that were docked in Piraeus. The Athenians agreed, in keeping with their posture of neutrality. Demetrius settled the members of his family in garrisoned Corinth, a more secure bolt-hole than Megara. Then he sailed to Cilicia, where he recovered other family members, who were made safe on Cyprus. Then he waited. One thing he had going for him was the near certainty that the post-Ipsus rapport between his enemies would not last.

While he waited, he continued to provoke Lysimachus. In 300 or 299 he sent a sizable raiding party to the Thracian Chersonese. It was a nasty little campaign, in the course of which Lysimachus killed thousands of his own men to quell a mutiny after Demetrius captured their baggage train.[4] Not one of Lysimachus's former coalition partners raised a finger to help him.

THE DEVELOPMENT OF SELEUCIS

Seleucus's first priority after Ipsus was to secure northern Syria. Within a few years—a remarkably few years—he had demolished Antigonea and started to build five major cities, which were named, in typical Macedonian fashion, after himself and members of his family. The "Syrian tetrapolis" consisted of Antioch with its port of Seleucia Pieria, and Apamea with its port of Laodicea; and the fifth foundation, Seleucia-on-the-Euphrates (also known as Zeugma), controlled the main Euphrates crossing. The cities were ringed with protective forts and were designed with security in mind: each of them had a strong acropolis, which was not entirely surrounded by the rest of the city, so that in an emergency the garrison could still communicate directly with the outside world. The area as a whole was called Seleucis and was to be the heart of his kingdom, both secure and splendid.[5]

Farther east, another Seleucia had already been started, not far north of Babylon. The ancient city had been badly damaged in the war of 311–309 and never fully recovered. Seleucia-on-the-Tigris was designed to supplement and partially replace Babylon as the center for trade routes from the east—for overland caravans from the Hindu Kush, or cargo that was offloaded at the head of the Persian Gulf. Babylon, on the Euphrates, was reduced to a lesser role and became more parochial, but it retained one of the most important Seleucid treasuries. Seleucia flourished, however, and within a short space of time the coastline of the Persian Gulf had become developed and important enough to the Seleucid economy that it became a satrapy in its own right.[6]

These foundations served a number of functions. First, as with all the foundations of Alexander the Great and his Successors, they pleased the native populations (mostly nomads and peasant farmers) by increasing land use and stimulating the local economy. Second, they pleased the local Greek and Macedonian settlers, many of whom (in Syria, at any rate) had been brought in by Antigonus, and so might have been inclined toward the Antigonid cause. Third, they attracted new settlers, to develop the economy and strengthen the army. Fourth, they had military and long-distance commercial functions as ports, on roads or river crossings, or near borders. In short, within the space of a few years Seleucus succeeded in developing the rich potential of the farmland of northern Syria and turning it into a center of commerce and culture. The magnitude of the project and the speed of its execution constituted regal display on an unprecedented scale.

Seleucis was also a front line against southern Syria, a reminder to Ptolemy that, sooner or later, an attempt would be made to drive him out of his illegally held Phoenician ports. No fewer than six wars were fought over the region between 274 and 168, when some kind of balance was imposed by the Romans, who were by then the power brokers throughout the Mediterranean.

MARRIAGE ALLIANCES

Ptolemy knew that his claim to southern Syria was provocative. Rifts began to appear in the coalition that had defeated Antigonus when in 300, in the face of saber rattling from his former friend Seleucus, Ptolemy approached Lysimachus for an alliance. Lysimachus was happy to agree. The main attraction for him was Ptolemy's navy, which he needed to facilitate his takeover of Demetrius's coastal possessions within Asia Minor, and generally to take on Demetrius in the Aegean. The pact was sealed by Lysimachus's taking Ptolemy's daughter Arsinoe as his wife. It would prove to be a fateful marriage, not least because of Arsinoe's ruthless ambition.[7]

The alliance between Ptolemy and Lysimachus left Seleucus isolated, surrounded by potential enemies, and in urgent need of a navy himself. To whom else could he turn except Demetrius, the old enemy? So, a couple of years later, Seleucus approached Demetrius for the hand of Stratonice, a prime dynastic catch—not just Demetrius's daughter, but also the granddaughter of Antipater and niece of Cassander. This was Seleucus's first foray, aged about fifty-five, into the Successors' endogamous marriage circus. No doubt he was as little averse to polygamy as the rest of the Macedonian dynasts, but as it happened, his Iranian wife, Apama, had died a year or two earlier. So, thanks to the antagonism between Seleucus and Ptolemy, Demetrius was back in the fold.

Demetrius understood Seleucus's need for a navy, and sailed to celebrate the wedding with an impressive fleet. Before picking up Stratonice and Phila from Cyprus, he found time to land a force in Cilicia and remove the last 1,200 talents of his father's bullion from the Cyinda treasury. Pleistarchus's protests to Seleucus fell on deaf ears: he needed the alliance of Demetrius more than the friendship of Pleistarchus. So Demetrius landed at Rhosus, where he was greeted as a king and an equal by Seleucus. The wedding celebrations took place on board Demetrius's enormous flagship, one of the largest vessels ever built up to that time.

By 298, then, two factions had already emerged: Lysimachus and Ptolemy against Seleucus and Demetrius. The new allies' attention was on Asia Minor and the eastern Mediterranean, which is why Cassander was not involved. He had problems of his own, with a new Boeotian–Aetolian alliance cutting him off from southern Greece. There may have been other reasons; Cassander had been plagued all his life by tuberculosis, and it is likely that by now the disease had a terminal grip on him. Under the circumstances, he preferred to wait and see what might fall his way as a result of these alliances.

As if to underline the aggressive purpose of these alliances, Seleucus and Demetrius wrote around to the Greek cities within Lysimachus's kingdom with assurances of their goodwill toward them. Before long, Demetrius turned his attention to his and Seleucus's other opponent, and carried out raids in southern Syria. War looked imminent, but

Ptolemy suspected that Seleucus would want peace for a while yet, to finish the consolidation of his kingdom. At Ptolemy's instigation, Seleucus brokered a pact of friendship between Demetrius and Ptolemy, centered on the betrothal of Demetrius to one of Ptolemy's daughters, called Ptolemais. War in the Middle East was averted, for the time being.

AN UNEASY PEACE

The peace that ensued, however, was marred by constant infringements. Immediately after the Rhosus wedding in 298, Seleucus took his new bride to the building site that was Antioch, and Demetrius turned once again to warfare. Having already probed Cilicia on his way to Rhosus, he now occupied it with his forces. Pleistarchus fled to his friend Lysimachus's court. Apart from this passive support, however, no one took up arms. Cassander should have helped his brother, but Demetrius sent Phila to Macedon to appease him. No doubt she pointed out the danger of going against the formidable new coalition of Demetrius and Seleucus, but the deciding factor was undoubtedly that Phila's advice matched his own policy of waiting on the sidelines. In fact, though, as we have already seen, Seleucus next brokered a marriage alliance between Demetrius and Ptolemy, so that there was actually a breathing space, with no large-scale fighting going on, except that Lysimachus's gradual takeover of Antigonid cities in Asia Minor continued.

Having eliminated Pleistarchus, Demetrius made Cilicia his headquarters from 298 to 296. These were vital years for him, and he used them well to build up his strength. The cedars of Lebanon were still being cut down for shipbuilding at Tyre and Sidon, and he had recruited a land army too, making use of the bullion he had taken from Cyinda, turned into coin at his new mint in Tyre. All the other Antigonid mints were in territory that was lost after Ipsus. Of course, this resurgence worried everyone else, including his erstwhile ally Seleucus, who now began to regret his part in allowing Demetrius to recover. He tried to bring Demetrius to heel by offering to buy Cilicia from him, and, when Demetrius refused, by demanding the surrender of Tyre and Sidon. Demetrius is said to have responded by saying that he would never pay for the privilege of having Seleucus as his son-in-law.[8]

By 296, however, his position in Cilicia had become untenable. He saw it only as a place to exploit, and his rule had not proved popular. And Lysimachus had already intervened militarily once, in an attempt to relieve a town that Demetrius had under siege. It is likely, though we have no direct evidence, that Seleucus was ready to abandon his supposed ally, and cooperate with Lysimachus to get rid of Demetrius. At any rate, when Demetrius withdrew from Cilicia and moved to Cyprus instead, Seleucus did nothing to help, and then, by agreement with Lysimachus, took Cilicia for himself. Lysimachus gave Pleistarchus a safer (and much smaller) realm in western Caria.[9] But Demetrius did not stay long on Cyprus. The situation in Greece was calling out for him.

INSTABILITY IN GREECE AND MACEDON

The Athenians' bid for neutrality had not gone very well. The problem with neutrality was that they automatically lost the benefactions of a protector king. Before long, several bad harvests stressed their neutrality beyond breaking point. They could hardly turn to Demetrius, so they asked Lysimachus for help. He was able to supply them with grain, but if he hoped for more—perhaps for an alliance—he was foiled. After a period of civic unrest the city fell under the control of the pro-Macedon faction, led by a man called Lachares. By 296, Lachares' opponents had left Athens and made Piraeus a democratic enclave, so that the city and the port were once again divided. Lachares declared a state of emergency and made himself the effective ruler of Athens. The schism in Athens tempted Demetrius. Perhaps, as in the 300s, he could make the city his headquarters again and recover Greece.

And Macedon too was in turmoil. Cassander died, as expected, of tuberculosis in 297. He had been regent since 315 and king since 305, and had kept Macedon's borders secure. No battles had been fought on Macedonian soil for twenty years, but his death ushered in two decades of instability and occasional chaos for Macedon. For all its inopportune and brutal start, then, Cassander's rule had been good for Macedon, and he had proved himself, after all, a worthy successor to his father. In eliminating all rivals to the throne, he was no more ruthless than many a Macedonian predecessor.

His eldest son inherited the throne as Philip IV, but also died of tuberculosis four months later. Philip's illness must already have been obvious, and before his death Cassander had arranged marriages for his younger sons, even though they were still teenagers, in an attempt to ensure a succession. Antipater took a daughter of Lysimachus, and Alexander a daughter of Ptolemy.

Antipater I and Alexander V reigned jointly, under the regency of their mother Thessalonice, but not amicably. The country fell apart, depending on where the two brothers found the most support: Alexander reigned in western Macedon and Antipater in the east, with the river Axius as the boundary between them. Macedon was divided between two squabbling teenagers, and civil war was imminent.

When Demetrius returned to Greece in 296, he must at least in part have wanted to be in a position to keep a close eye on events in Macedon. For years, he had maneuvered for the chance to make himself king of the homeland—the homeland he scarcely knew, since he had left there as a young child to join his father in Phrygia. But his immediate target was Athens, where he hoped (somewhat in vain, as it turned out) for help from Lachares' opponents. On the way, however, a storm destroyed many of his ships. On landing in Greece, he sent urgently to Tyre and Sidon for replacements, and occupied his time, while waiting for their arrival, by attacking some of the cities of the Peloponnese, very nearly losing his life in the course of a siege when a catapult bolt pierced his jaw and mouth.

The bulk of the new fleet had not yet arrived when he renewed his assault on Athens in 295. This time he was more successful, and cut off all the supply routes to the city. Before long, Athens was in the grip of a deadly famine. Anecdotes tell of a father fighting his son over the corpse of a mouse, and of the philosopher Epicurus counting out the daily ration of beans for the members of his commune.[10]

ATHENIAN HIGHER EDUCATION

Epicurus was not the only philosopher resident in Athens, which as yet had no rivals as the university town of the Greek world. His parents were Athenian settlers on Samos, and Epicurus had originally come to the city as a young man when all the Athenians left Samos in accordance with Alexander the Great's Exiles Decree. In 306 he returned and bought some property which he turned into a commune for himself and his followers, called "the Garden." Only a few years later, a young thinker from Citium in Cyprus, called Zeno, founded his own school; many of the school's lectures and discussions took place in one of the famous stoas of the Athenian agora, and so the school came to be known as the Stoa, or Stoicism.[11] Two older schools—the Academy originally founded by Plato, and the Aristotelian Lyceum—were still going strong, and since the city was the acknowledged cultural center of the world, it attracted philosophers and teachers of all other persuasions too. The most popular philosophers were superstars, with their lectures attracting audiences of hundreds or even thousands.

The new philosophies, of which the most successful were Epicureanism and Stoicism, differed from one another and argued, often with considerable rancor. Nevertheless, there was common ground. As we have seen when surveying the Hellenistic aesthetic, artists were increasingly focusing on the expression of individual emotions. A focus on the individual also characterized the philosophical schools. Philosophy climbed down from the abstract realms of Platonic metaphysics or Aristotelian polymathy, and learned also to appeal to a wider audience with promises of self-improvement. This is why we can still apply the names of the new Hellenistic schools to ordinary people; even though the meanings of the words have shifted over the ages, we still say that people are stoical or epicurean (or skeptical, or cynical), but not usually Platonist or Aristotelian. The new emphasis on the common man made provincial Athens a more congenial environment for most philosophers than the courts of kings.

All the schools set out to demonstrate how individual human beings should live and provided methods for achieving this goal. They all saw philosophy as the remedy for human ills, but differed in what they saw as the fundamental problems and in how to go about attaining enlightenment. The three main branches of philosophy in Hellenistic times were logic (understood as the way or ways of discovering the truth of any matter), physics (the nature of the world and the laws that govern it), and ethics (how to achieve happiness). The first two branches were subordinate to the third. For Epicurus, for instance, the point of understanding the nature of the world was to free your mind from fear, as an aid toward attaining mental tranquility.[12]

Philosophy was critically different, then, from today; it was not conceptual analysis, undertaken in libraries and classrooms, although all three branches of philosophy involved intricate and complex theories and argumentation. These are the aspects of ancient philosophy which primarily engage philosophers today, but in those days philosophy was a way of life as much as an academic discipline. Hence philosophers presented a public image that stressed poverty, or at least frugality, as a way of advertising the success of their teaching: they themselves had moved beyond the superficial values of the world, and could teach others to do so too. The pupils they wanted were those who already felt somewhat at odds with the world.

It is hard not to read this trend as a reaction to the violence and uncertainty of the times. Ordinary individuals were impotent to change the world at large, but they could at least try to change themselves and their inner worlds. There lay the appeal of the new philosophies. None of the schools, in this early period, encouraged their students to play an active part in politics. Philosophy was largely for dropouts, and so dovetailed with the escapism that we have already seen was a dominant feature of the literature of the time.

The great era of the philosophical schools lasted throughout the third and second centuries. Teaching and erudition began to be seen as professions in their own right, not mere eccentricities; schools disputed points great and small with one another; learning became systematic, spread around the Hellenistic world, and for the first time became valued as a way to get on in the world. This did little to alter elementary schooling, but gradually an intermediate stage evolved, between the elementary schools and attendance at the feet of a philosopher or a teacher of rhetoric. In his teens, then, a boy might learn grammar, rhetoric, logic, and geometry, as well as receiving further military training, to supplement the schooling of his younger years, with its emphasis on the three Rs and acculturation. Education was one of the prime engines of hellenization, and it is no surprise to find that Hellenistic gymnasia around the world expanded their curricula beyond physical fitness to encompass more aspects of Greek culture.

If there was originality within the philosophical schools, however, the same cannot be said of rhetoric, which began to form a major element in higher education. Quite early in the Hellenistic period, a canonical list was drawn up of the ten Athenian masters of rhetoric,[13] and their speeches were endlessly studied and imitated. Pedantic purists refused to use vocabulary or figures of speech which did not have precedents in the works of these masters. "Atticism," as their style was called (Attica being the district whose urban center was Athens), was worshipped as good in itself, and there were bitter fights, by word and occasionally fist, between its exponents and those of the florid Asianic style. Still, the schools of rhetoric flourished and polished their discipline, until writers of all stripes fell under their spell as much as orators and politicians.

But it must have been hard for even the philosophers resident in Athens to maintain their saintly detachment in the face of starvation; to many, it must have seemed the end of the world. Demetrius was poised to retake the city, and no one was coming to their help. Lachares did not give up easily, however. He quelled a near mutiny among his troops by robbing temples of their treasures and melting them down into bullion. Even the world-famous statue of Athena in the Parthenon, the symbol of Athenian greatness, was stripped of its golden robe. Ptolemy sent help in the form of a substantial fleet of 150 ships, but just as it approached Demetrius's replacement fleet hove into view, double the size of Ptolemy's fleet, which prudently withdrew. Lachares fled, and the starving Athenians opened their gates to Demetrius in April 295. They had insulted him in 301, and expected little mercy.

Demetrius staged a dramatic entry into Athens. Having ordered a general assembly in the Theater of Dionysus, he posted guards around the area, entered from the rear, and walked in silence down the steps, past the seated crowd, until he reached the stage. He announced the immediate distribution of plenty of grain—that was the good bit—but also the installation of garrisons not only in Athens and Piraeus, but in several outlying towns and fortresses. Now was not the time to let the ideology of freedom impede his progress. He also ensured that an oligarchy of his supporters formed the ruling elite. There could be little doubt that this time, his third period of residence in the city, he came not as a liberator but as an occupier of Athens.

The Fall of Demetrius

DEMETRIUS WAS BACK in Athens, and took immediate steps to regain other cities in Greece. His neighbors in Macedon and Asia Minor were too busy with their own affairs to intervene. The Peloponnesian cities were Demetrius's first targets in 294, but toward the end of his campaign there he was diverted by news from Macedon. The homeland was in the kind of trouble he had been waiting for. As soon as he could, he marched north.

In Macedon, Antipater, the elder of the two boy kings, had naturally assumed that, on attaining his majority, he would inherit the whole kingdom; Thessalonice, however, continued to insist on his sharing the kingdom with his brother. Antipater therefore had his mother murdered (an unusual crime even for the Macedonian royal family, and she was a half sister of Alexander the Great), expelled his brother from the western half of the kingdom, and made all Macedon his. Alexander accordingly invited Demetrius to help him recover the throne. Demetrius left his twenty-five-year-old son Antigonus Gonatas resident in Athens and in charge of affairs in Greece and marched north to take part in the War of the Brothers.

But it had taken him time to wrap things up in the south, and in the meantime Alexander had also looked for help elsewhere. Pyrrhus of Epirus, a great-nephew of Olympias and cousin of Alexander the Great, had been an enemy of Cassander, who had successfully supported his dynastic rival in Epirus. In 303 Demetrius had married one of his sisters, Deidameia, and so when Pyrrhus had fled from Epirus he had lived in exile in Demetrius's court and had fought on the Antigonid side at Ipsus, aged eighteen. In 299, as part of a short-lived attempt to get on with Ptolemy, Demetrius had sent him young Pyrrhus as a kind of hostage, a pledge of his goodwill. Pyrrhus had become close to Ptolemy, and had married one of his daughters. After the death of Deidameia in 298, Pyrrhus felt he no longer had any reason to be close to Demetrius, and it was as Ptolemy's ally, and with Ptolemy's financial help, that in 297 he reconquered Epirus. This was the powerful neighbor whom Alexander V had asked for help.

The price for Pyrrhus's help was enormous, but he was able to supply it quickly. He asked for, and received, the two cantons of Macedon that bordered his kingdom of Epirus, along with various other Macedonian dependencies that would serve his aim of developing Epirote rule in western Greece. These were mostly territories that had been annexed by Philip II and Cassander.

Pyrrhus easily drove Antipater out of western Macedon, but did no more. Lysimachus was Antipater's father-in-law, and Pyrrhus had no desire to provoke Lysimachus, even though he was currently busy quelling an uprising led by the warlike Getae. The threat of future intervention was enough for Lysimachus to persuade Pyrrhus to withdraw his troops—without, of course, abandoning his new territories. Pyrrhus's withdrawal paved the way for the two brothers to be reconciled. Lysimachus hoped he had done enough to secure Macedon against Demetrius's imminent arrival.

So when Demetrius reached Dium, on the borders of Macedon, Alexander thanked him and told him he was no longer needed. No one treated Demetrius like that—and certainly no Antipatrid teenager. Demetrius pretended that he was unconcerned and had other business to attend to down south. He invited the young king to a farewell banquet and had him killed. Minnows should not swim with sharks. In a show trial, forced on him by his insecurity, Demetrius gave it out before the Macedonian troops that he was acting in self-defense—that Alexander had been planning to murder him. It may have been true. There was so much mutual mistrust between them that, during the banquet, when Demetrius got up to leave the room, Alexander followed, not wanting to lose sight of him. At the doorway, Demetrius muttered to his guards as he passed: "Kill the man who follows me."[1]

Antipater abandoned his half of Macedon and fled to Thrace, where Lysimachus persuaded him that resistance was futile. Lysimachus quickly arranged a peace treaty with Demetrius; he knew from recent bitter experience how aggressive his new neighbor could be, and the situation gave him the leverage to persuade Demetrius to renounce his claim to the Greek cities of Asia Minor that had fallen to Lysimachus after Ipsus. But the peace made Antipater redundant, and Lysimachus had him killed, now or within a few years. It was the end of the Antipatrid line that had ruled Macedon, as viceroys and kings, for the best part of forty years.

DEMETRIUS I, KING OF MACEDON

The grail was his: Demetrius was king of Macedon. Immediately after the murder of Alexander V, the nobles present—members of Alexander's court, now surrounded by Demetrius's forces—agreed to his kingship, and he was duly acclaimed by the assembled army. But there were still hearts and minds to be won in Macedon itself, and Demetrius went about this by the traditional combination of action and words. He quelled an uprising in Thessaly and took steps to improve the security of central Greece, where the alliance between the Boeotians and Aetolians had been renewed in response to Demetrius's and his son's conquests in the south. In the Peloponnese, only the Spartans now held out against him, and they were no more than a nuisance.

At home, he played all the cards that supported his claim to the throne. He stressed his father's loyal service to the Argeads and the illegitimacy of the Antipatrid regime, and missed no opportunity to recall Cassander's murder of Alexander IV. His long marriage to Phila helped as well; as Cassander's sister, she provided an appearance of continuity, now that Cassander had no surviving descendants. Ironically, through Phila, Demetrius was the heir of those to whose ruin he and his father had devoted so much time and energy.

In order to help secure Thessaly, and to give himself another port, one of Demetrius's early acts as king was to found the city of Demetrias. The site, at the head of the Gulf of Pagasae (near modern Volos), was well chosen. The city was hard to assault, and served successive Macedonian kings for decades as one of the "Fetters of Greece":[2] as long as they controlled the heavily fortified ports of Demetrias, Chalcis, and Corinth (Piraeus was desirable too), they could move troops at will around the Greek mainland and restrict other shipping. And most commercial traffic in those days was seaborne.

A sign of how critical all this was for him was that he ignored what was going on elsewhere in the world—or maybe he just did not have the forces to cope. He had already, I think, effectively ceded the Asiatic Greek cities, and Lysimachus completed his takeover there by the end of 294. In the same year, Ptolemy, to his huge relief, regained Cyprus.

The defense of the island had been in the hands of Phila, but in the end she was pinned in Salamis and forced to surrender. Ptolemy courteously allowed all members of Demetrius's family safe conduct off the island and back to Macedon, laden with gifts and honors. The Ptolemies would now retain Cyprus until the Roman conquest of the island two hundred and fifty years later.

Lysimachus, as already mentioned, was chiefly occupied with a war against the Getae in northern Thrace, around the Danube. In 297 the warlike Getae had taken advantage of the fact that Lysimachus's attention was focused on Asia Minor to go to war. Lysimachus sent his son Agathocles to deal with the Getae, but it had not gone well: Agathocles had been captured, and Lysimachus had been forced to come to terms, which included marrying one of his daughters to the Getan king and returning territory he had occupied. But in 293, once he had more or less settled his affairs in Asia Minor, Lysimachus took to the field to recover the territory he had been forced to give up. Again, the war went badly; we know no details, but it is surely to the credit of the Getan king Dromichaetes that he was able twice to defeat as brilliant a general as Lysimachus. This time, it was Lysimachus himself who was taken prisoner. He was held at their capital, Helis (perhaps modern Sveshtari, where a tomb has been discovered which might be that of Dromichaetes and Lysimachus's nameless daughter).[3] It was the best part of a year before his captors were induced to let him go, and again Lysimachus lost territory to them, and had to leave hostages to ensure that he would not attack again. It was the last of his attempts to gain control of inner Thrace.

In 292, while Lysimachus was tied up, Demetrius, short on gratitude to the man who had so rapidly recognized his rulership of Macedon, took an expeditionary force into Asia Minor and Thrace. It was a sign of his future intentions, a declaration of war. Fortunately for Lysimachus, a united uprising by the central Greek leagues, backed by his friends Pyrrhus and Ptolemy, recalled Demetrius to Greece. As it happened, before he got back his son Antigonus Gonatas had succeeded in defeating the Boeotians and putting Thebes under siege (it fell the following year). But Demetrius was unable to return to his abandoned campaign, because Pyrrhus chose this moment to invade Thessaly. Demetrius advanced against him in strength; Pyrrhus, his work done, withdrew.

Pyrrhus's retreat was tactical; he had no intention of giving up his attempt to expand the frontiers of Epirus at Demetrius's expense. Two years later, in 290, he inflicted a serious defeat on Demetrius's forces in Aetolia (the victory was so spectacular that he was hailed as a second Alexander),[4] but lost the island of Corcyra (Corfu). The island was betrayed to Demetrius by Pyrrhus's ex-wife Lanassa (whose domain it was), allegedly because she was irritated at being ignored by her husband.[5] She married Demetrius instead. In 288, while Demetrius was laid low by illness, Pyrrhus seized the opportunity to invade Thessaly and Macedon. Demetrius hauled himself out of bed and drove Pyrrhus out.

The two kings had pummeled each other to exhaustion, and they made a peace which recognized the status quo in respect of Demetrius's possession of Corcyra and Pyrrhus's of the Macedonian dependencies given him by Alexander V in his hour of desperation. Demetrius was left in a powerful position. Macedon, though slimmer, was united under his rule; there was a treaty in place with his most formidable enemy; in central Greece, only the perennial hostility of the Aetolians remained; and he had done enough to secure the Peloponnese for the time being. He had the best fleet, and could call up a massive army. It was quite a turnaround for the Besieger, and he began to dream his father's dreams. Perhaps Demetrius was his own worst enemy.

DEMETRIUS'S PRIDE

The style of Demetrius's kingship was typically flamboyant, and he demanded obsequiousness from his subjects. An incident from 290 is particularly revealing. It was the year of the Pythian Games—the quadrennial festival and athletic games held at Delphi, second only to the Olympics in prestige. But the Aetolians controlled Delphi, and restricted access to the festival to their friends. A few weeks later, then, Demetrius came south to host alternate games in Athens.

He and Lanassa entered the city in a style that reminded many of Demetrius's outrageous behavior a dozen or so years earlier, when he had made the Parthenon his home and that of his concubines. They came, bringing grain for ever-hungry Athens, as Demetrius, the aptly named savior god, and his consort Demeter, the grain goddess. They were welcomed not only with incense and garlands and libations, but with an astonishing hymn that included the words: "While other gods are far away, or lack ears, or do not exist, or pay no attention to us, we see you present here, not in wood or stone, but in reality."[6] Obsequiousness indeed, but the point became clearer as the hymn went on to request of the king that he crush the Aetolian menace.

Many Athenians regretted such excesses, and all over the Greek world resentment built up against the new ruler. It was impossible for Demetrius to present himself as the leader the Greeks had been waiting for when he had to crack down hard on incipient rebellion and tax his subjects hard to pay for yet more war. Talk of the freedom of the Greek cities faded away, and between 291 and 285 Ptolemy deprived Demetrius of the Cycladic islands and the rest of his Aegean possessions, thus regaining the control over the entrance to the Aegean that he had lost in 306 and furthering his aim to control as much of the Aegean seaboard as he could. The promise of relief from taxes and a measure of respect for local councils was just as important in this enterprise as military muscle. Dominance in the Aegean was to serve successive Ptolemies well, both strategically and commercially.

Ptolemy also confirmed his control of Phoenicia by finally evicting Demetrius's garrisons from Sidon and Tyre. But these were pretty much Ptolemy's last actions; in 285, feeling the burden of his seventy-plus years, he stood down from the Egyptian throne in favor of Ptolemy II. Maybe he had a terminal illness, because only two years later he died—in his bed, remarkably enough for a Successor. But then "safety first" had been his motto, for most of his time as ruler of Egypt.

Despite these losses, Demetrius might have hung on in Macedon. But he was a natural autocrat, and that was not the Macedonian way. Demetrius never managed the kingly art of finding a balance between being loved and being hated, or at least feared. His subjects came to resent his luxurious ways and his unapproachability. Macedonian kings were supposed to make themselves available to petitions from their subjects, yet Demetrius was rumored on one occasion to have thrown a whole bundle of them into a river—or at least to be the sort of person who might.[7] This kind of talk, charging him with eastern-style monarchy, did his reputation no good. Nor did the fact that he wore a double crown, indicating rulership of Asia as well as Europe.[8]

Ignoring the rumbles of discontent, Demetrius began to prepare for a massive invasion of Asia. But the proud Macedonian barons resented their country's being thought of as no more than a launching point for eastern invasion; they did not want to be on the periphery of some vast Asian kingdom. It was all right when Philip and Alexander had done it, because that was for the greater glory of Macedon. But this war would be fought against fellow Macedonians, for the greater glory of an unpopular king. The idea of taking thousands more Macedonians east, following the tens of thousands who had already gone, did not go down well either, since the country was already somewhat depopulated.

But Demetrius was no Cassander, content with Macedon alone; he was as addicted to warfare as Alexander the Great. Just as Alexander had set out from Macedon and seized all Asia from the Persian king, so Demetrius intended at least to deprive Lysimachus of Asia Minor. But whereas Alexander had invaded Asia with about thirty-seven thousand men and no fleet to speak of, Demetrius was amassing a vast army, over a hundred thousand strong, while a fleet of five hundred warships was being prepared in the shipyards of Macedon and Greece. In typical Besieger style, some of these ships were larger than any vessel that had ever been built before, and he used the best naval architects available. The precise design of these ships is a matter of intelligent guesswork, but it will give some idea of their scale to say that, whereas a normal warship had three banks of rowers in some arrangement (hence its name, "trireme"), Demetrius was having a "fifteen" and a "sixteen" built.[9]

Naturally, Demetrius's preparations involved propaganda as well. Above all, he wielded the old, potent slogan of Greek freedom against Lysimachus. At a local level, a prominent public building in Pella displayed symbolic paintings, copies of which formed the wall paintings of a later Roman villa.[10] One of the panels of the painting depicted Demetrius's parents as king and queen of Asia, the idea being that he had inherited a natural claim, while other panels showed Macedon as the ruler of Asia by right of conquest. But history is littered with failed promises of manifest destiny.

EARLY HELLENISTIC RELIGIONS

Manifest or otherwise, Destiny, in its less implacable guise as Fortune, was to play a considerable role in the emotional life of the hellenized people of the new world the Successors were creating. But the rise of the cult of Fortune was only one of a number of new religious phenomena. The mobility of the early Hellenistic period uprooted people from their traditions and left them free, for the first time, to choose, to a greater extent than before, their own forms of worship. Not many decades earlier, Socrates had been taken to court for not worshipping the gods of the city; such a trial rapidly became unthinkable, as personal forms of religion proliferated alongside the old and new civic cults. In addition to ensuring that the gods protected their communities and their leaders, people simply wanted the gods to bless them as individuals.[11]

Greek religion was polytheistic, but one of the main innovations of the Hellenistic period was a henotheistic tendency. Influential philosophers earlier in the fourth century, such as Plato and Aristotle, had promoted a single supreme deity, and the idea found fertile soil. The fertility was due in part perhaps to increased intellectual sophistication, but mainly to social conditions, the larger world in which people now lived. In the past, deities and cults had often been tied to specific locations, even on occasion to specific families, but now more and more people were living away from their ancestral homes. New traditions were forged by the creation of clubs that combined religious and social purposes, always for relatively small congregations, but people were still worshipping at fewer shrines.

This reductionism was also aided by the strong cultural current in favor of individualism. We have already seen this current in both the aesthetic and the philosophy of the times. In religion, it meant not just that people increasingly settled on a smaller number of gods, those they found personally satisfying, but more importantly that they became more concerned with personal salvation. The cults that offered personal salvation, or at least a chance of a better afterlife, were known as the "mysteries"—that is, etymologically, "cults into which one was personally initiated." The most famous, in the early Hellenistic period, were the cult of Demeter and Persephone at the seaside town of Eleusis, near Athens, and the cult of the Great Gods on the beautiful north Aegean island of Samothrace. Both shrines were of considerable antiquity—it was said that Jason and the Argonauts had stopped at Samothrace and been initiated before continuing their quest for the Golden Fleece, and Demeter herself was supposed to have instigated the Eleusinian cult—but their heyday was the Hellenistic period. Samothrace in particular was graced by devotion and benefactions from several members of the Macedonian royal families. Philip II commissioned the first stone buildings in the sanctuary, Antipater had a remarkable stone pavilion built in the names of the two kings Philip III Arrhidaeus and Alexander IV, and Lysimachus's wife Arsinoe funded the construction of a unique circular, multistoried building, perhaps a hotel.[12]

One of the most successful new quasi-monotheistic cults was that of Sarapis, a healing god and worker of miracles. The development of his cult was attributed to Ptolemy I,[13] and the temple of Sarapis became one of the most splendid buildings in Alexandria. Sarapis already existed as a minor Egyptian deity (a sort of amalgam of Osiris and Apis, hence the name), but Ptolemy had the foresight to develop his cult in a European form. He borrowed the iconography of the god from the cult of Zeus of the Underworld in the Greek city of Sinope on the Black Sea. The cult of the new deity was conjoined, in a new form of mystery religion, with that of his sister-wife Isis. Devotees came to regard Sarapis and Isis as the primordial masculine and feminine principles of the universe. The combination of near monotheism with salvationism was irresistible, and a cult that Ptolemy originally intended to suit the multiculturalism of Alexandria spread throughout the entire known world.

The Olympian deities—Zeus and his extended family—continued to be worshipped both in private and in the public ceremonies of the Greek cities, and to be promoted by the Successors. Seleucus claimed immediate descent from Apollo; the Antigonids looked back to Heracles, and Ptolemy to Dionysus. But the Olympian religion seems to have exerted less of a hold over people's emotions. The Olympian deities had always been thought of in a quasi-anthropomorphic manner, but now abstractions increasingly began to gain cults; personality-free deities such as Fair Fame, Rumor, Peace, Victory, Shame—all received their altars, if they did not already have them.

By far the most widespread of these cults was that of Fortune. In a world of rapidly changing circumstances, the only certainty was uncertainty. Fortune was a great, irrational, female principle, and the spread of the worship of Sarapis and Isis around the world was helped by the early identification of Isis with Fortune. Demetrius of Phalerum wrote a book about Fortune in which he drew on current events to reveal the potency of the goddess: only a few decades earlier, the Persians had been rulers of the world, while the Macedonians were unknown, but Fortune had made the world topsy-turvy.[14] Seleucus adorned his new Syrian capital, Antioch, with a magnificent temple of Fortune, which contained a famous cult statue. Fortune was worshipped by private individuals, but also at a civic level, as the Fortune of entire cities or peoples (as Demetrius of Phalerum was speaking of the Fortune of the Persians and Macedonians). Wherever there were Greeks or hellenized peoples around the Mediterranean and beyond, the cult of Fortune was also to be found.

DEMETRIUS'S DOWNFALL

The scale of Demetrius's buildup indicated ambitions that threatened all the other kings, and they formed a coalition against him for what we could call the Fifth War of the Successors. Once again, an Antigonid was the enemy who united all the other Successor kings. Pyrrhus, "bombarded by letters from Lysimachus, Ptolemy and Seleucus,"[15] shrugged off the peace treaty he had made with Demetrius and joined the coalition. It was already clear that Demetrius did not stand a chance. It seems likely to me that he was suffering from megalomania.

Early in 288, while Ptolemy's admiral sailed for southern Greece with the intention of stirring the Greek cities to rebellion, Lysimachus and Pyrrhus attacked Macedon from, respectively, the east and the west. Pyrrhus employed the old Successor tactic of claiming that Alexander the Great had appeared to him in a dream and promised his aid. Demetrius left Gonatas to take care of the Ptolemaic threat in southern Greece and, unaware of Pyrrhus's treachery, concentrated his forces in the east to face Lysimachus. He learned just how unpopular he was when his Macedonian troops deserted, first to Lysimachus and then to Pyrrhus, when Demetrius heard of his invasion and turned to confront him.

It was the most effective coup imaginable. Demetrius was thrown out of his kingdom by the army, or its senior officers, after six years on the throne. But Macedon was left to endure, for a second time, the uncertainty of a dual kingship. Pyrrhus justified his rulership by citing his kinship to Alexander the Great (they were second cousins), and took western Macedon (and then Thessaly a few years later); Lysimachus gained the eastern kingdom—a significant gain for him, given the wealth of Macedon's natural resources there. For instance, with what he already had in Asia Minor, he now monopolized the most accessible sources of gold.

Demetrius adopted a lowly disguise and fled to Cassandreia. Elderly Phila saw the end and took poison. Her marriage to Demetrius had been long and apparently stable, despite his tempestuous career. She was clearly a formidable woman; even when she was young, her father had consulted her on official business, and she came to have her own court, Companions, and bodyguard, as well as cults in Athens and elsewhere. She was an early prototype of the powerful and independent queens of the later Hellenistic period.

From Cassandreia, Demetrius joined Gonatas in southern Greece. He was reduced once again to his fleet, his Companion Cavalry, and however many mercenaries he could afford to keep. Astonishingly, and with the help of his capacious treasury, he was able to keep himself relatively secure in Corinth, and over the next two years even built up his land army again. Athens seized the moment, however, and rose up against him in the spring of 286. Those of the Antigonid garrison who refused inducements to defect were defeated in battle. Ptolemy allowed Callias of Sphettus, an Athenian in his service, to detach a thousand elite troops from the Cyclades to protect the harvest against attacks by troops from Demetrius's other garrisons.

Demetrius arrived, with a larger army than expected, and the besieged Athenians sent for help from Pyrrhus. But then a Ptolemaic fleet appeared off Piraeus, so that Demetrius, who was in any case still insanely anxious to take the war to Asia, could see that he would be tied up in Athens for ages. He came to terms with Ptolemy and Pyrrhus, who appear to have been just as anxious not to fight. Athens would remain ungarrisoned, but Demetrius was allowed to keep his other garrisons in Piraeus and in fortresses nearby. As far as Athens was concerned, this made it a truce, not a treaty. When Pyrrhus arrived, he is said to have recommended that the Athenians never admit a king within their walls again.[16] Perhaps it was a warning against his own ambitions.

Demetrius left his remaining European possessions in the hands of Gonatas and set out immediately for Asia Minor. Disturbingly for Lysimachus, Ptolemy's Aegean fleet made no attempt to impede the invasion. Miletus defected to Demetrius, presumably by prearrangement, and gave him a first base. At Miletus, he was met by Eurydice, Ptolemy's ex-wife, and sister of Phila. She brought her daughter Ptolemais, to whom Demetrius had been betrothed in 298, and they now married. But the marriage was no kind of rapprochement with Ptolemy; things had changed in the twelve years since the couple were first betrothed. Eurydice was in exile, estranged from Ptolemy, and she had other designs. She saw alliance with Demetrius as a way to give her son a chance at power, since his prospects in Egypt were not good: Ptolemy had long favored his other wife Berenice and her offspring. The very next year, in fact, Ptolemy abdicated in favor of his son by Berenice, who became Ptolemy II. Eurydice's son was called Ptolemy Ceraunus, the Thunderbolt—named not "for his unpredictable and sinister character," as hostile propaganda claimed,[17] but for the power he wielded.

The campaigning season of 285 started well for Demetrius. He regained a few coastal towns, including Ephesus (presumably by treachery, if the Lysimachan fortifications briefly described earlier were already in place), and subsequently Lysimachus's governors in

Lydia and Caria surrendered their territories wholesale. There is no way to explain these rapid successes except by assuming that he was welcomed. Before Ipsus, Asia Minor had been under Antigonid rule for a long time, and had prospered; it seems that enough of the inhabitants wanted to turn back the clock.

Meanwhile, Pyrrhus invaded Thessaly, which drew Gonatas's attention northward, and Athens made an attempt to dislodge the Antigonid garrison in the Piraeus. The year before, they had persuaded one of the garrison commanders in Athens to defect with some of his men. They tried the same tactic again in Piraeus, but this time it ended in disaster. The man only pretended to go along with their plan. He opened the fortress gates to the approaching Athenian soldiers by night—but only to trap them inside and cut them down.

In Asia Minor, despite his first successes, Demetrius was losing the initiative. Lysimachus's son Agathocles was demonstrating that he had inherited his father's skills as a general. He drew Demetrius ever farther inland—the same strategy the Turks used in 1920–21 against the Greek invasion—while cutting him off from the coast by retaking the territories now in his rear that he had just taken himself, including Sardis and Miletus. Demetrius's fleet at Miletus either fled to safe refuges farther down the coast or surrendered. With their supply lines cut and their hopes rapidly fading, Demetrius's mercenaries began to desert him. Their commander claimed to be unconcerned, on the grounds that he could always find more men to recruit in Media, which he planned to reach via Armenia. By now he seems decidedly unbalanced; not content with being defeated by Agathocles, he was threatening Seleucus too, but with diminishing forces.

Demetrius was perhaps intending to encourage the often restless eastern satrapies to rise up and, with his help, overthrow Seleucus. But this was an unlikely scenario, not least because Seleucus had elevated his son Antiochus—"the only anchor for our storm-tossed house"[18]—to joint kingship in 294 or 293 and sent him east to quell any storm. In the longer term, it made sense to have a coruler for such a vast kingdom, and for the east, one who was half-Iranian and had been brought up in Babylon. At the same time, Seleucus gave Antiochus his wife Stratonice. Despite fanciful stories of illicit passion,[19] what was uppermost in his mind was probably to try to ensure stability within his household, since otherwise any son Stratonice might have borne him would have been a rival to Antiochus. It was also a way of keeping Demetrius within the family, so to speak, while simultaneously announcing a certain cooling of their relationship.

So no uprising took place in the eastern satrapies to aid Demetrius's plans. Instead of heading for Armenia, he turned south, with disease and desertion decimating his numbers. Agathocles let him cross the Taurus Mountains into Cilicia, and strengthened the fortresses on the passes against his return. He was Seleucus's problem now. Seleucus tolerated Demetrius's presence for a while, but had to take steps in the spring of 284 to contain him in the mountains. Demetrius reacted with some vigorous guerrilla warfare, and even threatened to enter Syria until he was laid low once again by illness.

While Demetrius lay sick, more and more of his men deserted. Even so, after he recovered, he kept pushing for a decisive battle. It was insanity; he had too few men. Seleucus refused to meet Demetrius in battle, preferring to wait for the low morale in the enemy camp to take its toll. The end, then, came with a whimper, not a bang. The two armies were close by, and Seleucus is said to have walked bareheaded himself up to Demetrius's lines to appeal to his men to lay down their arms. Recognizing that Seleucus was doing his best to spare their lives, they finally abandoned Demetrius.[20]

Seleucus put his former father-in-law under comfortable but closely guarded arrest in Apamea on the banks of the Orontes. While Gonatas petitioned Seleucus for his father's return, Lysimachus begged him to have the man put to death. Seleucus refused both requests, and accused Lysimachus of behaving like a barbarian.[21] In reality, however, he wanted Demetrius alive and in his keeping, in case he could use him in some way against his remaining adversaries. Humiliated by becoming no more than a pawn in others' games, Demetrius wrote to Greece, abdicating his kingship, such as it was, in favor of his son. By March 282 drink, and perhaps the illness that had been plaguing him for some years, took him to his grave. He was not much over fifty years of age. His ashes were released, and in due course of time Gonatas affirmed his kingship by the rite of burying the previous king.

Restless greed for imperial power had been Demetrius's undoing: he should have consolidated in Macedon and Greece rather than entertaining more grandiose dreams. He never truly had an opportunity for world conquest, the kind of gift of Fortune that came the way of Alexander, Antigonus, and, as we shall shortly see, Seleucus. Demetrius's reign had lasted only six years, but his pride would have been assuaged had he known that it would help his son Antigonus Gonatas later to legitimate his claim to the Macedonian throne. And then his descendants ruled the homeland until the dynasty's final overthrow by the Romans in 168 BCE.

The Last Successors

T HE THRACE THAT Lysimachus took over in 323 resembled Thessaly, the most backward of the Greek districts, about a hundred years earlier: it was split up by its terrain and history into separate cantons, each ruled by its own dynasty of chieftains, but tended toward some kind of unification whenever one chieftain got the better of his neighbors. Lysimachus's governorship happened to coincide with the peak of power of one such chieftain, Seuthes III, the Odrysian leader, who ruled from a richly endowed citadel at Seuthopolis.[1]

Seuthes held most of the immediate inland, reducing Lysimachus, on his arrival, to the coastline, where the Greek settlements were, and to fortresses on riverbanks as far upstream as possible. In theory, there was a nonaggression pact in place, but the news of Alexander the Great's death prompted Seuthes to full-scale rebellion. This was the first thing Lysimachus had to deal with when he took up his appointment. It was a serious conflict—serious enough to make it impossible for Lysimachus to help Antipater in the Lamian War. Lysimachus won, and forced Seuthes once again to recognize Macedonian suzerainty in Thrace, but it was not a decisive victory, and Seuthes retained much of the Thracian hinterland. Ten years later, encouraged by Antigonus the One-Eyed, he rose up again, only to be defeated once more by Lysimachus.

But Seuthes was only one of Lysimachus's recurrent problems. Beyond the Odrysians and the Haemus mountains, farther north around the Danube, were the Getae, a warlike tribe who made frequent incursions into Lysimachus's territory, with or without Seuthes' connivance and the help of other tribes. When Philip II had annexed

Thrace around 340, he had left the Getae unconquered and had simply come to some accommodation with them. For Lysimachus too, negotiation proved to be more effective than warfare.

Even the local Greeks were unfriendly. They inhabited outposts of the Greek world, and had long been accustomed to making their own way in a hostile environment; few felt the need to pay for protection, and anti-Macedonian politicians found a receptive audience. But taxing their wealth—earned chiefly from the trade in slaves and grain—was his only reliable source of revenue. Lysimachus had no choice but to use force to establish control, and to maintain it with garrisons. It was not a popular strategy.

The old picture, willfully perpetuated by the Greeks themselves, of the Thracians as primitive tribes ruled by warrior chieftains is a huge simplification. They certainly had a martial culture, but then so did the Macedonians—who also, like the Thracians, used Greek as their administrative language, employed Greek craftsmen and artisans, and were extremely wealthy in natural resources. If Seuthes had not been curbed by Lysimachus, he might have done for Thrace what Philip II did for Macedon. It is an index of Thracian martial prowess and resourcefulness that, although sandwiched between the Persian empire to the east, the equally expansionist Greek cities to the south, and the warlike Scythians to the north, they carved out and maintained their own culture and territory.

The constant warfare and his inability to dominate the inland tribes left Lysimachus perennially short of resources. He never fully controlled the interior, and essentially his province consisted of the Chersonese and the coastlines. But archaeology, so often our only resource for areas Greek writers were less interested in (as with Ai Khanum, we would not otherwise even know of the existence of Seuthopolis), has shown that, despite Lysimachus's failure to conquer the Thracian tribes, there was considerable cultural influence. The Macedonian presence nurtured rapid change, in terms of urbanization, monetization, and the exploitation of natural resources. Ironically, all these developments helped Seuthes defend his land against the very intruders who had brought them about.

LYSIMACHUS AT HIS PEAK

By around 310, however, Lysimachus had won sufficient security for him to focus on consolidation, as represented by his building his new capital, Lysimacheia; within a few years he was styling himself king, which also suggests that he felt he had subdued his core territory. By 302, he was free enough to devote time and energy to wider concerns than just Thrace. The rewards were immediate and impressive. He led the coalition forces to victory against the Antigonids at Ipsus, and added Asia Minor to his realm.

Since then, he had managed to secure his new territory (not least by a vigorous program of city foundation or refoundation and military colonization) and had grouped the Asiatic Greek cities into leagues, under governors of his choosing, to simplify administration.[2] In 284 he gained Paphlagonia and regained the independent city of Heraclea Pontica, where the ruler, his wife Amastris, had died under suspicious circumstances. In retaliation, Lysimachus killed his two stepsons as the alleged murderers, and reannexed the wealthy city. Most importantly, however, in 288 he added the eastern half of Macedon. He had a fabulous kingdom now, and it should have been enough, but for too long he had been kept busy in his miserable satrapy, fighting and negotiating with barbarians. For too long also, he had been no match for the other Successors in terms of wealth and ability to hire mercenaries, but he gained a fortune from the treasuries of Asia Minor, and was able to tap its resources for a generous annual income.

His rule was little harsher than that of his predecessors, but he maintained a firm control over the Greek cities within his domain. He did not want any trouble; he needed security. For by the middle of the 280s, Lysimachus, aged about seventy, was in a hurry. His building program included at least one Alexandria, and his coinage portrayed him as Alexander's heir, hinting at a hunger for further conquest. Ptolemy II was secure in Greater Egypt; Seleucus was a neighbor, but not one it would have been sensible to attack in the first instance. Antigonus Gonatas, however, held little more than a fleet and the Fetters of Greece—like his father after Ipsus, he was down but not quite out, clinging on to his few possessions with the help of his mercenaries—and Pyrrhus's possession of half of Macedon was an anomaly. Lysimachus's attention was inevitably drawn west.

The partitioners of Macedon had a peace treaty in place, but that was mere expediency. Pyrrhus found that his former allies, Ptolemy and the Aetolians, drifted away. The Aetolians were effectively bought off by Lysimachus's generosity, and Ptolemy was reluctant to antagonize Lysimachus, in case he ever needed his help against Seleucus in Syria. Lysimachus entered into an alliance with Athens, which completed Pyrrhus's exposure on the Greek mainland, and launched a propaganda campaign within Macedon, crudely depicting the Epirote as a foreign interloper.

In one of those volte-faces that characterize the entire period, Pyrrhus accordingly allied himself with Gonatas, as if to try to unite the Greek mainland against Lysimachus. Pyrrhus received some of Gonatas's mercenaries, but in 284, when it came to a confrontation, many of his men deserted to Lysimachus, who took over western Macedon and Thessaly. This not only restricted Pyrrhus to Epirus but drove a wedge between him and Gonatas. It was effectively the end of Pyrrhus's attempts to expand within the Greek mainland. Before long he turned his attentions west instead—and achieved considerable success for a while against the up-and-coming Romans. Called in to help the Greeks of southern Italy against galloping Roman imperialism, Pyrrhus actually managed to defeat the Romans in three successive battles, but still lost the war. The Romans always had more men on whom they could call, while Pyrrhus had been bled dry. That is why we use the term "Pyrrhic" for a victory that amounts to defeat.

A DIVIDED COURT

So Macedon had a new king, the fifth in ten years. Worse was to follow. In 287, Lysimacheia was badly damaged by an earthquake. It was soon rebuilt, but there were those who were inclined to read it as ominous that Lysimachus's new capital should fall.[3] Alarmed by his awesome power and evident ambitions, mighty enemies were lining up against him. All that was needed was a catalyst.

In 300, Ptolemy I had given his then teenaged daughter Arsinoe to the sexagenarian Lysimachus; in 293 or so, he had given Lysandra (previously married to Alexander V) to Lysimachus's son and heir Agathocles. Lysandra was a daughter of Ptolemy's first wife Eurydice, Arsinoe of his second, and preferred, wife Berenice. Ironically, Berenice, Eurydice's niece, had been in her retinue, and that is how she had come to Ptolemy's attention.

Long before 285, when Ptolemy named Ptolemy II as his successor, Berenice's faction at court had completely defeated that of Eurydice. It was a typical amphimetric dispute, the consequence of the Successors' propensity for polygamy: sons born of the same father but different mothers became rivals for the throne. Eurydice's son Ptolemy Ceraunus, who as the eldest son felt robbed of the Egyptian throne, was also currently resident at Lysimachus's court. He was living proof that the eldest son does not necessarily succeed to the throne.

Agathocles may have been disappointed that, while Ptolemy had abdicated in favor of his son and Seleucus had named Antiochus joint king, his own aged father had not seen fit to honor him in the same way. Even Antigonus had done as much for Demetrius. And Lysimachus, for his part, may have been concerned at Agathocles' royal pretensions, since he had named a city after himself and wore a diadem on his coins. The fact that he had done these things without his father's permission shows that he already had a semi-independent existence within Asia Minor, with his own treasury, mint, and presumably troops. His success in driving Demetrius out of Asia Minor had won him the allegiance of the Greek cities and of large numbers of prominent men, who formed, as it were, his court. But whatever the pretext—the occupation of the Egyptian throne by Arsinoe's brother may also have had something to do with it—Lysimachus now chose to favor the sons Arsinoe had borne him over Agathocles, his only son by Nicaea.

Agathocles rallied his supporters and launched a coup. Our sources are so scant for this period that we do not even know whether it came to battle. But, whether as a result of conflict or intrigue, Agathocles fell into his father's hands and was imprisoned. Before long, Lysimachus had him killed, possibly using Ceraunus as his hit man.[4] This terrible act did Lysimachus's cause no good, and he was faced with further unrest, which was brutally crushed. Those who survived the purge fled. Many found their way to Seleucus's court, including Lysandra; she hated her half sister Arsinoe as much as her mother hated Arsinoe's mother. Their appeals for help, sowing the seeds of renewed war, fell on fertile ground.

It was certainly a time for ambitions to be fulfilled. A man called Philetaerus, no friend of Arsinoe, was among those who found his way to Seleucus's court. Originally an Antigonid officer responsible for Pergamum, he had gone over to Lysimachus not long before Ipsus, and after the battle Lysimachus had reappointed him to the governorship of the city. One of the most important things about Pergamum was its relative impregnability; both Antigonus and Lysimachus kept one of their main treasuries there. At the time in question, the treasury held nine thousand talents (somewhat over five billion dollars). Philetaerus offered to draw on this to hire troops for Seleucus, on the understanding that, once Lysimachus was defeated, he could rule over an independent Pergamum. Seleucus agreed—a sound short-term decision, perhaps, but one that his successors would rue, since the Attalid kingdom of Pergamum prospered and soon came to challenge the Seleucids for much of Asia Minor. Its wealth and splendor may be gauged by the extant remains, and especially by the astonishing Altar of Zeus in the Pergamum Museum of Berlin, dating from the first quarter of the second century.[5] The kingdom survived until it was bequeathed to the people of Rome in 133 BCE.

LAST MAN STANDING

The chaos within Lysimachus's realm attracted Seleucus. He had spent the years since Ipsus stabilizing and securing his empire and he was now ready to extend it. Any of the Successors would have done the same if they had the resources of Seleucus and were handed such an opportunity—even if, like him, they were closer to eighty than seventy. As far as they were concerned, that was the whole point of having resources: to use them to gain more land and more resources. And Seleucus's propagandists had paved the way for grand imperialism; he had been born in the same year as Alexander, they said, and he had once rescued Alexander's diadem after an accident and briefly worn it. As well as spreading stories, he also had politicians promoting his interests in the Greek cities of Asia Minor.

Seleucus mustered his army, elephants and all (he had established a breeding farm at Apamea in Seleucis),[6] and in July 282 set out for Asia Minor. Ptolemy II, nominally Lysimachus's ally, did nothing, perhaps in the hope that Seleucus would at the same time rid him of his troublesome half brother. Seleucus crossed the Taurus well before winter set in and spent some time in winter camp on the Asia Minor side of the Taurus, within Lysimachus's kingdom. This was a bold strategy, but seems to have met with no opposition. The area must have been dominated by men loyal to Agathocles.

At the end of January 281, Seleucus took to the field, and at the same time sent his fleet on ahead to the west coast to lend help to his supporters in the Greek cities. He had softened the cities up by means of generous benefactions, and he used the old Antigonid gambit that they would find him a more congenial king than Lysimachus. A few of the cities did indeed erupt into factional strife, though more of them waited for the outcome of the inevitable decisive battle before committing themselves.

Seleucus's progress was unimpeded. Lysimachus had chosen to wait for him in western Asia Minor. This may have been a tactical decision, in order to be able to maintain some kind of control over the Asiatic Greek cities, but at the same time Lysimachus seems to have been helpless, and plagued by desertion. The decisive battle of the sixth and final war of the Successors was fought at Corupedium, the "Plain of Plenty" west of Sardis, in February 281. No details are known, but it was a complete victory for Seleucus. Aged Lysimachus died on the field. His wife Arsinoe persuaded an attendant to dress as her, while she slipped away from Ephesus (which had briefly borne her name), dressed in rags. The attendant was indeed killed, and Arsinoe fetched up in Macedon, in Cassandreia, where her late husband had been worshipped as a god and she could expect refuge. She took with her a considerable fortune and some of the mercenaries left over from Lysimachus's army, to improve the city's chances of remaining independent of Macedonian rule. Seleucus was the last of Alexander's Successors, and he was poised to fulfill the dream of empire on Alexander's scale.

THE CULT OF LIVING RULERS

The end of Lysimachus's rule in Asia Minor was widely welcomed by his former subjects—not so much because it had been especially harsh, but because, unluckily, it had seen almost constant warfare, after years of peace under Antigonus. Plutarch preserves a tale in which a peasant, digging a hole, is asked what he is doing; "Looking for Antigonus," he replies.[7] Lysimachus's demise and replacement promised peace; naturally, the cities were effusive toward their new master. The island of Lemnos even awarded Seleucus cult honors.

From time to time throughout this book we have met with the worship of the Successors, not just after their death, but, as with Seleucus in this instance, while they were still alive. Leaving aside the fact that, as a pharaoh, Ptolemy was recognized by at least the traditionalists among his native subjects as a god, he was also worshipped as Savior in Rhodes, as were Antigonus and Demetrius in Athens. Antigonus also received divine honors at Scepsis in northwestern Asia Minor, and Demetrius ended up with three cults in Athens. Alexander the Great demanded at the Olympic Games of 324 that all the Greek cities recognize his divinity, as a few already had of their own accord. During the brief period of Cassandreia's independence, Lysimachus was worshipped there, as he was also at Priene in Caria. Games were instituted in honor of Antigonus and Demetrius on the island of Delos. The awarding of divine honors to Alexander and the Successors was far from universal, but it was a widespread practice.[8]

Alexander and the Successors were not the first living individuals to be awarded divine honors. At the end of the fifth century, the Spartan general Lysander received cult honors as a savior for freeing the island of Samos from Athenian dominion. In the middle of the fourth century, Dionysius I, tyrant of the Greek city of Syracuse in Sicily, obliged his subjects to award him divine honors.[9] All that we find in the Successor period is a huge acceleration of the phenomenon, and that is easily explained by the extraordinary nature of the times.

Homer's *Odyssey*, written around the end of the eighth century BCE, was one of the foundation documents of Greek thinking about the gods. At one point Odysseus has been washed up on a shore, more dead than alive. He is rescued by the beautiful, fey princess Nausicaa, and he tells her that if he gets back home, "I will pray to you as a goddess for all my days, for you gave me life."[10] In a polytheistic world, the gods could take on all kinds of guises, and even appear as human beings. An embodied god was simultaneously divine and mortal. When an embodied god was recognized as such at the time (as opposed to with hindsight), it was, naturally, an intensely moving experience.

But how could you tell you were faced with a god? By his or her fruits, by the extraordinary, superhuman nature of what he or she was doing. The gods broke human barriers and saved people in extraordinary and unexpected ways. When Ptolemy saved Rhodes, or Demetrius Athens, they achieved something remarkable, even miraculous, and in so doing they proved that they were embodied gods, no less than Nausicaa in fiction. This is particularly clear in a decree from Scepsis, dating from 311: Antigonus is awarded divine honors precisely because he has brought peace and autonomy.[11] In almost every case, the awarding of divine honors to a Successor followed his winning a major victory.

The Successors stirred deep emotions. "He sat [on his horse] in the full realization of all that soldiers dream of—triumph; and as I looked up at him in the complete fruition of the success which his genius, courage, and confidence in his army had won, I thought that it must have been from such a scene that men in ancient days rose to the dignity of gods."[12] This description of Robert E. Lee at Chancellorsville, by one of his aides, captures a similar emotional experience. We might describe it simply as a reaction to military charisma, but the ancient Greeks would have described it as the presence of a god.

The fact that in Greek religion it was possible to merge the subjective and the objective in this way—so that if Lee is *perceived* as embodying divinity, he does embody divinity—helps to explain why such cults tended to last only a short time. When the first rush of emotion had passed, and especially when geopolitical circumstances had changed, it became possible to see the deified human being as no more than a human being, and to listen to those who had been skeptical from the start. The god had passed out of his temporary vehicle.

The deification of the Successors, then, was in origin a spontaneous emotional reaction to a life-saving or otherwise astonishing event. Hence it was not just cities that instituted cults, but there is evidence even of private worship.[13] All those who felt particularly touched by whatever remarkable event had just taken place were moved to give thanks. When a king himself ordered the institution of a cult, it was invariably the cult of a dead ancestor or of the dynasty as a whole, not of himself. It was others who recognized living kings as gods.

The kings played the part, however, in the ways they presented themselves. Hence, for instance, the array of headdresses we find on coins: lion scalp, elephant scalp, ram's horns, bull's horns, goat's horns, rayed diadem, winged diadem. Each evoked particular divine associations.[14] The very fact that some of them showed their own heads on their coinage was telling, since that was traditionally where a deity was portrayed. The Successors were well aware of the political advantages to be gained by their elevation to superhumanity, as were their ultimate heirs, the kings of early modern Europe, with their adherence to the belief in the divine right of kings.

The cult of rulers as gods was eased by a number of factors. First, there was hero worship; even successful athletes could receive cult honors after their deaths as heroes, to acknowledge that they had done something superhuman, even if not quite divine, and above all that they had benefited their community. Second, there was the long tradition, both in Macedon and the East, for kings to be regarded as especially favored by the gods and for majesty to be considered a reflection of divinity.[15]

Third, the basis of Greek religion was largely ritualistic, with little dogma involved. Long training in ritual had inculcated the essential attitude: you act "as if" the thing were real—as if the bread and wine were flesh and blood, as if the smoke of sacrifice really carried your prayers and petitions to the gods. Then the ritual acquires potency and emotional depth. It was only a small step to act as if a man were a god. It was not that he had to be one or the other; he could be both. Many readers may find this outrageous, and many scholars try to lessen its impact. Perhaps we should think of the Successors as receiving divine honors but not actually being thought of as gods. But in a religion founded on acts, the act of awarding divine honors is precisely a recognition of divinity.

Fourth, as mentioned also in the previous chapter, there was a certain weakening of and skepticism about the Olympian religion. A contemporary utopian writer, Euhemerus of Messene (a friend of Cassander), influentially revived the old fifth-century theory that the Olympian gods were no more than human beings who had achieved remarkable things—as Demeter, say, had discovered how to cultivate cereal crops, or Dionysus had discovered viticulture. In fact, he even specified "generals, admirals, and kings" as such gods in the making.[16] In the hymn the Athenians sang for Demetrius when he entered the city in 297, the Olympian gods are said to be remote. In a world at war, such a view is unsurprising: despite all their sacrifices and prayers, the Athenians were still starving—until Demetrius came and saved them.

If we shed Judeo-Christian preconceptions (especially monotheism, with its corollaries of divine omniscience and omnipotence), it is not difficult to understand the deification of the Successors as a spontaneous reaction to their superhuman and lifesaving achievements, aided and abetted by more than a soupçon of the desire to appease a power that could as readily destroy the city as save it. Nor is it hard to understand such a reaction; even in our own sophisticated times, people have been known to regard as gods whoever or whatever gives them the greatest rush of emotion. In an era of disillusionment, the orthodox churches often fail to deliver such ecstasy, and so exotic gurus and Elvis Presley become gods. In any case, the early Hellenistic world did not subscribe to Judeo-Christian principles; the Successors stirred deep enough emotions to pass as gods.

PTOLEMY CERAUNUS

Seleucus now held all Asia from the Aegean to Afghanistan—almost all the old Persian empire, apart from Greater Egypt and the territories he had ceded to Chandragupta. The Egyptian king must have felt himself to be the next target, especially since Seleucus incorporated Ceraunus into his court, indicating that he looked with favor on his claim to the Egyptian throne. By and large, the Asiatic Greek cities opportunistically welcomed Seleucus, though Lysimachan garrisons at Sardis and elsewhere had to be driven out.

Seleucus spent only a few months settling the present and planning for the future of Asia Minor before taking the next logical step. In the summer of 281, he crossed the Hellespont and marched on Lysimacheia to lay claim to Lysimachus's European possessions as well. With Thrace and Macedon, Seleucus would in effect rule the world. He was closer than even Antigonus ever got to emulating Alexander.

There was no army that could resist him—he was "the conqueror of conquerors"[17]—but even the leaders of vast armies are vulnerable as individuals. In September, while they were out riding together near Lysimacheia, Ceraunus treacherously killed Seleucus with his own hand. Ceraunus had decided to give up on Egypt—too tough a nut to crack—and take advantage of the current confusion to establish himself in Europe. Ironically, Seleucus had sheltered his own murderer. It was a wretched end for one of the most bold and enterprising of the Successors. At least, by making Antiochus joint king, he had left his empire as stable as it might be.

The last of the true Successors—the last of those who had known and ridden with Alexander the Great—both died in blood within a few months of each other. All four of the major post-Ipsus contenders had died within a few years: Ptolemy in 283, Demetrius in 282, Lysimachus and Seleucus in 281. The effect of this watershed would be the confirmation of the fundamental divisions of Alexander's empire, but it took a few years to become apparent. It was as though the original Successors' impetus continued by inertia for a few years, despite the fact that the kings of the next generation were more content to abide within their own borders. It was Macedon itself that bore the brunt of the final phases of the Successors' warfare.

Ceraunus had himself acclaimed king of Macedon at Lysimacheia by the assembled army. Not a few of the troops had worked for Lysimachus before being incorporated into Seleucus's army and felt no particular loyalty to Seleucus. Philetaerus bought Seleucus's body from Ceraunus and, after ceremonially cremating it at Pergamum, sent the ashes to Antiochus. After all, he was setting up an independent kingdom in territory that nominally belonged to Antiochus now. Antiochus had the bones interred in Seleucia Pieria, where a temple was constructed over them and the cult of the Seleucid royal house began.

But such genteel acts lay in the future. For the present, Antiochus was racing west to restore order in Asia Minor, which had been left without overall administration and with only scattered garrisons to defend it. But he was delayed on the way by an opportunistic rebellion in Syria, and Ptolemy seized the chance to add to his Asia Minor possessions. Only in 279 was Antiochus in a position to send an army into Asia Minor to stop the rot. In the two years since Corupedium and the deaths of Lysimachus and Seleucus, Ptolemy's forces had made major gains, and they now had effective control of a large slice of the Asia Minor coastline, from Lycia to Chios. Antiochus's general managed to check further expansion, but no more, and he marched north instead. He honored Seleucus's agreement with Philetaerus and left Pergamum alone, but invaded Bithynia, where Zipoetes was also taking advantage of the chaos to extend his borders. The repulse of the invasion did not bode well.

Meanwhile, in Europe, the quasi-pretender Gonatas tried to get to Macedon before the pretender Ceraunus, but was driven off. Ceraunus had already been proclaimed king by the army, and he now sought further legitimation. No doubt he reminded the Macedonians of his father's claim to be the illegitimate child of Philip II, as though there were good Argead blood in his veins. He also invested Arsinoe, Lysimachus's widow, in Cassandreia. The recovery of Cassandreia would demonstrate to the Macedonians his concern to pull the country back together again.

But then he had a better idea. Instead of trying to take Cassandreia, he offered to marry his half sister. This would not only gain him Cassandreia, but allow him to claim to be Lysimachus's heir and avenger. She finally agreed to the alliance—a fact that even the ancient authors found puzzling, since the marriage was so obviously doomed from the start. The tradition tells a chilling tale of a woman who wanted nothing more than to be queen of Macedon, and of an evil man foreswearing himself before the mightiest gods to persuade her of his sincerity when he said that he would recognize her sons as his heirs.[18]

Before long, the newlyweds fell out when Ceraunus butchered two of Arsinoe's three sons by Lysimachus, "in their mother's arms."[19] Arsinoe must have been foolish, or desperate, to believe that he would acknowledge them as his heirs; they were rivals. The eldest son had already fled, and soon his mother did the same. She went to Samothrace, and then to Egypt, where she later married her brother Ptolemy II, thus becoming a queen for the third time and introducing the Macedonian royal family to the pharaonic tradition of brother-sister marriage.

Ceraunus, free now to rule Macedon as he wished, did a good job of appeasing Pyrrhus and Ptolemy II. He loaned Pyrrhus troops for his imminent Italian campaign, and assured his half brother that he no longer had any designs on the Egyptian throne. Outside interference was the last thing he needed, since he had enough troubles from within, dealing with unruly barons and rival claimants to the throne. But Celtic tribes were on the prowl for land. They had been making a nuisance of themselves on the borders for many years; Cassander had had to deal with incursions or threatened incursions on several occasions. But recently the massive movement of land-hungry Celts had become a far more serious problem; they had already more or less brought to an end Odrysian rule in Thrace, for instance. Now, in 279, a monstrous band approached Macedon. Ceraunus thought he could handle the situation. They expected to be given a lot of money and sent to look for land elsewhere, but Ceraunus chose to face them in battle. The Macedonian army was cut to pieces, and Ceraunus's head displayed on a spear.

The Celts went on the rampage, but they lacked siegecraft. People huddled in terror in towns and fortresses while their land was plundered and spoiled. Cassandreia seized the opportunity to secede once again from Macedonian authority. Some of the Celts penetrated down into central Greece, but they were driven off by a combined Greek army led by the Aetolians. The massive horde dispersed; some established themselves in Thrace, while others, after ten years of brigandage on a grand scale in western Asia Minor, turned parts of Cappadocia and Phrygia into an independent kingdom called Galatia that lasted well into the Roman period.

ANTIGONUS GONATAS

Ceraunus had reigned for only two years and left no clear successor. Macedon descended into anarchy; five pretenders vied for the throne, and anyone who got it held it for no more than a few weeks. One of them, another Antipater (a nephew of Cassander), was derisively nicknamed "Etesias," because his reign lasted no longer than the season of the etesian winds (the modern *meltemi*)—about four months at the most, from late May.

Antiochus himself left Syria and came west. In return for acknowledging Ptolemy's possessions in Asia Minor and the Aegean, his fleet met with no opposition as it sailed to link up with his army in Sardis. Fortunately for Antiochus, Zipoetes had died, and his two sons were fighting over the kingdom. In fact, the Celts first entered Asia Minor at the invitation of one of the Bithynian brothers, to help him in his struggle. But even if Bithynia could be ignored for the present, the

Celts were at large in Antiochus's kingdom—and so was Antigonus Gonatas.

In view of his precarious position in Greece, where he had few possessions and many enemies (including a newly resurgent Sparta), and in view of the chaotic situation in Asia Minor, in 279 Gonatas decided, like his father before him, to extend into Asia Minor. The plan worked well, but perhaps not in the way he expected. When Antiochus arrived, they skirmished for a while, but then came to terms. The deal was that Gonatas would leave Asia to Antiochus, and Antiochus would not interfere in European affairs. This was a significant moment; if Gonatas could gain the throne, there would be, for the first time since Alexander's death, a balance of power, with none of the three kings inclined to try to take over the kingdom of one of the others. Gonatas and Antiochus sealed the peace between them by becoming double brothers-in-law: Antiochus was already married to Stratonice, Gonatas's sister, and Gonatas now married a sister of Antiochus.

Gonatas's first invasion of Macedon from Asia was a failure. But then in 277, apparently by sheer chance, he met a force of eighteen thousand Celts in Thrace on their way out of Greece. He lured them into an ambush near Lysimacheia and wiped them out. The rout was so thorough that Gonatas attributed his victory to Pan, the god of, among other things, panic. He later had his court poet write a hymn to Pan, and struck coins with the god's head on the obverse. Macedon lay open for Gonatas, now that he had eliminated the Celtic menace and could present himself as a successful warrior and their savior. In 276 (having expanded his army by hiring some of the defeated Celts) he drove out the last pretenders, regained Cassandreia and Thessaly, and had himself declared king. He took the year 283, when his imprisoned father had abdicated in his favor, as the official start of his reign. He died in 239, aged eighty, still on the throne of Macedon.

EPILOGUE

It is striking testimony to the endurance of Alexander's influence over the Successors that the attempt to emulate him died along with those who had actually known him. Of course, there was warfare to come, but it was limited. Successive Seleucids certainly wanted to take southern Syria from successive Ptolemies, but generally they did not expect to take Egypt as well; Pyrrhus drove Antigonus Gonatas out of Macedon for a couple of years, but the conflict was confined to the Greek mainland. The pattern of the three great Hellenistic kingdoms was fixed: Ptolemy had Greater Egypt, Antiochus had Asia, Gonatas had Macedon, and no one seemed to want the lot anymore. In the past, a frontier had been only temporary, as each king expected to try to expand his territory; now, greater respect was paid to natural borders of sea, river, mountain, and desert. Alexander's dream of a single Greek empire remained unfulfilled. In the end, the empire that spanned east and west was Roman.

The timetable of the Roman takeover tells its tale of ruthlessness. In 167, after long hostility, the kingdom of Macedon was replaced by four republics subject to Rome; twenty-one years later, the southern Greeks were finally quelled and the city of Corinth destroyed. In 133 Attalus III of Pergamum, fearing the consequences of Roman interest in Asia Minor, bequeathed his kingdom to the Roman people as a way of avoiding massive bloodshed. In 74 Nicomedes III of Bithynia followed suit. By 62 the last champion of Greek freedom, Mithradates VI of Pontus, had been forced to commit suicide, and the former Seleucid kingdom was split up into provinces of the burgeoning empire. In 58 the Romans annexed Cyprus, having already taken Cyrenaica from the Ptolemies about forty years earlier. In 30 the love affair of Cleopatra VII and Mark Antony doomed Egypt to following the other Successor kingdoms into extinction as a Roman province.

But even after the Roman conquest, there was still something essentially Greek about these eastern Roman provinces, and in due course of time (in 285 CE, and then more formally in 364) the Roman administration recognized this by dividing the empire into a western and an eastern half. The east, governed from Byzantium (now renamed Constantinopolis), outlasted the west by a thousand years, and came into conflict with successive powers from farther east: the Sasanians, the Arabs, and finally the Ottoman Turks. All these world-changing events were the legacy of Alexander and the Successors, since it was their energy and ambition that had created the Greek East.

But their legacy did not always involve conflict and loss of life. Much of the youthful energy of the new world they created was, it is true, absorbed by warfare, but there was still enough left to build on the past and create new ways of thinking about humankind and its role in the world, about how individuals might perfect themselves, about what counted as art and literature. Philosophy reached new heights of sophistication, while at the same time reaching out to ordinary people; artists worked with new canons of realism; science and technology progressed at a furious rate, often driven by the interminable wars.

The irony is that the Hellenistic age, which saw all this brilliance and high culture, was ushered in by the cynical brutality of Alexander and his Successors. But perhaps, for that very reason, this period of history can teach us to hope that even when things seem at their darkest, the forces of greed and destruction will not entirely win.

Time Line

History	Culture
323 death of Alexander III (11 June); negotiations in Babylon; death of Meleager; redistribution of satrapies; birth of Alexander IV; Philip III and Alexander IV joint kings of the Macedonian empire	ca. 325 Praxagoras of Cos (medical theory)
323–322 Greek rebellions in Greece (Lamian War) and in Bactria	
322 death of Leonnatus; Perdiccas pacifies Cappadocia and Lycaonia; Ptolemy annexes Cyrenaica; death of Demosthenes; Athens loses Samos	322 death of Aristotle; Theophrastus succeeds Aristotle as head of Lyceum; Hyperides' Funeral Oration (literature)
321 Perdiccas pacifies Pisidia; Ptolemy hijacks Alexander's corpse; Perdiccas marries Nicaea but woos Cleopatra; Adea marries Philip III; Antigonus flees to Greece	
320–319 First War of the Successors (Ptolemy, Antipater, Craterus vs. Perdiccas)	320–290 Menander of Athens (comedy); Crates of Thebes (philosophy)

320 Eumenes victorious in Asia Minor; death of Craterus; assassination of Perdiccas; Triparadeisus conference makes Antipater regent and Antigonus general of Asia; redistribution of satrapies; Ptolemy annexes southern Syria

ca. 320 Autolycus of Pitane (astronomy); Pyrrho of Elis (philosophy)

319 Antipater returns to Macedon with the kings; Antigonus defeats Eumenes and remaining Perdiccans; Polyperchon replaces Antipater as regent

319 choregic monuments of Thrasyllus and Nicias in Athens

318–316 Second War of the Successors (Antigonus and Cassander vs. Polyperchon and Eumenes)

318 Antigonus eliminates enemies in Asia Minor; Cassander joins Antigonus; Eumenes becomes Polyperchon's general in Asia; Polyperchon's declaration of freedom for the Greek cities

317–307 Demetrius of Phalerum rules Athens for Cassander

317 Philip III declares for Cassander; Antigonus defeats Eumenes in Iran

316 assassination of Philip III by Olympias; executions of Eumenes, Peithon, and Olympias; foundation of Cassandreia, Thessalonica

316–297 Cassander ruler of Macedon

315 Antigonus expels Seleucus from Babylon

315 death of Lysippus of Sicyon (portraiture, sculpture); birth of Aratus of Soli (literature)

315–301 Antigonus rules Asia and Asia Minor

315–311 Third War of the Successors (Lysimachus, Ptolemy, and Cassander vs. Antigonus, Demetrius, and Polyperchon)

History	Culture
315 Antigonus annexes Phoenicia; Proclamation of Tyre	
315–314 siege of Tyre; Polemaeus in Asia Minor	
313 Antigonus recovers Caria; Cyprus finally secured for Ptolemy; Lysimachus saves Thrace	313: Alexandria becomes Ptolemy's capital
313–312 Polemaeus in Greece	
312 Ptolemy invades Palestine; battle of Gaza	
311 Seleucus restored to Babylonia; Ptolemy abandons Palestine; "Peace of the Dynasts" between Antigonus, Ptolemy, Lysimachus, and Cassander; Antigonus foiled by Nabataeans	
311–309 Babylonian War (Seleucus vs. Antigonus and Demetrius)	
311–304 Seleucus secures eastern satrapies	
310 or 309 murder of Alexander IV by Cassander	ca. 310 circumnavigation of Britain by Pytheas of Massalia; foundation of Ptolemais in Egypt; Hecataeus of Abdera (ethnography); Duris of Samos and Timaeus of Tauromenium (historiography)
309 murder of Heracles by Polyperchon, of Cleopatra by Antigonus, and of Polemaeus by Ptolemy	309 foundation of Lysimacheia
309–308 Ptolemy's attempt on Greece	
307–301 Fourth War of the Successors (Antigonus and Demetrius vs. Ptolemy and Cassander, and subsequently Lysimachus and Seleucus too)	
307–304 Four-Year War in Greece (Cassander vs. Demetrius)	
307 Demetrius takes Athens	307 foundation of Antigonea

History	Culture
306 Demetrius takes Cyprus (siege of Salamis); Antigonus and Demetrius become kings	306 Epicurus founds his commune in Athens
305–304 siege of Rhodes; Antigonid invasion of Egypt repulsed; Ptolemy, Lysimachus, Cassander, and Seleucus become kings	ca. 305–260 tomb paintings at Aegae (Vergina) and Lefkadia
305–285 Ptolemy I king of Egypt	
305–281 Seleucus king of Asia	
304–303 Demetrius gains control of Greece	
302 Demetrius refounds Hellenic League; Demetrius and Cassander square off in Thessaly; Lysimachus and Prepelaus invade Asia Minor; Antigonus enters Asia Minor	
301 Ptolemy garrisons southern Syria; battle of Ipsus; death of Antigonus; Athens expels Demetrius	
301–294 Lysimachus consolidates Asia Minor	
	ca. 300 Zeno of Citium founds Stoic school of philosophy; Philitas of Cos (poetry); Dicaearchus of Messana (geography); Bion of Borysthenes (philosophy); Pella mosaics
	300–290 development of Seleucis; Fortune of Antioch (sculpture)
299 Demetrius raids Thrace	
298 Demetrius takes Cilicia	
297 death of Cassander; death of Philip IV; Pyrrhus recovers Epirus	
297–294 Antipater I and Alexander V kings of Macedon	
296 Seleucus annexes Cilicia	

History	Culture
295 Demetrius recovers Athens from Lachares	295 death of Apelles of Colophon (painting); Asclepiades of Samos (poetry)
294 Demetrius takes Macedon; deaths of Alexander V and Antipater I; Ptolemy regains Cyprus	
294–288 Demetrius king of Macedon	
294 or 293 Antiochus made coruler with Seleucus	
293–292 Lysimachus prisoner of Getae	ca. 293 foundation of Demetrias; foundation of Museum in Alexandria
292 Demetrius invades Asia Minor, returns to quell rebellion in Greece	
291–285 Ptolemy gains or regains Aegean possessions, as well as Tyre and Sidon	ca. 290 Euhemerus of Messene (fiction)
288–286 Fifth War of the Successors (Demetrius vs. Ptolemy, Pyrrhus, Lysimachus, and Seleucus)	
288 Lysimachus and Pyrrhus partition Macedon; suicide of Phila	
286–284 Demetrius in Asia Minor and Cilicia	
285 Ptolemy I abdicates in favor of Ptolemy II	ca. 285 birth of Archimedes of Syracuse (mathematics); translation of Septuagint begins in Alexandria; Zenodotus of Alexandria edits Homeric poems (literature)
284 Lysimachus takes western Macedon from Pyrrhus	
283 Ptolemy I dies; Demetrius abdicates in favor of Antigonus Gonatas	
283–282 civil war in Asia Minor; Lysimachus kills Agathocles	
282–281 Sixth War of the Successors	

History	Culture
282 Demetrius dies in captivity; Seleucus invades Asia Minor	
281 battle of Corupedium; death of Lysimachus; assassination of Seleucus by Ptolemy Ceraunus	
281–279 Ptolemy Ceraunus king of Macedon; Ptolemy II makes major gains in Asia Minor	
	ca. 280 Euclid's *Elements* (mathematics); Aristarchus of Samos develops heliocentric theory of the universe (astronomy); Theocritus, Callimachus, Posidippus (poetry)
279 Celtic invasion of Macedon and Greece; death of Ptolemy Ceraunus; Macedon descends into chaos; peace accord between Antigonus Gonatas and Antiochus I confirms division of empire	

Cast of Characters

The early Hellenistic period may be unfamiliar to some readers. Only one of its characters is a household name nowadays. In this book, I have held back from naming incidental characters—I could have mentioned seven Alexanders, for instance—but even so, some might feel rather overwhelmed. This feeling will pass as the book is read and the characters become familiar, but in the meantime here is a list of all the major historical characters, for reference. A few genealogical trees follow the list.

Adea: daughter of Cynnane; wife of Philip III Arrhidaeus; took the name Eurydice on marriage; allied herself and her husband against Polyperchon; forced to commit suicide by Olympias in 317.

Agathocles: son of Lysimachus by Nicaea; successful general, especially against Demetrius; fell out with Lysimachus and was killed by him in 283 or 282.

Alcetas: brother of Perdiccas, fought on after his death; defeated by Antigonus in 319 and later killed trying to escape from imprisonment.

Alexander, son of Polyperchon: joint leader of Polyperchon's viceregal forces; ally of Antigonus against Cassander in Greece; went over to Cassander's side in 315, but was soon assassinated.

Alexander III of Macedon (336–323), the Great: stabilized Macedon before heading east; conquered the Persian empire 334–330; his death in Babylon in 323 triggered the succession crisis.

Alexander IV of Macedon (323–ca. 309): son of Alexander III; killed by Cassander to prevent his coming of age.

Alexander V of Macedon (297–294): son of Cassander; ruler or coruler of Macedon with his brother Antipater I; killed by Demetrius.

Alexarchus: eccentric brother of Cassander, founded a utopian community on the Athos peninsula called Ouranopolis, the Heavenly City.

Amastris: Persian princess; married to Craterus at the mass Susa wedding of April 324; later married Dionysius, ruler of Heraclea Pontica; on his death, ruled as regent for her sons, in alliance with Antigonus; married Lysimachus in 302; killed, apparently by her sons, ca. 284.

Antigenes: commander of a crack infantry regiment; appointed satrap of Susiana in 320; brutally killed by Antigonus in 317 after Gabene.

Antigonus Gonatas: son of Demetrius Poliorcetes; king of Macedon 276–239.

Antigonus Monophthalmus (the One-Eyed): satrap of Phrygia for Alexander the Great; reappointed in 323 and then again in 320; in 320 also made Antipater's Royal General of Asia; used this position as a springboard to make himself ruler of all Asia by 314; died at Ipsus in 301.

Antiochus I of Asia (281–261): son of Seleucus; made coruler with responsibility for the eastern satrapies in 294 or 293.

Antipater: viceroy of Macedon during Alexander III's eastern campaigns; lost out to Perdiccas after Alexander's death, but regained the full regency in 320, only to die a year later of old age.

Antipater I of Macedon (297–294): son of Cassander, ruler or coruler of Macedon with his brother Alexander V; killed by Lysimachus ca. 293.

Apama: noble Iranian; married to Seleucus at the mass Susa wedding of April 324; unlike the other couples of the forced marriages, they stayed together; died ca. 300.

Aristonous: Bodyguard of Alexander the Great; fought for Perdiccas in the First War of the Successors; retired to Macedon, where he was killed by Cassander in 316.

Arrhidaeus: half brother of Alexander III, *see* **Philip III** of Macedon.

Arrhidaeus: Macedonian noble, responsible for the cortège containing Alexander's body; interim coregent in 320; awarded governorship of Hellespontine Phrygia in 320 but forced out by Antigonus in 319.

Arsinoe: daughter of Ptolemy I and Berenice; married successively to Lysimachus, Ptolemy Ceraunus (her half brother), and Ptolemy II (her full brother); first woman to be granted divine honors during her lifetime.

Asander: made satrap of Caria in 323 and reappointed in 320; originally an ally of Antigonus, but defected in 315; brought to heel by Antigonus in 313.

Attalus: originally an ally of Meleager, but soon joined Perdiccas; one of the rebels after Perdiccas's assassination; defeated by Antigonus in 319 and later killed trying to escape from imprisonment.

Barsine: noble Iranian mistress of Alexander the Great, by whom she had Heracles; killed by Polyperchon and Cassander in 309.

Berenice: first the mistress and later the preferred wife of Ptolemy I; mother of Ptolemy II and Arsinoe.

Cassander of Macedon (regent 316–305; king 305–297): son of Antipater; passed over for succession to regency; joined forces with Antigonus and seized Macedon in 316; married Thessalonice; killed Rhoxane and Alexander IV and was responsible for killing Heracles; joined anti-Antigonid alliance and helped defeat the Antigonids in 301.

Chandragupta (c. 360–298): founder of the Maurya empire of India; clashed with Seleucus and won large chunks of territory.

Cleitus: associate of Craterus and in command of the Macedonian navy in the Lamian War (323–322); at first loyal to Perdiccas but changed sides; awarded the satrapy of Lydia in 320 but forced out by Antigonus in 319; died after defeat by Antigonus in 318.

Cleomenes: born and bred in Egypt; appointed satrap, or perhaps financial administrator, of Egypt by Alexander in 331; killed by Ptolemy I in 322.

Cleopatra: sister of Alexander III of Macedon; wife of Alexander I of Molossia; ruled Molossia after his death; promised to Leonnatus, then Perdiccas, and later Ptolemy I; killed by Antigonus late in 309 or early in 308.

Craterus: one of Alexander's most trusted generals; Alexander's death found him in Cilicia; allied himself with Antipater for the Lamian War and then to deal with Perdiccas and Eumenes; died in battle with Eumenes in 320.

Cratesipolis: wife of Alexander, son of Polyperchon; after his death in 315, set up an independent enclave in Sicyon and Corinth; hung on there until Ptolemy I's takeover in 309.

Cynnane: half sister of Alexander III; mother of Adea; killed (by accident?) by Alcetas in 321.

Darius III: last Achaemenid king of the Persian empire; killed by his own men in 330 following defeat by Alexander the Great.

Deidameia: sister of Pyrrhus; once betrothed to Alexander IV, but married Demetrius Poliorcetes.

Demetrius of Phalerum: ruler of Athens 317–307 for Cassander; ousted by Demetrius Poliorcetes; fled eventually to Alexandria.

Demetrius Poliorcetes (the Besieger): flamboyant and erratic son and heir of Antigonus Monophthalmus; his father's right-hand man in the 300s; recovered after Ipsus and came to rule Macedon from 294 to 288; following an overambitious invasion of Asia, died in captivity under Seleucus's protection in 282.

Demosthenes: persistent opponent of Philip II and Alexander III, warning his fellow Athenians about Macedonian intentions for Athens and southern Greece; accused of embezzling some of Harpalus's money and exiled; returned just before the Lamian War, but his death was demanded by Antipater after victory in the war; committed suicide as a fugitive on the island of Calauria in 322, aged sixty-two.

Eumenes of Cardia: secretary and archivist to Philip II and Alexander III; awarded satrapy of Cappadocia in 323; fought on after Perdiccas's death until defeat by Antigonus in 319; allied himself to Antigonus in 318, but then soon to Polyperchon; killed by Antigonus in 317 after Gabene.

Eurydice: daughter of Antipater; first wife of Ptolemy I; mother of Ptolemy Ceraunus, Ptolemais, and Lysandra.

Eurydice: *see* **Adea**.

Harpalus: close associate of Alexander III, entrusted with the financial administration of the empire; on Alexander's return from India, absconded with a large amount of money, first to Tarsus and then to Athens, where his money helped finance the Lamian War; assassinated on Crete in 323.

Hephaestion: the closest friend, probable lover, and second-in-command of Alexander III; died in 324, probably from alcohol abuse, to Alexander's great grief.

Heracles: illegitimate son of Alexander III; never a contender for the Macedonian throne until 309, when Polyperchon set out to install him but treacherously killed him instead on Cassander's orders.

Iolaus (or Iollas): son of Antipater; cupbearer to Alexander the Great, and hence fell under suspicion of having poisoned him; died ca. 320; his tomb was desecrated by Olympias in 317.

Lachares: ruler of Athens from ca. 297 until defeat by Demetrius Poliorcetes in 295.

Lanassa: daughter of Agathocles, king of Syracuse; briefly married to Pyrrhus before marrying Demetrius.

Leonnatus: Bodyguard of Alexander the Great; outmaneuvered by Perdiccas in the power struggle following Alexander's death; sided with Antipater, while eyeing the Macedonian throne for himself, as husband of Cleopatra; killed in 323, early in the Lamian War.

Leosthenes: commander of the Greek forces in the Lamian War (323–322), during which he was killed.

Lysandra: daughter of Ptolemy I and Eurydice; married Alexander V and then Agathocles; fled to Seleucus's court during the civil war following Agathocles' execution by his father.

Lysimachus: Bodyguard of Alexander the Great; awarded Thrace in 323 and reappointed in 320; tied up in Thrace for many years, but emerged in the 300s and led the coalition forces against Antigonus and Demetrius at Ipsus in 301; gained Asia Minor and then took over Macedon as well in 284; his kingdom fell into civil war in 283; defeated and killed by Seleucus at Corupedium in 281.

Meleager: infantry commander under Alexander the Great; tried to seize power after Alexander's death in 323 but killed by Perdiccas.

Menander: Companion of Alexander the Great, appointed satrap of Lydia by Alexander in 331; reappointed after his death in 323 but replaced in 320.

Menander of Athens (ca. 344–292): foremost surviving author of New Comedy plays.

Menelaus: brother of Ptolemy I and governor of Cyprus from ca. 315 until defeat by Demetrius Poliorcetes in 306.

Nearchus of Crete: Alexander III's most trusted admiral; after Alexander's death joined Antigonus's court, and eventually became one of young Demetrius's advisers.

Neoptolemus: a Molossian prince in Alexander's court; ordered by Perdiccas to help Eumenes in Asia Minor, but instead joined Antipater's side; died in a battlefield duel with Eumenes in 320.

Nicaea: daughter of Antipater, married first to Perdiccas and then to Lysimachus; mother of Agathocles.

Nicanor: son of Antipater; appointed satrap of Cappadocia in 320 but forced out by Antigonus ca. 319; killed by Olympias in 317.

Nicanor: general of Cassander, garrison commander of Piraeus from 319 until 317, when he was executed by Cassander.

Olympias: wife (Philip II), mother (Alexander III), and grandmother (Alexander IV) of Macedonian kings; an enemy of Antipater, in exile in her native Epirus from 330; returned at Polyperchon's invitation in 317; killed by Cassander in 316.

Peithon: Bodyguard of Alexander the Great; appointed satrap of Media in 323; interim coregent in 320; too ambitious for his own good, he was killed by Antigonus in 316.

Perdiccas: Bodyguard of Alexander the Great; seized power after his death by gaining control of the two kings; the First War of the Successors was intended to curb his ambitions; assassinated by staff officers while invading Egypt in 320.

Peucestas: Bodyguard of Alexander the Great, appointed satrap of Persis in 323 and reappointed in 320; demoted by Antigonus as part of his settlement of the east in 316.

Phila: daughter of Antipater; married first to Craterus and then to Demetrius Poliorcetes; committed suicide in 288.

Philetaerus: governor or treasurer of Pergamum for Antigonus, then Lysimachus; fled to Seleucus in 283 during the civil war in Lysimachus's kingdom; with Seleucus's help, became the first ruler of independent Pergamum.

Philip II of Macedon (359–336): instigator of Macedonian greatness; unified and secured Macedon; hugely expanded its military capacity; planned to invade the Persian empire but was assassinated; his son Alexander III inherited the task.

Philip III of Macedon (323–317): birth name Arrhidaeus; mentally impaired half brother of Alexander the Great; a pawn in Meleager's, then Perdiccas's, then Adea's maneuvers; killed on Olympias's orders.

Philip IV of Macedon (297): son of Cassander, ruled for only a few months before dying.

Pleistarchus: younger brother of Cassander; one of Cassander's main generals in Greece from 313 onward; awarded Cilicia after Ipsus, but lost it to Demetrius in 298; established by Lysimachus as an independent dynast in Caria.

Polemaeus (called Ptolemaeus, i.e., Ptolemy, in some sources): nephew of Antigonus Monophthalmus and an extremely effective general in the 310s; briefly independent in central Greece 310–309 before being killed by Ptolemy I on Cos.

Polyperchon: Craterus's second-in-command in Cilicia at the time of Alexander's death; Antipater's deputy in Macedon 320–319; replaced Antipater as regent in 319; ally of Olympias; ousted by Cassander; reduced to some parts of the Peloponnese; tried to regain power by restoring Heracles in 309; died ca. 303.

Prepelaus: a general of Cassander from ca. 315; last heard of at Ipsus (301).

Ptolemais: daughter of Ptolemy I and Eurydice; became one of the many wives of Demetrius Poliorcetes.

Ptolemy I of Egypt (satrap 323–305; king 305–285): Bodyguard of Alexander the Great; awarded Egypt in 323 and reappointed in 320; pursued a policy of creating buffer zones around Egypt; successfully defended Egypt against two invasions (320, 306); expanded especially into the Aegean area, but an attempted takeover of Greece in 309 failed; abdicated in favor of his son Ptolemy II in 285 and died in 283.

Ptolemy II of Egypt (285–246): son of Ptolemy I by Berenice (and so not his eldest son).

Ptolemy Ceraunus: son of Ptolemy I by Eurydice (and so his eldest son); denied the throne by his father's preference of Berenice; in exile in Lysimachus's court, then Seleucus's; assassinated Seleucus and made himself king of Macedon (281–279); killed during Celtic invasion.

Pyrrhus of Epirus (306–302, 297–272): restless great-nephew of Olympias and second cousin of Alexander the Great; allied first with, then against Demetrius (then with, then against again); later a thorn in the side of the Romans and, briefly, king of Sicily.

Rhoxane (or Roxane): Bactrian princess who became Alexander III's first wife in 327; pregnant when he died, gave birth a few months later to Alexander IV; killed, along with her son, by Cassander ca. 309.

Seleucus I of Asia (305–281): after Alexander's death, rose rapidly thanks to alliances with Perdiccas, then Antipater; appointed satrap of Babylonia in 320; ousted by Antigonus in 316; made a dramatic return in 311; defended his province, and established his realm from the Euphrates eastward; after Ipsus, added Syria; after Corupedium, added Asia Minor; killed by Ptolemy Ceraunus while trying to add Macedon as well.

Seuthes III of Thrace (ca. 330– ca. 300): Lysimachus's bête noire, king of the Odrysians and effective ruler of inland Thrace.

Stratonice: daughter of Demetrius, granddaughter of Antipater, and niece of Cassander; married first to Seleucus and then to his son Antiochus.

Telesphorus: nephew of Antigonus; a not very successful general in Greece in 312; briefly independent in Elis.

Thessalonice: half sister of Alexander III; captured and subsequently married by Cassander in 316; failed to keep the peace between Antipater I and Alexander V; murdered by Antipater.

Zipoetes of Bithynia (327–280): ruler of independent Bithynia; subdued by Antigonus but resurgent after Ipsus.

Genealogies

None of these genealogies is complete. For fuller versions, and more trees, see F. W. Walbank et al. (eds), *The Cambridge Ancient History*, vol. 7.1: *The Hellenistic World* (2nd ed., Cambridge: Cambridge University Press, 1984), 484–91, or P. Green, *Alexander to Actium: The Historical Evolution of the Hellenistic Age* (Berkeley: University of California Press, 1990), 732–9.

Argeads

Philip II
|
seven wives, including:

Olympias of Epirus   Philinna of Larissa

Cleopatra   Alexander III the Great   Arrhidaeus (Philip III)
m. Alexander I   m. Rhoxane of Bactria   m. Adea (Eurydice)
of Epirus |
                        Alexander IV

Antigonids

Antigonus the One-Eyed
m. Stratonice

|

Demetrius the Besieger
m. six wives, including:

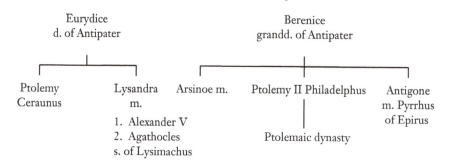

Phila	Deidameia	Ptolemais	Lanassa
d. of Antipater	sister of Pyrrhus	d. of Ptolemy I	d. of Agathocles
	of Epirus		of Syracuse

Antigonus Gonatas   Stratonice m. 1 Seleucus I
m. Phila, d. of Seleucus I   m. 2 Antiochus I

Ptolemies

Ptolemy I

|

four or five wives, including:

Eurydice   Berenice
d. of Antipater   grandd. of Antipater

Ptolemy   Lysandra   Arsinoe m.   Ptolemy II Philadelphus   Antigone
Ceraunus   m.   m. Pyrrhus
                 1. Alexander V   of Epirus
                 2. Agathocles
                 s. of Lysimachus   Ptolemaic dynasty

Note that Arsinoe, who married her brother Ptolemy II, had previously been married to Lysimachus and then to her half brother Ptolemy Ceraunus, while Ptolemy II had previously been married to another Arsinoe, the d. of Lysimachus.

Antipatrids

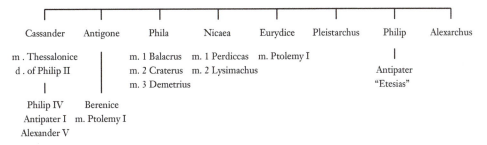

Antipater

at least thirteen children, including:

Cassander	Antigone	Phila	Nicaea	Eurydice	Pleistarchus	Philip	Alexarchus
m . Thessalonice d . of Philip II		m. 1 Balacrus m. 2 Craterus m. 3 Demetrius	m. 1 Perdiccas m. 2 Lysimachus	m. Ptolemy I		Antipater "Etesias"	
Philip IV Antipater I Alexander V	Berenice m. Ptolemy I						

The Molossian Royal House

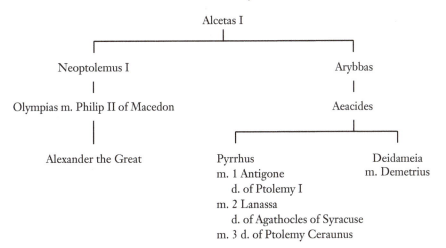

Alcetas I

Neoptolemus I — Arybbas

Olympias m. Philip II of Macedon — Aeacides

Alexander the Great

Pyrrhus
m. 1 Antigone
    d. of Ptolemy I
m. 2 Lanassa
    d. of Agathocles of Syracuse
m. 3 d. of Ptolemy Ceraunus

Deidameia
m. Demetrius

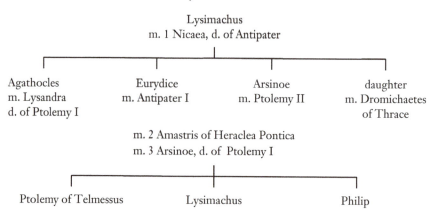

Lysimachids

Lysimachus
m. 1 Nicaea, d. of Antipater

Agathocles	Eurydice	Arsinoe	daughter
m. Lysandra	m. Antipater I	m. Ptolemy II	m. Dromichaetes
d. of Ptolemy I			of Thrace

m. 2 Amastris of Heraclea Pontica
m. 3 Arsinoe, d. of Ptolemy I

Ptolemy of Telmessus	Lysimachus	Philip

Notes

Abbreviations

Ager = Ager, S., 1996, *Interstate Arbitrations in the Greek World, 337–90 BC* (Berkeley: University of California Press).

Austin = Austin, M., 2006, *The Hellenistic World from Alexander to the Roman Conquest: A Selection of Ancient Sources in Translation* (2nd ed., Cambridge: Cambridge University Press).

Bagnall/Derow = Bagnall, R., and Derow, P., 2004, *The Hellenistic Period: Historical Texts in Translation* (2nd ed., Oxford: Blackwell) (1st ed. title: *Greek Historical Documents: The Hellenistic Period*).

Burstein = Burstein, S., 1985, *The Hellenistic Age from the Battle of Ipsos to the Death of Kleopatra VII* (Cambridge: Cambridge University Press).

Curtius = Quintus Curtius Rufus, *History of Alexander*.

DS = Diodorus of Sicily, *Library of History*.

FGrH = Jacoby, F., *Die Fragmente der griechischen Historiker* (Berlin: Weidmann, 1923–58; CD-ROM ed., Leiden: Brill, 2004).

Grant = Grant, F., 1953, *Hellenistic Religions: The Age of Syncretism* (Indianapolis: Bobbs-Merrill).

Harding = Harding, P., 1985, *From the End of the Peloponnesian War to the Battle of Ipsus* (Cambridge: Cambridge University Press).

Heckel/Yardley = Heckel, W., and Yardley, J. C., 2004, *Alexander the Great: Historical Texts in Translation* (Oxford: Blackwell).

Justin = Marcus Junianus Justinus, *Epitome of the Philippic History of Pompeius Trogus*

SSR = Giannantoni, G., 1990, *Socratis et Socraticorum Reliquiae*, 4 vols. (Naples: Bibliopolis).

Welles   = Welles, C. B., 1934/1974, *Royal Correspondence in the Hellenistic Period* (New Haven: Yale University Press; repr. Chicago: Ares).

Preface

1. Plutarch, *Life of Alexander* 8.2.
2. See I. Morris, "The Greater Athenian State," in Morris and Scheidel 2009, 99–177; and note that Polybius does not include the Athenian "empire" in his survey of empires prior to the Roman one (*Histories* 1.2).
3. Willa Cather, *O Pioneers!*, p. 44, Penguin ed.

Chapter 1

1. Arrian, *Anabasis* 24–6 relates this story, along with other glimpses of Alexander's last days; see also the other texts translated in Heckel/Yardley, 272–80.
2. The symptoms are described by Plutarch, *Life of Alexander* 73–7, and Arrian, *Anabasis* 24–6. The main innocent suggestions are malaria (Engels 1978a; Hammond 1989b, 304–5), peritonitis (Ashton/Parkinson 1990), acute surgical complications (Battersby 2007), and encephalitis (Marr/Calisher 2003). Bosworth 1971 cannot rule out poisoning on historical grounds, nor can Schep 2009 on medical grounds. We owe accurate knowledge of the time of Alexander's death to Depuydt 1997.
3. Curtius 10.10.14.
4. Plutarch, *Life of Agesilaus* 15.4.
5. On Hyperides: Ps.-Plutarch, *Lives of the Ten Orators* 849f. On Cassander: Plutarch, *Life of Alexander* 74.2–3. The story sounds over-melodramatic, but it may contain an element of truth.
6. On this document, the *Royal Ephemerides* or *Royal Journal*, see especially Bosworth 1971 and Hammond 1988. Another version of its value as propaganda is given by Heckel 2007. The view that it was a much later forgery is argued by, e.g., L. Pearson, "The Diary and Letters of Alexander the Great," *Historia* 3 (1955), 429–55; repr. in Griffith 1966, 1–27. in Griffith 1966.
7. DS 16.93.7; Justin 9.6.5–6.
8. "Satrapy" is the term for a province of the Achaemenid empire; a "satrap" was the governor of a satrapy.
9. For Alexander's innovatory style of kingship, see Fredricksmeyer 2000 and Spawforth 2007; for Alexander's attitude toward easterners, Bosworth 1980.
10. Carney 2001. Guesses began in antiquity: see e.g. Plutarch, *Life of Alexander* 77.5; DS 18.2.2.
11. Bosworth 2000; Heckel 1988; text in Heckel/Yardley, 281–89. Heckel skillfully argued for a date early in 316 for the forgery, but Bosworth's 308 seems more plausible.

12. A talent was the largest unit of Greek currency. In this book I have assumed that one talent had a spending power equivalent to $600,000. Greek money was not on the whole fiduciary, but worth its weight; the primary meaning of "talent" is a weight—close to 26 kgs (somewhat over 57 lbs). The breakdown is as follows: 36,000 obols = 6,000 drachmas = 60 minas = 1 talent. A mercenary soldier in the period covered in this book might expect to receive at most 2 drachmas a day, to cover all his expenses; see Griffith 1935/1984, 294–307.

13. DS 18.4.1–6. Some scholars doubt the authenticity of all or some of the "Last Plans": see e.g. Hampl in Griffith 1966. But see e.g. Hammond 1989b, 281–85.

14. See Fraser 1996.

15. DS 18.8.2–7; Justin 13.5.2–7; Curtius 10.2.4.

16. DS 18.8.4.

17. Justin 13.1.12, clearly speaking with hindsight.

18. Arrian, *Anabasis* 7.26.3; Curtius 10.5.5; Justin 12.15.8; DS 17.117.4.

Chapter 2

1. On this practice in Persia, see Briant 2002, 302–15; in Macedon, Hammond 1989a, 54–5.

2. Slightly distorted in Curtius 10.5.16.

3. This percolation is presented by Curtius (10.6–10) as the physical presence of ordinary troops in the meeting room. None of our other sources for these events (Justin 13.2–4; DS 18.2–3; Arrian, *After Alexander* fr.1.1–8) contains this feature, and I judge it to be a dramatic or distorted way of representing the percolation. Otherwise I have broadly followed Curtius's account. There are, however, serious difficulties with Curtius and all the sources, not least that, implausibly, none of them has the meeting paying any attention to Arrhidaeus until forced to do so. The extant accounts read more like dramatizations of the main issues than reliable accounts of who proposed what. Other discussions of the Babylon meetings: Atkinson/Yardley 2009; Bosworth 2002, ch. 2; Errington 1970; Meeus 2008; Romm 2011, ch. 2.

4. Curtius 10.5.4.

5. Bosworth 1992, 75–9.

6. Arrian, *After Alexander* fr. 1.3; for the meaning of the Greek phrase, see Anson 1992, Hammond 1985, and Meeus 2009a.

7. Justin 13.4.4.

8. Errington 1970.

9. For full details, see DS 18.3; Curtius 10.1–4; Arrian, *After Alexander* fr. 1.5–8; Dexippus fr. 1; with Appendix 2 in Heckel 1988.

10. On the preserved Argead tombs at Vergina, the modern village near the site of ancient Aegae, see especially Andronicos, tempered by Borza 1990, 253–66, and by Borza/Palagia 2007.

11. Carney, *Olympias*, 61.

Chapter 3

1. R. G. Kent, *Old Persian: Grammar, Texts, Lexicon* (2nd ed., New Haven: Yale University Press, 1953), 151–2. Alternatively: http://www.livius.org/aa-ac/achaemenians/XPh.html.
2. Curtius 9.7.11.
3. DS 18.7.1.
4. DS 18.7.2.
5. See especially Billows 1990, 292–305; Billows 1995, 146–82; Briant 1978/1982; Fraser 1996. For the general connection between empire building and mass migration, see Pagden 2001.
6. See Lecuyot in Cribb and Herrmann 2007, 155–62. For the city's history, see Holt 1999. The site has apparently been pillaged and badly damaged by the Taliban in recent years.
7. The inscription is Burstein 49; it can also be found at Holt 1999, 175.
8. The guild is first heard of in an inscription of 287 BCE, but as an already well-established organization: *IG* II² 1132.
9. Holt 1999, 44.
10. Robertson 1993, 73.
11. On Pytheas, see B. Cunliffe, *The Extraordinary Voyage of Pytheas the Greek* (New York: Penguin Books, 2003).
12. *Koinē* was such an important feature of the new world that the scholarly term "Hellenistic" for the entire period from Alexander's death in 323 until the death of the last of the Macedonian rulers in 30 BCE is derived from the Greek verb meaning "to speak Greek."
13. The few fragments of Manetho have been collected as *FGrH* 609, those of Berossus as *FGrH* 680. On both historians, see J. Dillery, "Greek Historians of the Near East: Clio's 'Other' Sons," in J. Marincola (ed.), *A Companion to Greek and Roman Historiography*, vol. 1 (Oxford: Blackwell, 2007), 221–30.
14. Main literary sources for the Lamian War: DS 18.8–18; Plutarch, *Life of Phocion* 23–9, *Life of Demosthenes* 27–31; Hyperides 6 (*Funeral Speech*).
15. The evidence for this incident is difficult to interpret: see Carney 2006, 67–8.
16. Arrian, *After Alexander* fr. 12 (cf. Plutarch, *Life of Pyrrhus* 8.2).
17. Hyperides 6 (*Funeral Speech*).
18. Plutarch, *Life of Demosthenes* 30.5.
19. The historian Polybius's description of mercenaries at 13.6.4. See also Niccolò Machiavelli, *The Prince*, ch. 12: "Such troops are disunited, ambitious, insubordinate, treacherous, insolent among friends, cowardly before foes, and without fear of God or faith with man" (trans. N. H. Thomson).
20. Text and discussion of the tablet in Jordan 1980.
21. On polygamy etc., see Ogden 1999.

Chapter 4

1. e.g. Inarus of Egypt in 454 (Ctesias fr. 14.39 Lenfant); Ariobarzanes in 362 (Harpocration s.v. "Ariobarzanes").

2. Pausanias, *Guide to Greece* 1.6.3.

3. We are fortunate to have the text of the revised constitution: *SEG* 9.1, translated as Austin 29 and Harding 126. Cyrenaica did not entirely shake off its political troubles, but it stayed in Ptolemaic hands until the Romans took it over in 96 BCE.

4. Arrian, *After Alexander* fr. 1.22–3; Polyaenus, *Stratagems* 8.60.

5. Bosworth 1993, 425.

6. This is a much-discussed episode of Alexander's life. See e.g. Cartledge 2004, 265–70; Lane Fox 1973, 200–18. Texts in Heckel/Yardley, 217–22.

7. Full description at DS 18.26–27. See Miller 1986 for discussion of the catafalque, and Erskine 2002 for the whole episode.

8. DS 18.27.4.

9. Aelian, *Miscellany* 12.64.

10. On Alexandria's Alexander artwork, see Stewart 1993, Index s.v. "Alexandria."

11. A particularly good study of Ptolemy's quest for legitimacy is Bingen 2007, ch. 1.

12. Eumenes' dream: DS 18.60.4–6; Seleucus's dream: DS 19.90.4; Seleucus and Apollo: Justin 15.4.2–6.

13. What little remains of his history is collected as *FGrH* 138.

14. Craterus's monument: Plutarch, *Life of Alexander* 40.5; the inscribed base of the bronze group has been preserved: *Fouilles de Delphes* 3.4.2, no. 137. Craterus's pretensions: Arrian, *After Alexander* fr. 19. Leonnatus's pretensions: Arrian, *After Alexander* fr. 12 (cf. Plutarch, *Life of Pyrrhus* 8.2). On the Mosaic, see Stewart 1993 130–50. On Alcetas's tomb, Stewart 1993, 312. On the topic of legitimation in general, Meeus 2009c.

15. On Alexander's postmortem influence, see also Errington 1976; Goukowsky 1978/1981; Lianou 2010; Meeus 2009c; Stewart 1993.

16. The starting point for further discussion is Cartledge 2000.

17. J. K. Davies in Walbank et al. 1984, 306.

18. Plutarch tells the most famous story at *Life of Alexander* 14.2–5. The complete texts can be found at *SSR* V B 31–49.

19. *SSR* V H 70.

20. Diogenes Laertius, *Lives of Eminent Philosophers* 10.119; Epicurus, *Vatican Sayings* 58.

21. Posidippus 63 Austin/Bastianini.

22. Posidippus 55 Austin/Bastianini; translation by Kathryn Gutzwiller.

23. *Palatine Anthology* 12.46; translation by Kathryn Gutzwiller.

24. On the education of women in the Hellenistic period, see Pomeroy 1977.

25. Women as benefactors: Burstein 45. Women holding public office: H. W. Pleket, *Epigraphica*, vol. 2: *Texts on the Social History of the Greek World* (Leiden: Brill, 1969), nos. 2, 5, 170. Women signing their own marriage contracts: *P.Tebt.* 104.

26. Thucydides, *The Peloponnesian War* 3.82.8; see the perspicacious remarks of J. de Romilly in ch. 3 of *The Rise and Fall of States According to Greek Authors* (Ann Arbor: University of Michigan Press, 1977).

Chapter 5

1. Within the forty years covered by this book, Agathocles made himself supreme in Syracuse and then in Sicily as a whole, and nearly defeated the Carthaginians in North Africa. In 304, after finally defeating his rivals, he declared himself king of Syracuse. He died in 289. A little farther north, the Romans were forcing all the northern Italian tribes to submit to their rule. The Greeks of the south would be next.
2. Plutarch, *Life of Eumenes* 7.4–7.
3. On Philip's military innovations, see Hammond 1989a, ch. 6.
4. Polybius, *Histories* 5.84.3; for war elephants in the ancient world, see Scullard 1974; Epplett 2007.
5. For the claim that Egypt was now spear-won land, see DS 18.39.5, 20.76.7.
6. Schlumberger 1969.
7. Adea Eurydice's actions at Triparadeisus are difficult to reconstruct from the conflicting sources; see e.g. Carney 2000, 132–34.
8. DS 18.39.2. For fuller details of the distribution of satrapies, see DS 18.39.5–6 and Arrian, *After Alexander* fr. 1.34–8 (= Austin 30).
9. Arrian, *After Alexander* fr. 1.34.

Chapter 6

1. Plutarch, *Life of Eumenes* 11.3–5.
2. DS 19.16.
3. DS 18.58.2.
4. DS 18.56.8.
5. On the Greek cities in the early Hellenistic period, see especially Billows 1990, ch. 6; Billows 2003; Chamoux 2003, ch. 6; Dixon 2007; Gruen 1993; Shipley 2000, 186–207.
6. Polybius, *Histories* 15.24.4.
7. Many examples in Welles.
8. Bagnall/Derow 14, dating from 283.
9. See Chaniotis 2005, 116–17.
10. McNicoll and Milner 1997, 103.
11. See Chamoux 2003, 209–10, for discussion of a document from 206 BCE, showing how hard it was for a small town to pay for building its own defenses.
12. Austin 54; Bagnall/Derow 13.

Chapter 7

1. There is a detailed account of Polyperchon's Megalopolis campaign in DS 18.70–71.
2. Plutarch, *On the Fortune of Alexander* 338a.
3. See Murray 2012.
4. Theophrastus, *Characters* 8.6.
5. e.g. Aristophanes, *Acharnians* 628–58, *Frogs* 389–90.
6. Vitruvius, *On Architecture* 7.5.2–3; see Pollitt, ch. 9.
7. Green 1990, 234. The translation of Theocritus that, to my mind, best captures his spirit is that of Robert Wells, *Theocritus: The Idylls* (New York: Carcanet, 1988).
8. Pliny, *Natural History* 34.65.
9. Aelian, *Miscellany* 2.3; Pliny, *Natural History* 35.95.
10. DS 19.11.6; Aelian, *Miscellany* 13.36. The lunar crater Ariadaeus is named, or misnamed, after Philip III Arrhidaeus.
11. More details in DS 19.51.2–5.
12. The identity of the occupants of Tomb 2 is extremely controversial. I follow the most recent work on the subject, that of Borza and Palagia 2007, but the alternative view, that the tomb's main occupant was Philip II himself (along with his seventh and last wife), promulgated by the tomb's original excavator, Andronicos, is still extremely popular, and is naturally enough the default position for tourists. On the hunt painting, see Saatsoglou-Paliadeli 2007.
13. For some of the later history of the city, see Mark Mazower, *Salonica, City of Ghosts* (London: HarperCollins, 2005).

Chapter 8

1. The main ancient sources are DS 18.58–63, 73, 19.12–5, 17–32, 34.7–8, 37–44; Plutarch, *Life of Eumenes* 13–9. My discussion is indebted above all to Bosworth 2002, ch. 4.
2. DS 19.12.3–13.5 contains more details of Eumenes' departure, or escape, from Babylonia.
3. DS 19.41.1.
4. Curtius 4.15.7.
5. DS 19.46.1.
6. DS 19.48.3.
7. Details of Chandragupta's administration may be found in Mookerji 1966/1999.
8. They are preserved as *FGrH* 715.
9. If it was a drunken rampage. The destruction of the palace may have been an act of policy; archaeology has revealed that the rooms were emptied of their treasures before the fire was set. See e.g. Fredricksmeyer 2000, 145–9.
10. Phylarchus fr. 12 (*FGrH* 81 F12).

11. The evidence for Antigonus's administration of Asia is exiguous. Billows 1990, chs. 7 and 8, has made the most of it.
12. Arrian, *Anabasis* 2.4.8–9; Curtius 4.1.13–14.

Chapter 9

1. DS 19.56.2.
2. Ps.-Aristotle, *Oeconomica* 1345b–1346a; for the assignation of this passage to Antigonus's times, see Billows 1990, 289–90; for further discussion of the passage, Aperghis 2004b, 117–35.
3. *SIG³* 344 = Welles 3, Ager 13, Austin 48.
4. Theophrastus, *Inquiry into Plants* 4.8.4.
5. DS 19.90.4; see also Appian, *Syrian History* 56.
6. Text at DS 19.61.1–3 = Austin 35.
7. DS 19.63.2.
8. DS 19.63.4.
9. An inscription has survived, *IG* II² 450, that places Asander in Athens in the winter of 314/313, but whether his visit preceded or followed Prepelaus's expedition to Caria is uncertain.

Chapter 10

1. Plutarch, *Life of Demetrius* 6.1.
2. Details of the Nabataean campaign can be found in DS 19.94–100.2.
3. *The Devil's Dictionary* (1911), s.v.
4. Text in Austin 38–9; Bagnall/Derow 6; Harding 132.
5. Plutarch, *Life of Demetrius* 7.3.
6. AD (Astronomical Diaries) 1–309, obv. 9, available at http://www.livius.org/cg-cm/chronicles/bchp-diadochi/diadochi_06.html.
7. ABC (*Assyrian and Babylonian Chronicles*) 10: rev. 23–25, available at http://www.livius.org/di-dn/diadochi/diadochi_t23.html.
8. Plutarch, *Life of Demetrius* 19.4

Chapter 11

1. DS 19.105.4.
2. As late as 305 in Egypt: *P.Dem. Louvre* 2427, 2440.
3. Plutarch, *On Spinelessness* 530d. There has been speculation in the press that the new royal grave discovered at Aegae/Vergina in 2009 is that of Heracles (see e.g. http://www.ekathimerini.com/4dcgi/_w_articles_politics_0_31/08/2009_110269), but it is far too soon to tell.
4. "A monument to the rewards of carefully limited ambitions" is Green's description (quoted in Ellis 1994, 66).

5. DS 20.37.2.
6. See Dixon 2007, 173–75.
7. For more on Cleopatra, see Carney 2000a, and Meeus 2009.
8. DS 20.106.2–3.
9. Habicht 1997, 153–54.
10. Plutarch, *Life of Demetrius* 10.3.
11. On the library, see Canfora 1990; Collins 2000; Erskine 1995.
12. The definitive account of Alexandria is Fraser 1972; Green 1990, ch. 6, is considerably shorter.
13. On the Septuagint, see Collins 2000.
14. The famous earlier fire, in the time of Julius Caesar, did not, as is usually thought, damage the main library. See Canfora, 66–70.
15. P.-A. Beaulieu in Briant and Joannès 2006, 17–36.
16. See e.g. Plato, *Timaeus* 22a–23b.
17. Theocritus's *Idyll* 17 in praise of Ptolemy II is a prime example.
18. "In the populous land of Egypt there is a crowd of bookish scribblers who get fed as they argue away interminably in the birdcage of the Muses," said the satirist Timon of Phlius (fr. 60 Wachsmuth; fr. 12 Diels).

Chapter 12

1. *IG* II² 469.9–10. A photograph of this decree is available, thanks to the Oxford University Centre for the Study of Ancient Documents, at http://www.csad.ox.ac.uk/CSAD/Images/200/Image286.html.
2. See P. Anderson, "The Divisions of Cyprus," *London Review of Books* 30.8 (April 24, 2008), 7–16; or online at http://www.lrb.co.uk/v30/n08/perry-anderson/the-divisions-of-cyprus.
3. Plutarch, *Life of Demetrius* 17.5; see also Appian, *Syrian History* 54; DS 20.53.2.
4. Plutarch, *Life of Demetrius* 25.4; see also Plutarch, *Precepts of Statecraft* 823c–d; Phylarchus fr. 31 (*FGrH* 81 F31). For discussion, see Hauben 1974.
5. Bosworth 2002, 246.
6. The nature of Hellenistic monarchy is, naturally, much debated. See especially Austin 1986; Bosworth 2002, ch. 7; Bringmann 1994; Beston 2000; Chamoux 2003, ch. 7; Gruen 1985; Ma 2003; Smith 1988; Walbank 1984.
7. Niccolò Machiavelli, *The Prince*, ch. 14 (trans. N. H. Thomson).
8. Plutarch, *Life of Demetrius* 42.3.
9. Plutarch, *Whether Old Men Should Engage in Politics* 790a.
10. Appian, *Syrian History* 61.
11. Durrell's *Reflections on a Marine Venus* (London: Faber and Faber, 1953) contains a spirited account of the siege, in a chapter perhaps unfortunately titled "The Sunny Colossus." Durrell is not unsound, but Berthold (1984, 66–80) is better.

12. Polybius, *Histories* 12.13.11. On Hellenistic technology in general, Lloyd 1973, ch. 7, but for technical details, see Oleson 2008. Demetrius's snail was reconstructed in theory by A. Rehm, "Antike Automobile," *Philologus* 317 (1937), 317–30.

13. Plutarch, *Life of Demetrius* 24.1.

14. e.g. DS 22.92.3, Plutarch, *Life of Demetrius* 2.2.

15. *The Flatterer*, fr. 4 Arnott; Athenaeus, *The Learned Banqueters* 587d. The line is addressed to a soldier, who in Menander's comedies of the period was often a Demetrius look-alike. See S. Lape, *Reproducing Athens: Menander's Comedy, Democratic Culture, and the Hellenistic City* (Princeton: Princeton University Press, 2004), 61–3.

16. Heckel 1992, 188.

17. A fragmentary constitution of the league survives: *IG* IV² 1.68 = Austin 50; Harding 138; Bagnall/Derow 8; Ager 14.

18. Plutarch, *Life of Demetrius* 3.

Chapter 13

1. Studies stressing or discussing Seleucid continuation of Achaemenid practices: Aperghis 2008; Briant 1990, 2010; Briant and Joannès 2006; Kuhrt and Sherwin-White 1988, 1994; McKenzie 1994; Sherwin-White and Kuhrt 1993; Tuplin 2008; Wolski 1984. For continuity in Ptolemaic Egypt: Manning 2010.

2. Curtius 9.1.1–2.

3. This paragraph skates over considerable debate about the degree of constitutionalism in early Macedon. See especially Adams 1986; Anson, 1985, 1991, 2008; Borza 1990 (ch. 10); Carlier 2000; Errington 1974, 1978, 1990 (ch. 6); Greenwalt 2010; Hammond 1989, 1993, 1999, 2000; Hammond and Walbank 1988; Hatzopoulos 1996; Lock 1977; Mooren 1983, 1998; O'Neil 1999, 2000.

4. Leriche in Cribb and Herrmann 2007, 131, 134.

5. Some idea of the increasing importance of gymnasia, and the increasing civic power wielded by their directors, is given by a second-century inscription from Macedon: Austin 137 = Bagnall/Derow 78.

6. Eddy 1961, 19.

7. More detailed studies of taxation in early Ptolemaic Egypt: Bingen 2007 and Thompson 1997; in early Seleucid Asia: Aperghis 2004b.

8. e.g. Polybius, *Histories* 30.26.9 on Antiochus IV (175–64).

9. *P.Tebt.* III 703 (= Bagnall/Derow 103, Burstein 101, Austin 319) gives a good impression of what a minor official was expected to do to ensure the system's smooth and profitable running. *P.Rev.* (= Bagnall/Derow 114, Austin 296–97) is another vital document for understanding the Ptolemaic taxation system; commentary in Bingen 2007, 157–88.

10. It is, of course, hard to be exact about such figures. See Manning 2010, 125–27.

11. Jenkins 1967, 59.

12. e.g. *P.Col.Zen.* II 66 = Bagnall/Derow 137, Austin 307; *P.Ryl.* IV 563 = Bagnall/Derow 90; *P.Lond.* 1954 = Austin 302; *P.Cairo Zen.* 59451 = Austin 308.

Chapter 14

1. Will 1984, 61.
2. Plutarch, *Life of Demetrius* 30.1.
3. Athenaeus, *The Learned Banqueters* 98d.
4. Polyaenus, *Stratagems* 4.12.1. See Bosworth 2002, 248–49, for dating this episode during the raids described by Plutarch, *Life of Demetrius* 31.2.
5. See Grainger 1990a.
6. Polybius, *Histories* 5.46.7, 54.12.
7. Most of the story of this remarkable woman lies outside the period covered in this book, but see Carney 2000a, 173–77; Macurdy 1932/1985, 111–30; S. Burstein, "Arsinoe II Philadelphos: A Revisionist View," in W. L. Adams and E. N. Borza (eds), *Philip II, Alexander the Great and the Macedonian Heritage* (Washington, DC: University Press of America, 1982), 197–212.
8. Plutarch, *Life of Demetrius* 33.1.
9. Where, in typical Successor fashion, he renamed the city he made his seat: Heraclea became Pleistarcheia. The defensive walls built probably by Pleistarchus are among the best preserved early Hellenistic fortifications: see McNicoll and Milner 1997, 75–81.
10. Plutarch, *Life of Demetrius* 34.2.
11. A stoa was a building containing offices and/or meeting rooms, but consisting most prominently of a long, covered colonnade designed for shelter from the elements; the stoas were therefore popular meeting places. The reconstructed Stoa of Attalus in the Athenian agora gives the best impression.
12. The therapeutic aspect of Hellenistic philosophy has only recently become more accepted within scholarly circles, thanks especially to Hadot 2002; Sharples 2006 is a good product of the new thinking.
13. Antiphon, Andocides, Lysias, Isocrates, Isaeus, Demosthenes, Aeschines, Lycurgus, Hyperides, and Deinarchus.

Chapter 15

1. Plutarch, *Life of Demetrius* 36.12.
2. The expression was coined by a later Macedonian king, Philip V (222–179), according to Polybius, *Histories* 18.11.5.
3. Delev 2000.
4. Plutarch, *Life of Pyrrhus* 8.2.
5. Plutarch, *Life of Pyrrhus* 10.5.
6. Duris of Samos, fr. 13 Jacoby; full text at Austin 43, Burstein 7, Grant p. 67.

7. Plutarch, *Life of Demetrius* 42.2.

8. Plutarch, *Life of Demetrius* 41.3.

9. Plutarch, *Life of Demetrius* 43.5. On the whole subject, see Murray 2012.

10. The villa of P. Fannius Synistor at Boscoreale: see Billows 1995, 45–55.

11. On Hellenistic religious developments, see especially Chamoux 2003, ch. 9; Mikalson 2006; Potter 2003; Shipley 2000, 153–76.

12. On Samothrace, see Cole 1984; on Eleusis, Mylonas 1961.

13. Plutarch, *On Isis and Osiris* 361f–362a; Tacitus, *Histories* 4.83–4 (= Austin 300).

14. Demetrius of Phalerum fr. 82a Stork/van Ophuijsen/Dorandi.

15. Lund 1992, 98.

16. Plutarch, *Life of Pyrrhus* 12.4.

17. Memnon of Heraclea, fr. 1.5.6 Jacoby. A later Hellenistic king was also named Ceraunus: Seleucus III Ceraunus, king of Syria from 226 to 223.

18. So Plutarch has Seleucus describe him (*Life of Demetrius* 38), with a hint at the significance of the anchor symbol to their line. It was said to be a Seleucid birthmark, passed down through the generations, as predicted by the anchor seal ring the god Apollo had given to Seleucus's mother after impregnating her with Seleucus.

19. Plutarch, *Life of Demetrius* 38.7; Appian, 59–61.

20. Plutarch, *Life of Demetrius* 49.2.

21. Plutarch, *Life of Demetrius* 51.3.

Chapter 16

1. There is an excellent account of the excavations at Seuthopolis in Dimitrov and Čičikova 1978.

2. The evidence for Lysimachus's administration is regrettably scant. See Lund 1992, ch. 5, for more on the topic.

3. Justin 17.1.3.

4. Memnon of Heraclea, fr. 1.5.6 Jacoby.

5. On the sculptures of Pergamum, see Pollitt 1986, ch.4.

6. Strabo, *Geography* 16.2.10.

7. Plutarch, *Life of Phocion* 29.1.

8. This is a very controversial topic, with views ranging from skepticism to acceptance of the idea that men could be gods. See especially Badian 1981; Balsdon 1950/1966; Bosworth 2003b; Cawkwell 1994; Chaniotis 2003; Dreyer 2009; Fredricksmeyer 1979, 1981; Green 1990 (ch. 23), 2003; Habicht 1970; Hamilton 1984; Sanders 1991.

9. For Lysander, see Plutarch, *Life of Lysander* 18, based on Duris of Samos. For Dionysius, see DS 16.20.6 with Sanders 1991. For further pre-Alexandrian possibilities, see Fredricksmeyer 1979 and 1981.

10. Homer, *Odyssey* 8.467–8.

11. *OGIS* 6 = Austin 39.

12. Sir Frederick Maurice (ed.), *An Aide de Camp of Life: Being the Papers of Colonel Charles Marshall, Assistant Adjutant General on the Staff of Robert E. Lee* (London: Little, Brown, 1927), 173.
13. The evidence for private cult of rulers is slight, but see Smith 1988, 11.1–2.
14. Smith 1988, 39–41.
15. For this view in Greek literature (though certainly later than the Successors), see Diotogenes, *On Kingship* fr. 2, pp. 73–4 in H. Thesleff's *The Pythagorean Texts of the Hellenistic Period* (Åbo: Åbo University Press, 1965). For Achaemenid Persia, see e.g. Briant 2002, 240–41; for Macedon, Hammond 1989a, 21–2.
16. Euhemerus T4e Jacoby. For more on Euhemerus, see Ferguson 1975 (ch. 7) and Gutzwiller 2007, 189–90; for the fifth-century origins of the idea, see Prodicus of Ceos fr. 5 Diels/Kranz.
17. Justin 17.2.1.
18. Justin 24.2.
19. Justin 24. 3.7; after an unsuccessful bid for the Macedonian throne, the surviving son (another Ptolemy) became an independent dynast based in the city of Telmessus in Pisidia.

Bibliography

There are good reasons for the length of this bibliography. The loss of nearly all our literary sources for the era of the Successors, and the patchiness and unreliability of the sources that remain, mean that the period is a playground for scholars. My job in this book is to reach as wide an audience as possible. This means that I have not gone into scholarly controversies, nor have I generally interrupted the flow of the book with other arguments and positions. The notes have largely been restricted to referencing quotations and alerting the reader to major controversies. The list that follows, then, is intended to be full enough to guide any reader who wants to go on to read more detailed and more nuanced accounts. I have omitted many books and even more articles, especially if they were written in a language other than English. I have marked with an asterisk those works which seem to me to be indispensable, or at least the most useful of their class. The ancient sources are, of course, all essential.

ANCIENT SOURCES

Among the lost sources for the era of Alexander the Great and his Successors, the greatest loss is the work of Hieronymus of Cardia, an eyewitness attached to the courts, in turn, of Eumenes (possibly a cousin), Antigonus Monophthalmus, Demetrius Poliorcetes, and Antigonus Gonatas. See J. Hornblower, *Hieronymus of Cardia* (Oxford: Oxford University Press, 1981), and J. Roisman, 'Hieronymus of Cardia: Causation and Bias from Alexander to His Successors', in. E. Carney and D. Ogden (eds), *Philip II and Alexander the Great: Father and Son, Lives and Afterlives* (New York: Oxford University Press, 2010), 135–48.

The most important literary source that remains is Diodorus of Sicily (late first cent. BCE). Books 18–20 of his *Library of History* constitute the only continuous narrative of the age of the Successors, though after 302 BCE his work remains only in pitiful fragments. But others add substance in the form of alternative traditions or corroboration: Appian, *Syrian History* 52–64 (second cent. CE = *Roman History* 11.52–64); Q. Curtius Rufus, *The History of Alexander* (first cent. CE), book 10; Justin (M. Junianus Justinus, perhaps third cent. CE), digest of books 13–17 of the *Philippic History* of Pompeius Trogus (late first cent. BCE); Cornelius Nepos (first cent. BCE), *Lives of Eumenes, Phocion*; Plutarch (first/second cent. CE), *Lives of Alexander, Eumenes, Demetrius, Demosthenes, Phocion, Pyrrhus*; Polyaenus (2nd cent. CE), *Stratagems*, esp. book 4.

A number of fragmentary histories are also relevant, of which the most important is that of Arrian (L. Flavius Arrianus, second cent. CE), *After Alexander* (fragments, and lamentably brief summary by Photius of Constantinople, ninth cent. CE). Others include P. Herennius Dexippus (third cent. CE), *After Alexander* (fragments, and summary by Photius of Constantinople, ninth cent. CE); Duris of Samos (fourth/third cent. BCE); Memnon of Heraclea Pontica (second cent. CE); and Philochorus of Athens (fourth/third cent. BCE). These fragments are collected in F. Jacoby, *Die Fragmente der griechischen Historiker* (Berlin: Weidmann, 1923–58; CD-ROM ed, Leiden: Brill, 2004): Arrian is *FGrH* 156; Dexippus is *FGrH* 100; Duris is *FGrH* 76; Hieronymus is *FGrH* 154; Memnon is *FGrH* 434; Philochorus is *FGrH* 328. Jacoby's monumental work is currently being revised under the editorship of I. Worthington, to be published in various formats by Brill.

Arrian's fragments are also collected in the second volume of the Teubner Arrian, edited by A. Roos and G. Wirth (1967). Two recently discovered fragments have not yet been incorporated into either Jacoby or the Teubner text. The best versions of these two fragments can be found in, respectively, A. B. Bosworth, "Eumenes, Neoptolemus and *PSI* XII 1284," *Greek, Roman, and Byzantine Studies* 19 (1978), 227–37, and B. Dreyer, "The Arrian Parchment in Gothenburg: New Digital Processing Methods and Initial Results," in W. Heckel et al. (eds.), *Alexander's Empire: Formulation to Decay* (Claremont: Regina, 2007), 245–63. There is a translation of and brief historical commentary on a few of the fragments by W. Goralski, "Arrian's *Events after Alexander*: Summary of Photius and Selected Fragments," *Ancient World* 19 (1989), 81–108.

TRANSLATIONS OF LITERARY SOURCES

Translations of the relevant works by Appian, Diodorus, Nepos, and Plutarch can most easily be found in the Loeb Classical Library series, published by Harvard University Press. These translations tend to be a bit old-fashioned, however; in fact, those of Diodorus and Appian are out of copyright, and also available on the Web. Otherwise, for Curtius: *Quintus Curtius Rufus: The History of Alexander*, trans. by J. C. Yardley, introduction by W. Heckel (London: Penguin, 1984). And for Justin: *Justin: Epitome of the Philippic History of Pompeius Trogus*, trans. by J. C. Yardley, introduction by R. Develin (Atlanta: Scholars Press, 1994).

Excerpts from the literary sources, along with translations of inscriptions, cuneiform texts, and papyri, have been collected in a number of sourcebooks:

Ager, S., 1996, *Interstate Arbitrations in the Greek World, 337–90 BC* (Berkeley: University of California Press). [inscriptions and literary sources]

*Austin, M., 2006, *The Hellenistic World from Alexander to the Roman Conquest: A Selection of Ancient Sources in Translation* (2nd ed., Cambridge: Cambridge University Press). [literary sources, inscriptions, papyri]

Bagnall, R., and Derow, P., 2004, *The Hellenistic Period: Historical Texts in Translation* (2nd ed., Oxford: Blackwell) (1st ed. title: *Greek Historical Documents: The Hellenistic Period*). [inscriptions and papyri]

Burstein, S., 1985, *The Hellenistic Age from the Battle of Ipsos to the Death of Kleopatra VII* (Cambridge: Cambridge University Press). [literary sources, inscriptions, papyri]

Grant, F., 1953, *Hellenistic Religions: The Age of Syncretism* (Indianapolis: Bobbs-Merrill). [inscriptions and literary sources]

Harding, P., 1985, *From the End of the Peloponnesian War to the Battle of Ipsus* (Cambridge: Cambridge University Press). [inscriptions and literary sources]

*Heckel, W., n.d., *The Successors of Alexander the Great: A Sourcebook* (http://www.ucalgary.ca/~heckelw/grst341/Sourcebook.pdf). [almost entirely literary sources]

Heckel, W., and Yardley, J. C., 2004, *Alexander the Great: Historical Texts in Translation* (Oxford: Blackwell). [literary sources]

Inwood, B., and Gerson, L., 1997, *Hellenistic Philosophy: Introductory Readings* (2nd ed., Indianapolis: Hackett). [literary sources]

Sage, M., 1996, *Warfare in Ancient Greece: A Sourcebook* (London: Routledge). [literary sources, inscriptions, papyri]

Van der Spek, R., and Finkel, I., n.d., *Babylonian Chronicles of the Hellenistic Period* (http://www.livius.org/cg-cm/chronicles/chronoo.html). [cuneiform sources]

Welles, C. B., 1934/1974, *Royal Correspondence in the Hellenistic Period* (New Haven: Yale University Press; repr. Chicago: Ares). [inscriptions]

Dating the Early Hellenistic Period

The dating of events in the first dozen years of this period is highly complex and controversial. There are two basic dating schemes, but many scholars nowadays tweak one or the other rather than adopt either wholesale. For a good introduction, see P. Wheatley, "An Introduction to the Chronological Problems in Early Diadoch Sources and Scholarship," in W. Heckel et al. (eds.), *Alexander's Empire: Formulation to Decay* (Claremont: Regina, 2007), 179–92. In this book, I have followed the most recent work on this intractable problem, which is that of T. Boiy in his *Between High and Low: A Chronology of the Early Hellenistic Period* (Berlin: Verlag Antike, 2008). Boiy also includes a definitive bibliography (up to 2007), to which the interested reader is referred.

SECONDARY LITERATURE

Abel, F.-M., 1937, "L'expédition des grecs à Pétra en 312 avant J.-C.," *Revue Biblique* 46, 373–91.

Adams, W. L., 1983, "The Dynamics of Internal Macedonian Politics in the Time of Cassander," *Ancient Macedonia* 3, 2–30.

Adams, W. L., 1984, "Antipater and Cassander: Generalship on Restricted Resources in the Fourth Century," *Ancient World* 10, 79–88.

Adams, W. L., 1986, "Macedonian Kingship and the Right of Petition," *Ancient Macedonia* 4, 43–52.

Adams, W. L., 1991, "Cassander, Alexander IV and the Tombs at Vergina," *Ancient World* 22, 27–33.

Adams, W. L., 1997, "The Successors of Alexander," in L. Tritle (ed.), *The Greek World in the Fourth Century* (London: Routledge), 228–48.

*Adams, W. L., 2004, *Alexander the Great: Legacy of a Conqueror* (London: Longman).

Adams, W. L., 2006, "The Hellenistic Kingdoms," in Bugh 2006a, 28–51.

Alcock, S., et al. (eds.), 2001, *Empires: Perspectives from Archaeology and History* (Cambridge: Cambridge University Press).

*Algra, K., et al. (eds.), 1999, *The Cambridge History of Hellenistic Philosophy* (Cambridge: Cambridge University Press).

Andronicos, M., 1992, *Vergina: The Royal Tombs* (Athens: Athenon).

Anson, E., 1977, "The Siege of Nora: A Source Conflict," *Greek, Roman, and Byzantine Studies* 18, 251–56.

Anson, E., 1985, "Macedonia's Alleged Constitutionalism," *Classical Journal* 80, 303–16.

Anson, E., 1986, "Diodorus and the Date of Triparadeisus," *American Journal of Philology* 107, 208–17.

Anson, E., 1988, "Antigonus, the Satrap of Phrygia," *Historia* 37, 471–77.

Anson, E., 1990, "Neoptolemus and Armenia," *Ancient History Bulletin* 4, 125–28.

Anson, E., 1991, "The Evolution of the Macedonian Army Assembly (330–315 BC)," *Historia* 40, 230–47.

Anson, E., 1992, "Craterus and the *Prostasia*," *Classical Philology* 87, 38–43.

Anson, E., 2004, *Eumenes of Cardia: A Greek among Macedonians* (Leiden: Brill).

Anson, E., 2006, "The Chronology of the Third Diadoch War," *Phoenix* 60, 226–35.

Anson, E., 2008, "Macedonian Judicial Assemblies," *Classical Philology* 103, 135–49.

Aperghis, G. G., 2004a, "City Building and the Seleukid Royal Economy," in Z. Archibald et al. (eds.), *Making, Moving and Managing: The New World of Ancient Economies, 323–31 BC* (Oxford: Oxbow), 27–43.

*Aperghis, G. G., 2004b, *The Seleukid Royal Economy: The Finances and Financial Administration of the Seleukid Empire* (Cambridge: Cambridge University Press).

Aperghis, G. G., 2008, "Managing an Empire—Teacher and Pupil," in S. Darbandi and A. Zournatzi (eds.), *Ancient Greece and Ancient Iran: Cross-Cultural Encounters* (Athens: National Hellenic Research Foundation), 137–47.

Archibald, Z., 1998, *The Odrysian Kingdom of Thrace: Orpheus Unmasked* (Oxford: Oxford University Press).

Ashton, N., 1977, "The *Naumachia* near Amorgos in 322 BC," *Annual of the Bristish School at Athens* 72, 1–11.

Ashton, N., 1983, "The Lamian War—A False Start?," *Antichthon* 17, 47–63.

Ashton, N., 1993, "Craterus from 324 to 321 BC," *Ancient Macedonia* 5, 125–31.

Ashton, N., and Parkinson, S., 1990, "The Death of Alexander the Great: A Clinical Reappraisal," in A. M. Tamis (ed.), *Macedonian Hellenism* (Melbourne: River Seine), 27–36.

*Atkinson, J. (ed.), and Yardley, J. C. (trans.), 2009, *Curtius Rufus: Histories of Alexander the Great, Book 10* (Oxford: Oxford University Press).

*Austin, M., 1986, "Hellenistic Kings, War and the Economy," *Classical Quarterly* n.s. 36, 450–66.

Austin, M., 2001, "War and Culture in the Seleucid Empire," in T. Bekker-Nielsen and L. Hannestad (eds.), *War as a Cultural and Social Force: Essays in Warfare in Antiquity* (Cophenhagen: Royal Danish Academy of Science and Letters), 90–109.

*Austin, M., 2003, "The Seleukids and Asia," in Erskine 2003, 121–33.

*Badian, E., 1961/1966, "Harpalus," *Journal of Hellenic Studies* 81 (1961), 16–43 (repr. in Griffith 1966, 206–33).

Badian, E., 1962/1964, "The Struggle for the Succession to Alexander the Great" (a review article originally published in *Gnomon* 34), in id., *Studies in Greek and Roman History* (Oxford: Blackwell), 262–69.

Badian, E., 1981, "The Deification of Alexander the Great," in H. J. Dell (ed.), *Ancient Macedonian Studies in Honor of Charles F. Edson* (Thessaloniki: Institute for Balkan Studies), 27–71.

Bagnall, R., 1976, *The Administration of the Ptolemaic Possessions outside Egypt* (Leiden: Brill).

*Bagnall, R., 1984, "The Origins of Ptolemaic Cleruchs," *Bulletin of the American Society of Papyrologists* 21, 7–20.

Bagnall, R., 1997, "Decolonizing Ptolemaic Egypt," in Cartledge et al. 1997, 225–41.

Baker, P., 2003, "Warfare," in Erskine 2003, 373–88.

Balsdon, J. P. V. D., 1950/1966, "The "Divinity" of Alexander," *Historia* 1, 363–88 (repr. in Griffith 1966, 179–204).

Barr-Sharrar, B., and Borza, E. (eds.), 1982, *Macedonia and Greece in Late Classical and Hellenistic Times* (Washington, D.C.: National Gallery of Art = Studies in the History of Art, vol. 10).

Battersby, C., 2007, "What Killed Alexander the Great?," *The Australian and New Zealand Journal of Surgery* 77, 85–7.

Bayliss, A., 2006, "Antigonus the One-Eyed's Return to Asia in 322: A New Restoration for a *Rasura* in *IG* II² 682," *Zeitschrift für Papyrologie und Epigraphik* 155, 108–26.

Baynham, E., 1994, "Antipater: Manager of Kings," in Worthington 1994a, 331–56.

Baynham, E., 2003, "Antipater and Athens," in Palagia/Tracy 2003, 23–9.

Bengtson, H., 1987, *Die Diadochen: Die Nachfolger Alexanders des Grossen (323–281 v. Chr.)* (Munich: Beck).

Bennett, B., and Roberts, M., 2008/2009, *The Wars of the Successors, 323–281* BC, vol. 1: *Commanders and Campaigns;* vol. 2: *Battles and Tactics* (Barnsley: Pen & Sword).

Berlin, A., 1997, "Between Large Forces: Palestine in the Hellenistic Period," *Biblical Archaeologist* 60, 2–51.

*Berthold, R., 1984, *Rhodes in the Hellenistic Age* (Ithaca, N.Y.: Cornell University Press).

Beston, P., 2000, "Hellenistic Military Leadership," in H. van Wees (ed.), *War and Violence in Ancient Greece* (London/Swansea: Duckworth/The Classical Press of Wales), 315–35.

Billows, R., 1989, "Anatolian Dynasts: The Case of the Macedonian Eupolemos in Karia," *Classical Antiquity* 8, 173–206.

*Billows, R., 1990, *Antigonos the One-Eyed and the Creation of the Hellenistic State* (Berkeley: University of California Press).

*Billows, R., 1995, *Kings and Colonists: Aspects of Macedonian Imperialism* (Leiden: Brill, 1995).

Billows, R., 2003, "Cities," in Erskine 2003, 196–215.

*Bingen, J., 2007, *Hellenistic Egypt: Monarchy, Society, Economy, Culture*, ed. R. Bagnall (Berkeley: University of California Press).

Boiy, T., 2010, "Royal and Satrapal Armies in Babylon during the Second Diadoch War. The *Chronicle of the Successors* on the Events during the Seventh Year of Philip Arrhidaeus (= 317/316 BC)," *Journal of Hellenic Studies* 130, 1–13.

*Borza, E., 1990, *In the Shadow of Olympus: The Emergence of Macedon* (Princeton: Princeton University Press).

Borza, E., and Palagia, O., 2007, "The Chronology of the Macedonian Royal Tombs at Vergina," *Jahrbuch des Deutschen Archäologischen Instituts* 122, 81–126.

Borza, E., and Reames-Zimmerman, J., 2000, "Some New Thoughts on the Death of Alexander the Great," *Ancient World* 31, 22–30.

*Bosworth, A. B., 1971, "The Death of Alexander the Great: Rumour and Propaganda," *Classical Quarterly* n.s. 21, 112–36.

Bosworth, A. B., 1980, "Alexander and the Iranians," *Journal of Hellenic Studies* 100, 1–21.

Bosworth, A. B., 1988, *Conquest and Empire: The Reign of Alexander the Great* (Cambridge: Cambridge University Press).

Bosworth, A. B., 1992, "Philip III Arrhidaeus and the Chronology of the Successors," *Chiron* 22, 56–81.

Bosworth, A. B., 1993, "Perdiccas and the Kings," *Classical Quarterly* n.s. 43, 420–27.

Bosworth, A. B., 2000, "Ptolemy and the Will of Alexander," in Bosworth/Baynham 2000, 207–41.

*Bosworth, A. B., 2002, *The Legacy of Alexander: Politics, Warfare, and Propaganda under the Successors* (Oxford: Oxford University Press).

Bosworth, A. B., 2003, "Why Did Athens Lose the Lamian War?," in Palagia/Tracy 2003, 14–22.

Bosworth, A. B., and Baynham, E. (eds.), 2000, *Alexander the Great in Fact and Fiction* (Oxford: Oxford University Press).

Bowen, J., 1972, *A History of Western Education*, vol. 1: *The Ancient World: Orient and Mediterranean, 2000 BC–AD 1054* (London: Methuen).

Braund, D., 2003, "After Alexander: The Emergence of the Hellenistic World," in Erskine 2003, 19–34.

Breebaart, A., 1967, "King Seleucus I, Antiochus, and Stratonice," *Mnemosyne* ser. 4, 20, 154–64.

Briant, P., 1973, *Antigone le Borgne: Les débuts de sa carrière et les problèmes de l'assemblée macédonienne* (Paris: Centre de Recherches d'Histoire Ancienne).

Briant, P., 1978/1982, "Colonisation hellénistique et peuples indigènes. La phase d'installation," *Klio* 60, 57–92 (repr. in id., *Roi, tributs et paysans: Études sur les formations tributaires du Moyen-Orient ancien* (Besançon: Université de Besançon), 227–62).

Briant, P., 1985, "Iraniens d'Asie Mineure après la chute de l'empire achéménide," *Dialogues d'histoire ancienne* 11, 167–95.

Briant, P., 1990, "The Seleucid Kingdom and the Achaemenid Empire," in P. Bilde et al. (eds.), *Religion and Religious Practice in the Seleucid Kingdom* (Aarhus: Aarhus University Press), 40–65.

Briant, P., 2002, *From Cyrus to Alexander: A History of the Persian Empire*, trans. P. Daniels (Winona Lake, Ind.: Eisenbrauns).

Briant, P., and Joannès, F. (eds.), 2006, *La transition entre l'empire achéménide et les royaumes hellénistiques* (Paris: de Boccard).

*Briant, P., 2010, *Alexander the Great and His Empire: A Short Introduction*, trans. A. Kuhrt (Princeton: Princeton University Press).

*Bringmann, K., 1994, "The King as Benefactor: Some Remarks on Ideal Kingship in the Age of Hellenism," in Bulloch et al. 1994, 7–24.

Brunt, P., 1975, "Alexander, Barsine and Heracles," *Rivista di Filologia e d'Instruzione Classica* 103, 22–34.

Bugh, G. (ed.), 2006a, *The Cambridge Companion to the Hellenistic World* (Cambridge: Cambridge University Press).

Bugh, G., 2006b, "Hellenistic Military Developments," in Bugh 2006a, 265–94.

Bulloch, A., et al. (eds.), 1994, *Images and Ideologies: Self-Definition in the Hellenistic World* (Berkeley: University of California Press, 1994).

Burn, L., 2005, *Hellenistic Art from Alexander the Great to Augustus* (Los Angeles: Getty Publications).

Burstein, S., 1974, *Outpost of Hellenism: The Emergence of Heraclea on the Black Sea* (Berkeley: University of California Press).

Burstein, S., 1980, "Lysimachus and the Greek Cities of Asia: The Case of Miletus," *Ancient World* 3, 73–9.

Burstein, S., 1984, "Lysimachus the *Gazophylax*: A Modern Scholarly Myth?," in W. Heckel and R. Sullivan (eds.), *Ancient Coins of the Graeco-Roman World* (Waterloo: Wilfred Laurier University Press), 57–68.

Burstein, S., 1986a, "Lysimachus and the Greek Cities: The Early Years," *Ancient World* 14, 19–24.

Burstein, S., 1986b, "Lysimachus and the Greek Cities: A Problem in Interpretation," *Ancient Macedonia* 4, 133–38.

Burstein, S., 2003/2008, "The Legacy of Alexander: New Ways of Being Greek in the Hellenistic Period," in W. Heckel and L. Tritle (eds.), *Crossroads of History: The Age of Alexander* (Claremont: Regina), 217–42 (repr. as "Greek Identity in the

Hellenistic Period," in K. Zacharia (ed.), *Hellenisms: Culture, Identity, and Ethnicity from Antiquity to Modernity* (Aldershot: Ashgate), 59–77).

Canfora, L., 1990, *The Vanished Library: A Wonder of the Ancient World* (Berkeley: University of California Press).

Carlier, P., 2000, "Homeric and Macedonian Kingship," in R. Brock and S. Hodkinson (eds.), *Alternatives to Athens: Varieties of Political Organization and Community in Ancient Greece* (Oxford: Oxford University Press), 259–68.

Carlsen, J., et al. (eds.), 1993, *Alexander the Great: Reality and Myth* (Rome: "L'Erma" di Bretschneider).

Carney, E., 1983, "Regicide in Macedonia," *La Parola del Passato* 38, 260–72.

Carney, E., 1994, "Olympias, Adea Eurydice, and the End of the Argead Dynasty," in Worthington 1994a, 357–80.

Carney, E., 1995, "Women and *Basileia*: Legitimacy and Female Political Action in Macedonia," *Classical Journal* 90, 367–91.

Carney, E., 1999, "The Curious Death of the Antipatrid Dynasty," *Ancient Macedonia* 6, 209–16.

*Carney, E., 2000a, *Women and Monarchy in Macedonia* (Norman: University of Oklahoma Press).

Carney, E., 2000b, "The Initiation of Cult for Royal Macedonian Women," *Classical Philology* 95, 21–43.

Carney, E., 2001, "The Trouble with Philip Arrhidaeus," *Ancient History Bulletin* 15, 63–89.

Carney, E., 2004, "Women and Military Leadership in Macedonia," *Ancient World* 35, 184–95.

*Carney, E., 2006, *Olympias, Mother of Alexander the Great* (London: Routledge).

Carney, E., and Ogden, D. (eds.), 2010, *Philip II and Alexander the Great: Father and Son, Lives and Afterlives* (New York: Oxford University Press).

Cartledge, P., 2000, "Greek Political Thought: The Historical Context," in C. Rowe and M. Schofield (eds.), *The Cambridge History of Greek and Roman Political Thought* (Cambridge: Cambridge University Press), 11–22.

Cartledge, P., 2004, *Alexander the Great: The Hunt for a New Past* (London: Macmillan).

Cartledge, P., et al. (eds.), 1997, *Hellenistic Constructs: Essays in Culture, History, and Historiography* (Berkeley: University of California Press).

Cawkwell, G., 1994, "The Deification of Alexander the Great: A Note," in Worthington 1994a, 293–306.

*Chamoux, F., 2003, *Hellenistic Civilization*, trans. M. Roussel (Oxford: Blackwell).

Champion, J., 2009, *Pyrrhus of Epirus* (Barnsley: Pen & Sword).

Chaniotis, A., 2003, "The Divinity of Hellenistic Rulers," in Erskine 2003, 431–45.

*Chaniotis, A., 2005, *War in the Hellenistic World* (Oxford: Blackwell).

Clarysse, W., 1985, "Greeks and Egyptians in the Ptolemaic Army and Administration," *Aegyptus* 65, 57–66.

Cohen, G., 1978, *The Seleucid Colonies: Studies in Founding, Administration and Organization* (Wiesbaden: Steiner = Historia Einzelschriften 30).

Cole, S.G., 1984, *Theoi Megaloi: The Cult of the Great Gods at Samothrace* (Leiden: Brill).

Collins, A., 2001, "The Office of Chiliarch under Alexander and the Successors," *Phoenix* 55, 259–83.

Collins, N., 1997, "The Various Fathers of Ptolemy I," *Mnemosyne* ser. 4, 50, 436–76.

*Collins, N., 2000, *The Library in Alexandria and the Bible in Greek* (Leiden: Brill).

Connor, P. (ed.), 1994, *Ancient Macedonia: An Australian Symposium* (Sydney: Meditarch = *Mediterranean Archaeology* 7, 1–126).

*Cribb, J., and Herrmann, G. (eds.), 2007, *After Alexander: Central Asia before Islam* (Oxford: Oxford University Press = *Proceedings of the British Academy* 133).

Decleva Caizzi, F., 1994, "The Porch and the Garden: Early Hellenistic Images of the Philosophical Life," in Bulloch et al. 1994, 303–29.

Delev, P., 2000, "Lysimachus, the Getae and Archaeology," *Classical Quarterly* n.s. 50, 384–401.

Delev, P., 2003, "Lysimachus and the Third War of the Successors (314–311 BC)," in H. Angelova (ed.), *Thracia Pontica VI.2* (Sofia: Center for Underwater Archaeology), 63–70.

Depuydt, L., 1997, "The Time of Death of Alexander the Great: 11 June 323 BC (−322), ca. 4:00–5:00 PM," *Die Welt des Orients* 28, 117–35 (with an appendix in id., *From Xerxes' Murder (465) to Arridaios' Execution (317): Updates to Achaemenid Chronology* (Oxford: Archaeopress, 2008), 47–51).

Devine, A. M., 1984, "Diodorus' Account of the Battle of Gaza," *Acta Classica* 27, 31–40.

Devine, A. M., 1985a, "Diodorus' Account of the Battle of Paraitacene (317 B.C.)," *Ancient World* 12, 75–86.

Devine, A. M., 1985b, "Diodorus' Account of the Battle of Gabiene," *Ancient World* 12, 87–96.

Dimitrov, D., and Čičikova, M., 1978, *The Thracian City of Seuthopolis*, trans. M. P. Alexieva (Oxford: Archaeopress).

*Dixon, M., 2007, "Corinth, Greek Freedom, and the Diadochoi, 323–301 BC," in Heckel et al. 2007, 151–78.

Dmitriev, S., 2004, "Alexander's Exiles Decree," *Klio* 86, 34–81.

Dmitriev, S., 2007, "The Last Marriage and the Death of Lysimachus," *Greek, Roman, and Byzantine Studies* 47, 135–49.

Dreyer, B., 2009, "Heroes, Cults, and Divinity," in Heckel/Tritle 2009, 218–34.

Eckstein, A., 2009, "Hellenistic Monarchy in Theory and Practice," in R. Balot (ed.), *A Companion to Greek and Roman Political Thought* (Oxford: Blackwell), 247–65.

*Eddy, S., 1961, *The King Is Dead: Studies in the Near Eastern Resistance to Hellenism 334–31 BC* (Lincoln: University of Nebraska Press).

Ehrenberg, V., 1969, *The Greek State* (2nd ed., London: Methuen).

Ellis, W., 1994, *Ptolemy of Egypt* (London: Routledge).

Engels, D., 1978a, "A Note on the Death of Alexander," *Classical Philology* 73, 224–28.

Engels, D., 1978b, *Alexander the Great and the Logistics of the Macedonian Army* (Berkeley: University of California Press).

Epplett, C., 2007, "War Elephants in the Hellenistic World," in Heckel et al. 2007, 209–32.

Errington, R. M., 1970, "From Babylon to Triparadeisos: 323–320 BC," *Journal of Hellenic Studies* 90, 49–77.

Errington, R. M., 1974, "Macedonian 'Royal Style' and Its Historical Significance," *Journal of Hellenic Studies* 94, 20–37.

Errington, R. M., 1976, "Alexander in the Hellenistic World," in E. Badian (ed.), *Alexandre le Grand: Image et réalité* (Geneva: Fondation Hardt), 137–79.

Errington, R. M., 1977, "Diodorus Siculus and the Chronology of the Early Diadochi," *Hermes* 105, 478–504.

Errington, R. M., 1978, "The Nature of the Macedonian State under the Monarchy," *Chiron* 8, 77–133.

Errington, R. M., 1990, *A History of Macedonia*, trans. C. Errington (Berkeley: University of California Press).

*Errington, R. M., 2008, *A History of the Hellenistic World* (Oxford: Blackwell).

*Erskine, A., 1995, "Culture and Power in Ptolemaic Egypt: The Museum and Library of Alexandria," *Greece and Rome* 42, 38–48.

*Erskine, A., 2002, "Life after Death: Alexandria and the Body of Alexander," *Greece and Rome* 49, 163–79.

Erskine, A. (ed.), 2003, *A Companion to the Hellenistic World* (Oxford: Blackwell).

Ferguson, J., 1973, *The Heritage of Hellenism* (London: Thames and Hudson).

Ferguson, J., 1975, *Utopias in the Classical World* (London: Thames and Hudson).

Ferguson, W. S., 1948, "Demetrius Poliorcetes and the Hellenic League," *Hesperia* 17, 112–36.

Fraser, P., 1972, *Ptolemaic Alexandria*, 3 vols. (Oxford: Oxford University Press).

Fraser, P., 1996, *Cities of Alexander the Great* (Oxford: Oxford University Press).

Fredricksmeyer, E., 1979, "Divine Honors for Philip II," *Transactions of the American Philological Association* 109, 39–61.

Fredricksmeyer, E., 1981, "On the Background of the Ruler Cult," in H. J. Dell (ed.), *Ancient Macedonian Studies in Honor of Charles F. Edson* (Thessaloniki: Institute for Balkan Studies), 145–56.

Fredricksmeyer, E., 2000, "Alexander the Great and the Kingdom of Asia," in Bosworth/Baynham 2000, 136–66.

Frösén, J. (ed.), 1997, *Early Hellenistic Athens: Symptoms of a Change* (Helsinki: Finnish Institute at Athens).

Gabbert, J., 1997, *Antigonos II Gonatas: A Political Biography* (London: Routledge).

Garlan, Y., 1984, "War and Siegecraft," in Walbank et al. 1984, 353–62.

Goukowsky, P., 1978/1981, *Essai sur les origines du mythe d'Alexandre, 336–270 av. J.-C.*, 2 vols. (Nancy: Université de Nancy).

Grainger, J., 1990a, *The Cities of Seleukid Syria* (Oxford: Oxford University Press).

*Grainger, J., 1990b, *Seleukos Nikator: Constructing a Hellenistic Kingdom* (London: Routledge).

*Grainger, J., 1992, *Hellenistic Phoenicia* (Oxford: Oxford University Press).

Grainger, J., 1999, *The League of the Aetolians* (Leiden: Brill).

Grainger, J., 2007, *Alexander the Great Failure: The Collapse of the Macedonian Empire* (New York: Continuum).

*Green, P., 1990, *Alexander to Actium: The Historical Evolution of the Hellenistic Age* (Berkeley: University of California Press).

Green, P., 1991, *Alexander of Macedon, 356–323 BC: A Historical Biography* (Berkeley: University of California Press).

*Green, P. (ed.), 1993, *Hellenistic History and Culture* (Berkeley: University of California Press).

Green, P., 2003, "Delivering the Go(o)ds: Demetrius Poliorcetes and Hellenistic Divine Kingship," in G. Bakewell and J. Sickinger (eds.), *Gestures: Essays in Ancient History, Literature and Philosophy Presented to Alan L. Boegehold* (Oxford: Oxbow, 2003), 258–77.

Green, P., 2007, *The Hellenistic Age: A Short History* (New York: The Modern Library).

Greenwalt, W., 1984, "The Search for Arrhidaeus," *Ancient World* 10, 69–77.

Greenwalt, W., 1988, "Argaeus, Ptolemy II and Alexander's Corpse," *Ancient History Bulletin* 2, 39–41.

Greenwalt, W., 1989, "Polygamy and Succession in Argead Macedonia," *Arethusa* 22, 19–43.

Greenwalt, W., 1999, "Argead Name Changes," *Ancient Macedonia* 6, 453–62.

Greenwalt, W., 2010, "Argead *Dunasteia* during the Reigns of Philip II and Alexander III: Aristotle Reconsidered," in Carney/Ogden 2010, 151–63 (and endnotes).

Griffith, G. T., 1935/1984, *The Mercenaries of the Hellenistic World* (Cambridge: Cambridge University Press; repr. Chicago: Ares Press).

Griffith, G. T. (ed.), 1966, *Alexander the Great: The Main Problems* (Cambridge: Heffer).

Gruen, E., 1985, "The Coronation of the Diadochoi," in J. Eadie and J. Ober (eds.), *The Craft of the Ancient Historian: Essays in Honor of C. G. Starr* (Lanham: University Press of America), 253–71.

Gruen, E., 1993, "The Polis in the Hellenistic World," in R. Rosen and J. Farrell (eds.), *Nomodeiktes: Studies in Honor of Martin Ostwald* (Ann Arbor: University of Michigan Press), 339–54.

*Gutzwiller, K., 2007, *A Guide to Hellenistic Literature* (Oxford: Blackwell).

Habicht, C., 1970, *Gottmenschentum und griechische Städte* (2nd ed., Munich: Beck).

*Habicht, C., 1997, *Athens from Alexander to Antony*, trans. D. Schneider (Cambridge: Harvard University Press).

Hadley, R. A., 1974, "Royal Propaganda of Seleucus I and Lysimachus," *Journal of Hellenic Studies* 94, 50–65.

Hadot, P., 2002, "The Hellenistic Schools," ch. 7 (pp. 91–145) of *What Is Ancient Philosophy?*, trans. M. Chase (Cambridge: Harvard University Press).

Hahm, D., 2000, "Kings and Constitutions: Hellenistic Theories," in C. Rowe and M. Schofield (eds.), *The Cambridge History of Greek and Roman Political Thought* (Cambridge: Cambridge University Press), 457–76.

Hamilton, J. R., 1984, "The Origins of Ruler-Cult," *Prudentia* 16, 3–16.

Hammond, N. G. L., 1984, "Alexander's Veterans after His Death," *Greek, Roman, and Byzantine Studies* 25, 51–61.

Hammond, N. G. L., 1985, "Some Macedonian Offices c. 336–309 BC," *Journal of Hellenic Studies* 105, 156–60.

Hammond, N. G. L., 1988, "The Royal Journal of Alexander," *Historia* 37, 129–50.

Hammond, N. G. L., 1989a, *The Macedonian State: The Origins, Institutions, and History* (Oxford: Oxford University Press).

Hammond, N. G. L., 1989b, *Alexander the Great: King, Commander and Statesman* (2nd ed., Bristol: Bristol Classical Press).

Hammond, N. G. L., 1989c, "Arms and the King: The Insignia of Alexander the Great," *Phoenix* 43, 217–24.

Hammond, N. G. L., 1993, "The Macedonian Imprint on the Hellenistic World," in Green 1993, 12–23 (with a response by E. Borza, 23–35).

Hammond, N. G. L., 1999, "The Nature of the Hellenistic States," *Ancient Macedonia* 6, 483–88.

Hammond, N. G. L., 2000, "The Continuity of Macedonian Institutions and the Macedonian Kingdoms of the Hellenistic Era," *Historia* 49, 141–60.

*Hammond, N. G. L., Griffith, G. T., and Walbank, F. W., 1972/1979/1988, *A History of Macedonia*, 3 vols. (Oxford: Oxford University Press). The third volume, by Hammond and Walbank, is of most relevance to this book.

Hatzopoulos, M., 1996, *Macedonian Institutions under the Kings: A Historical and Epigraphical Study*, 2 vols. (Athens: Center for Greek and Roman Antiquity).

Hauben, H., 1974, "A Royal Toast in 302 BC," *Ancient Society* 5, 105–17.

Hauben, H., 1977a, "The First War of the Successors (321 BC): Chronological and Historical Problems," *Ancient Society* 8, 85–120.

Hauben, H., 1977b, "Rhodes, Alexander and the Diadochi from 333/2–304 BC," *Historia* 26, 307–39.

Heckel, W., 1982, "The Career of Antigenes," *Symbolae Osloenses* 57, 57–67.

Heckel, W., 1985, "The Macedonian Veterans in Kilikia," *Liverpool Classical Monthly* 10, 109–10.

Heckel, W., 1988, *The Last Days and Testament of Alexander the Great: A Prosopographic Study* (Stuttgart: Steiner = *Historia* Einzelschriften 56).

*Heckel, W., 1992, *The Marshals of Alexander's Empire* (London: Routledge, 1992). [Much of the material of this book is repeated in id., *Who's Who in the Age of Alexander: Prosopography of Alexander's Empire* (Oxford: Blackwell, 2006).]

Heckel, W., 1999, "The Politics of Antipatros, 324–319 BC," *Ancient Macedonia* 6, 489–98.

Heckel, W., 2002, "The Politics of Distrust: Alexander and His Successors," in D. Ogden (ed.), *The Hellenistic World: New Perspectives* (London: Duckworth), 81–95.

Heckel, W., 2007, "The Earliest Evidence for the Plot to Poison Alexander," in Heckel et al. 2007, 265–75.

*Heckel, W., and Tritle, L. (eds.), 2009, *Alexander the Great: A New History* (Oxford: Wiley-Blackwell).

Heckel, W., et al. (eds.), 2007, *Alexander's Empire: Formulation to Decay* (Claremont: Regina).

Herman, G., 1980–81, "The 'Friends' of the Early Hellenistic Rulers: Servants or Officials?" *Talanta* 12–13, 103–49.

Herman, G., 1997, "The Court Society of the Hellenistic Age," in Cartledge et al. 1997, 199–224.

Hölbl, G., 2000, *A History of the Ptolemaic Empire*, trans. T. Saavedra (London: Routledge).

Holt, F., 1988, *Alexander the Great and Bactria: The Formation of a Greek Frontier in Central Asia* (Leiden: Brill).

Holt, F., 1999, *Thundering Zeus: The Making of Hellenistic Bactria* (Berkeley: University of California Press).

Hope Simpson, R., 1954, "The Political Circumstances of the Peace of 311 BC," *Journal of Hellenic Studies* 74, 25–31.

Hope Simpson, R., 1955, "Ptolemaeus' Invasion of Greece in 313 BC," *Mnemosyne* ser. 4, 8, 34–7.

Hope Simpson, R., 1957, "Antigonus, Polyperchon and the Macedonian Regency," *Historia* 6, 371–73.

Hope Simpson, R., 1959, "Antigonus the One-Eyed and the Greeks," *Historia* 8, 385–409.

Howe, S., 2002, *Empire: A Very Short Introduction* (Oxford: Oxford University Press).

*Hughes Fowler, B., 1989, *The Hellenistic Aesthetic* (Madison: University of Wisconsin Press).

Hunter, R., 2003, "Literature and Its Contexts," in Erskine 2003, 477–93.

Invernizzi, A., 1996, "Seleucia on the Tigris: Centre and Periphery in Seleucid Asia," in P. Bilde et al. (eds.), *Centre and Periphery in the Hellenistic World* (2nd ed., Aarhus: Aarhus University Press), 230–50.

Jenkins, G., 1967, "The Monetary Systems in the Early Hellenistic Time with Special Regard to the Economic Policy of the Ptolemaic Kings," in A. Kindler (ed.), *Proceedings of the International Numismatic Convention, Jerusalem 1963* (Tel Aviv: Schocken), 53–74.

Johnson, C., 2000, "Ptolemy I's Epiklesis *Soter*: Origin and Definition," *Ancient History Bulletin* 14, 101–6.

Johnson, C., 2002, "*OGIS* 98 and the Divinization of the Ptolemies," *Historia* 5, 112–16.

Jones, A. H. M., 1940, *The Greek City from Alexander to Justinian* (Oxford: Oxford University Press).

Jordan, D., 1980, "Two Inscribed Lead Tablets from a Well in the Athenian Kerameikos," *Mitteilungen des Deutschen Archäologischen Instituts: Athenische Abteilung* 95, 225–39.

Kertész, I., 1974, "Ptolemy I and the Battle of Gaza," *Studia Aegyptica*, 231–41.

Koenen, L., 1994, "The Ptolemaic King as a Religious Figure," in Bulloch et al. 1994, 25–115.

Kuhrt, A., 1996, "The Seleucid Kings and Babylonia: New Perspectives," in P. Bilde et al. (eds.), *Aspects of Hellenistic Kingship* (Aarhus: Aarhus University Press), 41–54.

Kuhrt, A., and Sherwin-White, S., 1994, "The Transition from Achaemenid to Seleucid Rule in Babylonia: Revolution or Evolution?," *Achaemenid History* 8, 311–27.

*Kuhrt, A., and Sherwin-White, S. (eds.), 1988, *Hellenism in the East: The Interaction of Greek and Non-Greek Civilizations from Syria to Central Asia after Alexander* (Berkeley: University of California Press).

Landucci Gattinoni, F., 1992, *Lisimaco di Tracia: Un sovrano nella prospettiva del primo ellenismo* (Milan: Jaca, 1992).

Landucci Gattinoni, F., 2003, *L'arte del potere: Vita e opere di Cassandro di Macedonia* (Stuttgart: Steiner = *Historia* Einzelschriften 171).

Landucci Gattinoni, F., 2009, "Cassander's Wife and Heirs," in Wheatley/Hannah 2009, 261–75.

Landucci Gattinoni, F., 2010, "Cassander and the Legacy of Philip II and Alexander III in Diodorus' *Library*," in Carney/Ogden 2010, 113–21 (and endnotes).

*Lane Fox, R., 1973, *Alexander the Great* (London: Allen Lane).

Lattimore, S., 1997, "Art and Architecture," in L. Tritle (ed.), *The Greek World in the Fourth Century* (London: Routledge, 1997), 249–82.

Launey, M., 1949/1950, *Recherches sur les armées hellénistiques*, 2 vols. (Paris: Bibliothèque des écoles françaises d'Athènes et de Rome).

Lianou, M., 2010, "The Role of the Argeadai in the Legitimation of the Ptolemaic Dynasty," in Carney/Ogden 2010, 123–33 (and endnotes).

Lightfoot, J., 2000, "Sophisticates and Solecisms: Greek Literature after the Classical Period," in O. Taplin (ed.), *Literature in the Greek World* (Oxford: Oxford University Press), 199–238.

Ling, R., 1984, *The Cambridge Ancient History: Plates to Volume VII Part 1* (Cambridge: Cambridge University Press).

*Lloyd, G. E. R., 1973, *Greek Science after Aristotle* (New York: Norton).

Lock, R., 1977, "The Macedonian Army Assembly in the Time of Alexander the Great," *Classical Philology* 72, 91–107.

*Lund, H., 1992, *Lysimachus: A Study in Early Hellenistic Kingship* (London: Routledge).

Ma, J., 2000, "Fighting Poleis of the Hellenistic World," in H. van Wees (ed.), *War and Violence in Ancient Greece* (London/Swansea: Duckworth/The Classical Press of Wales), 337–76.

Ma, J., 2003, "Kings," in Erskine 2003, 177–95.

Macurdy, G., 1929, "The Political Activities and the Name of Cratesipolis," *American Journal of Philology* 50, 273–78.

Macurdy, G., 1932a/1985, *Hellenistic Queens: A Study of Woman-Power in Macedonia, Seleucid Syria, and Ptolemaic Egypt* (Baltimore: Johns Hopkins University Press; repr. Chicago: Ares).

Macurdy, G., 1932b, "Roxane and Alexander IV in Epirus," *Journal of Hellenic Studies* 52, 256–61.

Manning, J., 2003, *Land and Power in Ptolemaic Egypt: The Structure of Land Tenure* (Cambridge: Cambridge University Press).

*Manning, J., 2007, "Hellenistic Egypt," in W. Scheidel et al. (eds.), *The Cambridge Economic History of the Greco-Roman World* (Cambridge: Cambridge University Press), 434–59.

*Manning, J., 2010, *The Last Pharaohs: Egypt under the Ptolemies, 305–30 BC* (Princeton: Princeton University Press).

Marr, J., and Calisher, C., 2003, "Alexander the Great and West Nile Virus Encephalitis," *Emerging Infectious Diseases* 12, 1599–1603.

Marsden, E., 1969, *Greek and Roman Artillery: Historical Development* (Oxford: Oxford University Press).

Martin, L., 1987, *Hellenistic Religions: An Introduction* (New York: Oxford University Press).

Martin, T., 1996, "Adeimantos of Lampsakos and Demetrios Poliorketes' Fraudulent Peace of 302 BC," in R. Wallace and E. Harris (eds.), *Transitions to Empire: Essays in Greco-Roman History, 360–146, in Honor of E. Badian* (Norman: University of Oklahoma Press), 179–90.

McKechnie, P., 1999, "Manipulation of Themes in Quintus Curtius Rufus Book 10," *Historia* 48, 44–60.

McKenzie, L., 1994, "Patterns in Seleucid Administration: Macedonian or Near Eastern?," in Connor 1994, 61–68.

McNicoll, A., and Milner, N., 1997, *Hellenistic Fortifications from the Aegean to the Euphrates* (Oxford: Oxford University Press).

*Meeus, A., 2008, "The Power Struggle of the Diadochoi in Babylonia, 323 BC," *Ancient Society* 38, 39–82.

Meeus, A., 2009a, "Some Institutional Problems concerning the Succession to Alexander the Great: *Prostasia* and Chiliarchy," *Historia* 58, 287–310.

Meeus, A., 2009b, "Kleopatra and the Diadochoi," in P. van Nuffelen (ed.), *Faces of Hellenism: Studies in the History of the Eastern Mediterranean (4th Century BC–5th Century AD)* (Leuven: Peeters), 63–92.

Meeus, A., 2009c, "Alexander's Image in the Age of the Successors," in Heckel/Tritle 2009, 235–50.

Mendels, D., 1984/1998, "Aetolia 331–301: Frustration, Political Power, and Survival," *Historia* 33, 129–80 (repr. in id., *Identity, Religion and Historiography: Studies in Hellenistic History* (Sheffield: Sheffield Academic Press), 36–100).

Merker, I., 1979, "Lysimachus—Thessalian or Macedonian?" *Chiron* 9, 31–6.

*Migeotte, L., 2009, *The Economy of the Greek Cities from the Archaic Period to the Early Roman Empire*, trans. J. Lloyd (Berkeley: University of California Press).

Mikalson, J., 1998, *Religion in Hellenistic Athens* (Berkeley: University of California Press, 1998).

*Mikalson, J., 2006, "Greek Religion: Continuity and Change in the Hellenistic Period," in Bugh 2006a, 208–22.

Miller, S., 1986, "Alexander's Funeral Cart," *Ancient Macedonia* 4, 401–11.

Miller, S., 1993, *The Tomb of Lyson and Kallikles: A Painted Macedonian Tomb* (Mainz am Rhein: von Zabern).

Mitchell, L., 2007, "Born to Rule? Succession in the Argead Royal House," in Heckel et al. 2007, 61–74.

Mookerji, R. K., 1966/1999, *Chandragupta Maurya and His Times*, 4th ed. (New Delhi: South Asia Books; repr. Delhi: Banarsidass).

Mooren, L., 1983, "The Nature of the Hellenistic Monarchy," in E. Van't Dack et al. (eds.), *Egypt and the Hellenistic World* (Leuven: Peeters), 205–40.

Mooren, L., 1998, "Kings and Courtiers: Political Decision-Making in the Hellenistic States," in W. Schuller (ed.), *Politische Theorie und Praxis im Altertum* (Darmstadt: Wissenschaftliche Buchgesellschaft), 122–33.

Morris, I., and Scheidel, W., 2009, *The Dynamics of Ancient Empires: State Power from Assyria to Byzantium* (Oxford: Oxford University Press).

Morrison, J. S., 1987, "Athenian Sea-Power in 323/2 BC: Dream and Reality," *Journal of Hellenic Studies* 107, 88–97.

Mueller, K., 2006, *Settlements of the Ptolemies: City Foundation and New Settlement in the Hellenistic World* (Leuven: Peeters).

Murray, W., 2012, *The Age of Titans: Big Ships and the Exercise of Naval Power during the Hellenistic Age* (New York: Oxford University Press).

Musti, D., 1984, "Syria and the East," in Walbank et al. 1984, 175–220.

Mylonas, G., 1961, *Eleusis and the Eleusinian Mysteries* (London: Routledge & Kegan Paul).

Nielsen, I., 1994, *Hellenistic Palaces: Tradition and Renewal* (Aarhus: Aarhus University Press).

*Ogden, D., 1999, *Polygamy, Prostitutes and Death: The Hellenistic Dynasties* (London: Duckworth).

*Oleson, J. (ed.), 2008, *The Oxford Handbook of Engineering and Technology in the Classical World* (Oxford: Oxford University Press).

*Oliver, G., 2007, *War, Food, and Politics in Early Hellenistic Athens* (Oxford: Oxford University Press).

O'Neil, J., 1999, "Political Trials under Alexander the Great and His Successors," *Antichthon* 33, 28–47.

O'Neil, J., 2000, "Royal Authority and City Law under Alexander and His Hellenistic Successors," *Classical Quarterly* n.s. 50, 424–31.

O'Sullivan, L., 2008, "*Le Roi Soleil*: Demetrius Poliorcetes and the Dawn of the Sun King," *Antichthon* 42, 78–99.

*O'Sullivan, L., 2009, *The Regime of Demetrius of Phalerum in Athens, 317–307 BC: A Philosopher in Politics* (Leiden: Brill).

Pagden, A., 2001, *Peoples and Empires: A Short History of European Migration, Exploration and Conquest from Greece to the Present* (London: Modern Library, 2001).

*Palagia, O., and Tracy, S. (eds.), 2003, *The Macedonians in Athens, 322–229 BC* (Oxford: Oxbow).

Paspalas, S., 2005, "Philip Arrhidaios at Court—An Ill-Advised Persianism? Macedonian Royal Display in the Wake of Alexander," *Klio* 87, 72–101.

*Pollitt, J. J., 1986, *Art in the Hellenistic Age* (Cambridge: Cambridge University Press).

Pomeroy, S., 1977, "*Technikai kai Mousikai*: The Education of Women in the Fourth Century and in the Hellenistic Period," *American Journal of Ancient History* 2, 51–68.

*Potter, D., 2003, "Hellenistic Religion," in Erskine 2003, 407–30.

Potts, D., 1990, *The Arabian Gulf in Antiquity*, vol. 2: *From Alexander the Great to the Coming of Islam* (Oxford: Oxford University Press).

Von Reden, S., 2001, "The Politics of Monetization in Third-Century BC Egypt," in A. Meadows and K. Shipton (eds.), *Money and Its Uses in the Ancient Greek World* (Oxford: Oxford University Press), 65–76.

Von Reden, S., 2007, *Money in Ptolemaic Egypt from the Macedonian Conquest to the End of the Third Century BC* (Cambridge: Cambridge University Press).

Ridgway, B., 2001, *Hellenistic Sculpture*, vol. 1: *The Styles of ca. 331–200 BC* (Madison: University of Wisconsin Press).

Robert, L., 1966/2007, "Sur un décret d'Ilion et sur un papyrus concernant des cultes royaux," in A. Samuel (ed.), *Essays in Honor of C. B. Welles* (New Haven: American Society of Papyrologists), 175–210 (repr. in id., *Choix d'écrits*, ed. D. Rousset (Paris: Les Belles Lettres), 569–601).

Robertson, M., 1993, "What Is '"Hellenistic' about Hellenistic Art?," in Green 1993, 67–90 (with a response by J. J. Pollitt, 90–103).

Rodgers, W., 1937, *Greek and Roman Naval Warfare: A Study of Strategy, Tactics, and Ship Design from Salamis (480 BC) to Actium (31 BC)* (Annapolis: Naval Institute Press).

Roisman, J. (ed.), 2003, *Brill's Companion to Alexander the Great* (Leiden: Brill).

*Romm, J., 2011, *Ghost on the Throne: The War for the Corpse, Crown and Empire of Alexander the Great* (New York: Simon & Schuster).

Rostovtzeff, M., 1941, *The Social and Economic History of the Hellenistic World*, 3 vols. (London: Oxford University Press).

Rowlandson, J., 2003, "Town and Country in Ptolemaic Egypt," in Erskine 2003, 249–63.

Roy, J., 1998, "The Masculinity of the Hellenistic King," in L. Foxhall and J. Salmon (eds.), *When Men Were Men: Masculinity, Power and Identity in Classical Antiquity* (London: Routledge), 111–35.

Saatsoglou-Paliadeli, C., 2007, "La peinture de la chasse de Vergina," in S. Deschamps-Lequime (ed.), *Peinture et couleur dans le monde grec antique* (Paris: Musée de Louvre), 47–55.

Sabin, P., 2007, "Land Battles," in P. Sabin et al. (eds.), *The Cambridge History of Greek and Roman Warfare* (Cambridge: Cambridge University Press), 399–433.

Samuel, A., 1993, "The Ptolemies and the Ideology of Kingship," in Green 1993, 168–92 (with a response by D. Delia, 192–204).

Sanders, L., 1991, "Dionysius I of Syracuse and the Origins of Ruler Cult in the Greek World," *Historia* 40, 275–87.

Scharfe, H., 1971, "The Maurya Dynasty and the Seleucids," *Zeitschrift für vergleichende Sprachforschung* 85, 211–25.

Schep, L., 2009, "The Death of Alexander the Great: Reconsidering Poison," in Wheatley/Hannah 2009, 227–36.

Schlumberger, D., 1969, "Triparadisos," *Bulletin du Musée de Beyrouth* 22, 147–49.

Schober, L., 1981, *Untersuchungen zur Geschichte Babyloniens und der oberen Satrapien von 323–303 v. Chr.* (Frankfurt: Lang).

Scullard, H., 1974, *The Elephant in the Greek and Roman World* (Ithaca: Cornell University Press).

Seibert, J., 1983, *Das Zeitalter der Diadochen* (Darmstadt: Wissenschaftliche Buchgesellschaft).

Seyrig, H., 1988, "Seleucus I and the Foundation of Hellenistic Syria," in W. A. Ward (ed.), *The Role of the Phoenicians in the Interaction of Mediterranean Civilizations* (Beirut: American University of Beirut), 53–63.

Sfameni Gasparro, G., 1997, "*Daimôn* and *Tuchê* in the Hellenistic Religious Experience," in P. Bilde et al. (eds.), *Conventional Values of the Hellenistic Greeks* (Aarhus: Aarhus University Press), 67–109.

Sharples, I., 1994, "Curtius' Treatment of Arrhidaeus," in Connor 1994, 53–60.

Sharples, R., 2006, "Philosophy for Life," in Bugh 2006a, 223–40.

Shear, T. L., 1978, *Kallias of Sphettos and the Revolt of Athens in 286 BC* (Princeton: American School of Classical Studies at Athens = *Hesperia* supp. 17).

Sherwin-White, S., and Kuhrt, A., 1993, *From Samarkhand to Sardis: A New Approach to the Seleucid Empire* (Berkeley: University of California Press).

*Shipley, G., 2000, *The Greek World after Alexander, 323–30 BC* (London: Routledge).

Shipley, G., and Hansen, M., 2006, "The Polis and Federalism," in Bugh 2006a, 52–72.

*Smith, R. R. R., 1988, *Hellenistic Royal Portraits* (Oxford: Oxford University Press).

De Souza, P., 2007, "Naval Battles and Sieges," in P. Sabin et al. (eds.), *The Cambridge History of Greek and Roman Warfare* (Cambridge: Cambridge University Press), 434–60.

*Spawforth, A., 2007, "The Court of Alexander the Great between Europe and Asia," in id. (ed.), *The Court and Court Society in Ancient Monarchies* (Cambridge: Cambridge University Press), 82–120.

*Stewart, A., 1993, *Faces of Power: Alexander's Image and Hellenistic Politics* (Berkeley: University of California Press, 1993).

Stewart, A., 2006, "Hellenistic Art: Two Dozen Innovations," in Bugh 2006a, 158–85.

Stoneman, R., 1991, *The Greek Alexander Romance* (London: Penguin).

Taylor, M., 1998, "When the Peiraieus and the City Are Reunited," *Zeitschrift für Papyrologie und Epigraphik* 123, 207–12.

*Thompson, D., 1997, "The Infrastructure of Splendour: Census and Taxes in Ptolemaic Egypt," in Cartledge et al. 1997, 242–57.

*Thompson, D., 2001, "Hellenistic Hellenes: The Case of Ptolemaic Egypt," in I. Malkin (ed.), *Ancient Perceptions of Greek Ethnicity* (Washington, DC: Center for Hellenic Studies), 301–22.

*Thompson, D., 2003, "The Ptolemies and Egypt," in Erskine 2003, 105–20.

Tuplin, C., 2008, "The Seleucids and Their Achaemenid Predecessors: A Persian Inheritance?," in S. Darbandi and A. Zournatzi (eds.), *Ancient Greece and Ancient Iran: Cross-Cultural Encounters* (Athens: National Hellenic Research Foundation), 109–36.

Turner, E., 1984, "Ptolemaic Egypt," in Walbank et al. 1984, 118–74.

*Van der Spek, R., 2007, "The Hellenistic Near East," in W. Scheidel et al. (eds.), *The Cambridge Economic History of the Greco-Roman World* (Cambridge: Cambridge University Press), 409–33.

Van Straten, F., 1994, "Images of Gods and Men in a Changing Society: Self-Identity in Hellenistic Religion," in Bulloch et al. 1994, 248–64.

*Walbank, F. W., 1984, "Monarchies and Monarchic Ideas," in id. et al. 1984, 62–100.

Walbank, F. W., 1992, *The Hellenistic World* (2nd ed., London: Fontana).

Walbank, F. W., et al. (eds.), 1984, *The Cambridge Ancient History*, vol. 7 Part 1: *The Hellenistic World* (2nd ed., Cambridge: Cambridge University Press).

Wehrli, C., 1964, "Phila, fille d'Antipater et épouse de Démétrios, roi des Macédoniens," *Historia* 13, 140–46.

Wheatley, P., 1995, "Ptolemy Soter's Annexation of Syria 320 BC," *Classical Quarterly* n.s. 45, 433–40.

Wheatley, P., 1997, "The Lifespan of Demetrius Poliorcetes," *Historia* 46, 19–27.

Wheatley, P., 1998a, "The Date of Polyperchon's Invasion of Macedonia and Murder of Herakles," *Antichthon* 32, 12–23.

Wheatley, P., 1998b, "The Chronology of the Third Diadoch War," *Phoenix* 52, 257–81.

Wheatley, P., 2001, "The Antigonid Campaign in Cyprus, 306 BC," *Ancient Society* 31, 133–56.

Wheatley, P., 2002, "Antigonus Monophthalmus in Babylonia, 310–308 BC," *Journal of Near Eastern Studies* 61, 39–47.

Wheatley, P., 2009a, "The Diadochi, or Successors to Alexander," in Heckel/Tritle 2009, 53–68.

Wheatley, P., 2009b, "The Besieger in Syria 314–312 BC. Historiographic and Chronological Notes," in Wheatley/Hannah 2009, 323–33.

Wheatley, P., and Hannah, R. (eds.), 2009, *Alexander and His Successors: Essays from the Antipodes* (Claremont: Regina).

Will, E., 1984, "The Succession to Alexander" and "The Formation of the Hellenistic Kingdoms," trans. F. McDonagh, in Walbank et al. 1984, 23–61, 101–17.

Williams, J., 1984, "A Note on Athenian Chronology, 319/8–318/7 BC," *Hermes* 112, 300–5.

Williams, J., 1989, "Demades' Last Years, 323/2–319/8 BC: A 'Revisionist' Interpretation," *Ancient World* 19, 19–30.

Wolski, J., 1984, "Les Séleucides et l'héritage d'Alexandre le Grand en Iran," in B. Virgilio (ed.), *Studi Ellenistici*, vol. 1 (Pisa: Giardini), 9–20.

Worthington, I. (ed.), 1994a, *Ventures into Greek History* (Oxford: Oxford University Press).

Worthington, I., 1994b, "Alexander and Athens in 324/3 BC: On the Greek Attitude to the Macedonian Hegemony," in Connor 1994, 45–51.

Worthington, I., 1994c, "The Harpalus Affair and the Greek Response to the Macedonian Hegemony," in id. 1994a, 307–30.

*Worthington, I. (ed.), 2002, *Alexander the Great: A Reader* (London: Routledge).

Index